The Routledge Introduction to Twentieth- and Twenty-First-Century Canadian Poetry

When asked the question "what is the power of poetry?" writer Ian Williams said "poetry punctures the surface." Williams's statement—that poetry matters and that it does something—is at the heart of this book. Building from this core idea that poetry perforates the everyday to give greater range to our lives and our thinking, the practical and pedagogical aim of this book is twofold: the first aim is to provide students with an introduction to the key cultural, political, and historical events that inform twentieth- and twenty-first-century Canadian poetry; and to familiarize those same readers with poetic movements, trends, and forms of the same time period. This book addresses the aesthetic and social contexts of Canadian poetry written in the twentieth and twenty-first centuries: it models for its readers the critical and theoretical discourses needed to understand the contexts of literary production in Canada. Put differently, readers need a sense of the "where" and "how" of poetic production to help situate them in the "what" of poetry itself. In addition to offering a historically contextualized overview of significant movements, developments, and poets of this time period, this book also familiarizes readers with key moments of reflection and rupture, such as the effects of economic and ecological crisis, global conflicts, and debates around appropriation of culture. This book is built on the premise that poetry in Canada does not happen outside of political, social, and cultural contexts.

Erin Wunker is Associate Professor of Canadian literature at Dalhousie University, which is located in Mi'kma'ki, the ancestral and unceded territory of the Mi'kmaq Peoples. Her areas of research and teaching include Canadian poetry and poetics, feminist and affect theory, and creative nonfiction with a focus on the personal essay and autotheory. She is the author of *Notes from a Feminist Killjoy: Essays on Everyday Life* (2016). With Sina Queyras and Geneviève Robichaud she edited *Avant Desire: A Nicole Brossard Reader* (2020). With Hannah McGregor and Julie Rak she edited *Refuse: CanLit in Ruins* (2018). With Bart Vautour, Travis V. Mason, and Christl Verduyn she edited *Public Poetics: Critical Issues in Canadian Poetry and Poetics* (2015). She is currently working on a creative non-fiction project about boredom, anxiety, and care work.

Routledge Introductions to Canadian Literature

Series Editors:
Robert Lecker, *McGill University*
Lorraine York, *McMaster University*

Routledge Introductions to Canadian Literature is a series that provides critical introductions to important trends, issues, authors, historical, cultural and intellectual contexts in Canadian Literature. The series draws on the work of experts in the field to provide a detailed but accessible commentary on those works or conceptual issues which are taught with undergraduate students in mind but also graduate students and instructors.

The Routledge Introduction to Canadian Fantastic Literature
Allan Weiss

The Routledge Introduction to Auto/biography in Canada
Sonja Boon, Laurie McNeill, Julie Rak, and Candida Rifkind

The Routledge Introduction to Gender and Sexuality in Literature in Canada
Linda Morra

The Routledge Introduction to the Canadian Short Story
Maria Löschnigg

The Routledge Introduction to Twentieth- and Twenty-First-Century Canadian Poetry
Erin Wunker

For more information about this series, please visit: https://www.routledge.com/Routledge-Introductions-to-Canadian-Literature/book-series/RICL

The Routledge Introduction to Twentieth- and Twenty-First-Century Canadian Poetry

Erin Wunker

NEW YORK AND LONDON

Cover image: Marlene Creates

Fire and Water, Nova Scotia 1985
burnt wood from a forest fire area and driftwood from the Atlantic shore,
488 x 488 cm or 335 x 670 cm floor space
Dalhousie Art Gallery, gift of the Canada Council Art Bank, 2002
Photo: Steve Farmer

First published 2023
by Routledge
605 Third Avenue, New York, NY 10158

and by Routledge
4 Park Square, Milton Park, Abingdon, Oxon, OX14 4RN

Routledge is an imprint of the Taylor & Francis Group, an informa business

ISBN: 978-0-367-37167-8 (hbk)
ISBN: 978-0-367-37166-1 (pbk)
ISBN: 978-0-429-35296-6 (ebk)

DOI: 10.4324/9780429352966

Typeset in Bembo
by Newgen Publishing UK

Contents

Preface

> Are we to have a Primer of Canadian Literature, and a Primer of Australian? ... [T]hese things are not only absurd; they are also retarding.
>
> (Matthew Arnold, 1886 in response to recently published *Primer of American Literature*)

> A national literature is an essential element in the formation of a national character.
>
> (Rev. E.H. Dewart, *Selections from Canadian Poets*, 1867, 369)

> Do you speak your language?
> I stare—I just said: how are you?
> I thought English was my language
> apparently it isn't
> I thought Halkomelem was gibberish
> the devil's language
> that's what the nuns said
> apparently not
> Some white guy sets me straight:
> *Aboriginal people are losing languages*
> Funny, I thought I had it just a moment ago
> maybe it's in Gramma's old shoebox
> maybe it's sandwiched between papers
> in plastic bags hidden under mom's bed
> Hey, has anyone seen my language?
>
> (Lee Maracle from "Language," *Talking to the Diaspora*, 2015)

Poetry has the power both to reinforce and to disrupt the status quo. Each of the epigraphs above attests to this claim, albeit in substantially different ways. Taken together, the words of Matthew Arnold, Rev. E.H. Dewart, and Lee Maracle triangulate divergent ways in which literature—perhaps especially poetry—has been made central to discourses about country and "belonging" in Canada. Dewart, an Irish-born Canadian Methodist minister, editor, and author, stakes a claim for the constitutive potential of literature: for him it is *essential* to nation-building, and it comes with the attendant assumption that nation-building is a positively coded project. English poet and cultural critic Matthew Arnold also subscribes to the power of literature, but Arnold undermines the impetus towards organizing literature along with the development of new nations. Arnold's disdain demonstrates an assumed hierarchy: literature has power *if* and *when* the nation is perceived to have power. Finally, and potently, Stó:lō poet and writer Lee Maracle complicates these two competing claims. The Indigenous speaker's wry observations work from the lyric perspective. Enjambment layers self-reflection upon colonial imposition: for the poet's interlocutors, English isn't the speaker's language, nor is Halkomelem, which is both infantilized and demonized. Here, the lyric perspective situates the reader in relation to the Indigenous speaker; we listen to the speaker's incredulity. We witness as the speaker is set straight by "some white guy." We catalogue with the speaker where the lost language may be and, like the speaker, the reader is left looking over her shoulder. *Hey, has anyone seen my language?* Maracle's speaker requires the reader to either nod in recognition at the absurdity of the exchange or to dismiss it due to a misunderstanding or disagreement with the speaker. Either the reader comprehends the irony offered by the Indigenous speaker, or the reader remains bound to colonial logics. This, Maracle shows, is the power of poetry. Poetry invites the reader to consider how language is working to shape our thinking.

The cultural histories of poetry in Canada offer rich sites from which to think through belonging, nation, and other claims, perhaps especially in the relatively recent past of the twentieth and twenty-first centuries. Yet, there is no straight path we readers may trace to form any sense of "the" origins of poetry in Canada to the present moment. In Canada, a country with a colonial history that continues to influence and shape the present, the savvy reader might begin by asking what indeed is meant by "origins"? How do students, poets, and literary historians alike plot a beginning to poetry that calls itself "Canadian" on lands that have been home to different nations of Indigenous Peoples for thousands of years? Indeed, when poetic traditions accompany settler cultures, how can we pretend that a new locale represents an easy or obvious poetic break? What assumptions are made about literary value when a scholar places a date on a poet's work along with the designation of "first"? These are a few of the initial questions I ask you to think through with me in this *The Routledge Introduction to Twentieth- and Twenty-First-Century Canadian Poetry*. For, while it may seem strange at the outset to ask historical questions of a text whose task it is to plot out a more recent past, in Canada and in Canadian literary culture, questions of origins and of beginnings, as well as questions of perspective and place remain of crucial importance well into the twenty-first century.

A note on the notion of literary "origins" in this part of Turtle Island[1]

In his crucial pedagogical text, *Elements of Indigenous Style*, the late Gregory Younging puts it plainly: questions of "beginnings" and of "origins" are fraught in Canada. Canada is a country with a history of imperial imposition dominated by the logics of settler colonialism, and this settler-colonial history has tended to erase, efface, or displace the millennia-long presence of Indigenous Peoples, cultures, and histories on these lands. Literature offers a particularly rich place from which to encounter these complications in the present. As Younging suggests, on these lands now called Canada, writing was one of the initial ways Europeans described encounters with Indigenous Peoples. Those texts, many of which were revised for a general readership, informed social engagement, trade and commerce, and eventually state policy. Significantly, Younging underscores that early writing was *about* Indigenous Peoples and written *by* explorers, missionaries, anthropologists, in addition to literary writers. "Most of these writings," Younging tells us, "referred to Indigenous Peoples as an inferior, vanishing race—a description that is degrading and offensive to most Indigenous Peoples for obvious reasons, and inaccurate in ways that still escape some Canadian publishers and editors today" (8). Younging explains that while most of the texts and literature written about Indigenous Peoples provided "little insight into the cultural realities" of their diverse lives, their narratives were enormously influential in shaping settler perceptions of Indigenous Peoples as "primitive and underdeveloped" (8). Texts from the early writers who were explorers or were sent on settlement and "civilizing" missions are perhaps best categorized as presenting themselves as documentary or non-fiction writing. The texts of these writers, such as Jacques Cartier (1534), Samuel de Champlain (1604), the Jesuits (1611), and Samuel Hearne (1769), informed the literary tropes that are still present in a broader collection of literary texts.[2] While these persistent tropes sometimes get cast as "foundational" to Canadian cultural production, others are consistently expunged from literary-critical accounts that seek to name the "foundational." For example, as Mi'kmaq interdisciplinary artist and poet Michelle Sylliboy argues, poetics are inherent in the Komqwejwi'kasikl writing system of her ancestors, which has been in use for thirteen thousand years (1). Yet, these works have not been contemplated as originary or foundational literary texts in Canada. The settlers did not recognize them as such. Colonialism forcibly attempted to interrupt Indigenous poetics on these lands.

What gets taken up as literature worthy of serious thought, as well as what is demarcated as "poetry," is bound up in questions of value. Thus, when Dewart, an Irish-born settler clergyman, argues for the necessity of a national literature in the project of nation-building, we would do well to contemplate what is hailed into that "formative" gesture. Where does Dewart locate evidence of a burgeoning literary culture? Significantly, in *Selections from Canadian Poets* (1864), Dewart is looking only to the poetic production of settlers largely working in Anglo-American traditions. It is our job as readers and scholars to ponder this decision, just as it is our job to weigh the response of English poet Matthew Arnold. To speak of "origins" without taking account of the complexities of settler-colonial culture is to avoid this fact of history.

One of the goals of this book is to track *how* the idea and aspiration of "a national literature" has been taken up, disrupted, recapitulated, and/or rejected by poets in the twentieth and twenty-first centuries. Stó:lō writer Lee Maracle's statement about the complicated and fractious nature of language is clear: in countries with histories of colonialism, language is both a tool of oppression and a tool for freedom. Maracle's tongue-in-cheek critique of "some white guy" telling an Indigenous woman about her own history is both funny and searing. His remarks—that English is not her language, and that "Aboriginal people are losing their languages"—suggest that she, the Indigenous woman, is to blame for both her ignorance and her carelessness. Maracle renders the rhetorical gymnastics implicated in colonial narrative impulses to erase and reframe Indigenous presence as poetics. Published in a collection called *Talking to the Diaspora*, Maracle reminds readers that, unless they are Indigenous, all Canadians are part of the global diaspora. Her poetic assertion is both intervention and an act of refusal. Published in 2015, the same year that the Truth and Reconciliation Commission of Canada published its findings on systematic state violence against Indigenous Peoples, Maracle reminds all settlers that "Canada" is comprised of many nations. How does Indigenous nationhood and sovereignty work in relation to a call for "a national literature"? Maracle's collection marks a recent period in the history of Canada when Indigenous activism has been impossible to ignore. From the winter of 2012 when *Idle No More* introduced the performative and communal power of the Round Dance to what felt like every public square and mall in Canada; to the sustained public outcry following the acquittals of both Gerald Stanley and Raymond Cormier for the murders of Colton Boushie and Tina Fontaine; to the work of the Water Protectors from Shubenacadie to Unist'ot'en, Indigenous activists are on the front lines of justice issues, and poets are a central part of that justice work.

While actively eschewing a literary-critical impulse for origin stories and pointing to "foundational" narratives, it is also a challenge to characterize the aesthetic modes and prevailing zeitgeist of any given era, to say the least. And, in some ways, it is folly. Literary historians can look back and, with the help of archival material and close reading, make observations, projections, and even revelations about what the poets themselves were doing at a particular period of time, and speculate—sometimes with excellent resources and a good measure of surety—why poets were working through those modes. Books such as this one can reflect and project certain through lines and evolving conversations across communities, coteries, and contexts. But ultimately, the poems are always there and always have been, and what they *do* happens whether we are paying attention or not. A line break will not stop a war, for example, but it will be there on the page engaging with atrocity or subverting a prevailing mode of representation, and if we encounter it and give it time, it may well work on us.

One of the acrobatics of a book such as this one is to both demonstrate for readers that poetry does things, and that those things—many and various—have been happening for as long as poetry has happened. And, at the same time, any story of the poetic scene at a given time is only ever going to be partial. There are a great many anthologies of Canadian literature generally, and Canadian poetry specifically, and nearly all of these anthologies contain editorial introductions or prefaces which frame the aims of the specific anthology. Rather than try to reproduce many of the same stories of poetries in Canada, I instead attempt to add to the archive by offering additional angles, contexts, and poets. My hope is that, rather than be disappointed by the absence of some expected figures, readers instead catch the spirit of this text. My aim here is to demonstrate the fact of Canada's settler-colonial history, acknowledge that in some key moments literary culture has been and remains bound up in those histories, and to go from there.

Poetry *does* things. Poetry was a place from which complex and often paradoxical arguments about nation were staged leading up to and shortly after Canadian Confederation. Poetry was also a means for tracing wandering trajectories of poets who had to leave Canada to write and live elsewhere. Between the First World War and the Second World War, poetry was a tool for articulating a collective mode of action, for reflecting on asymmetrical power relations. Poetry was a place from which the shifting aesthetics and politics of modernism, transnationalism, and identity were explored. After the Second World War, poetry shifted alongside the changing conditions of modernity and what has come to be called post-modernity. Indeed, poetry continues to change alongside changing conditions. And all the time, Indigenous Poetics have persisted and endured attempts at erasure. Poetry is a means of intergenerational connection, a site of discursive engagement, and a place of experimentation. Poetry, we might conclude, like other modes of cultural production, is constantly in flux, always giving readers a sense or a snapshot of some of the prevailing preoccupations or perspectives of the poet in their context.

In this *The Routledge Introduction to Twentieth- and Twenty-First-Century Canadian Poetry*, I organize each chapter around key historical and cultural moments that affect poetic production and are reflected in poetry. Most chapters delineate a temporal era bounded by major political and social events. Of course, poets don't just write in single eras and the poetic practices of poets change across time too. In Chapter 5, I eschew the temporally bound framework followed by the other chapters to engage in a different kind of history of Indigenous Poetics that builds to our current moment that Younging recognizes (along with many others) as one in which Indigenous Peoples "are currently in a process of cultural reclamation and rejuvenation" (101). While I want to make clear and amplify the insistence that "Indigenous Literatures are their own canon and not a subgroup of CanLit," I include this chapter here to show the relationality (often a relation of disproportionate power relations) of settler-Canadian Poetics with Indigenous Poetics.

After providing readers with some historical and cultural inroads into the periods under consideration, I move to a collection of "Case Studies" to think through the context in specific poetic examples. The poets whose work I focus on in the case studies are not necessarily the most obvious choices. In some cases, they are poets whose work might be considered canonical or mainstream. In other words, there are case studies of poets whose work is regularly anthologized. There are also case studies of poets who may surprise some readers, especially those with an established knowledge of the field. The aim here is not to shock, but rather to expand discourse around and about poets writing poetry in Canada while constructing a text that does more than list poets publishing in each era. Rather, my use of a "Case Study" model rather than the compiling of a more generalized (and therefore attenuated) survey seeks to show a number or points through which changes happen in Canadian poetry. I eschew an impulse towards a substantively threadbare encyclopaedic consolidation across decades in favour of a relatively small number of useful examples rooted in context. For each era, subject, or poetic trajectory covered here, there are scholarly accounts available for further study. I encourage readers to search out those accounts.

Acknowledgements

Work on this book began shortly before the Covid-19 pandemic shut down the world. Suddenly, well-laid plans for library trips, stretches of quiet research and writing time, and space to read and think were gone. Instead, like many colleagues and students, I learned to "pivot" to online learning. Research hours were given over to learning how to make dynamic in-person lectures (which I had previously just thought of as "lectures") work in a recorded medium. Waking hours were given over to learning how to be an elementary school teacher for our child. Access to research libraries was restricted. Access to colleagues was limited to interfaces. My experience is not unique, not even in my household. Instead, my experience is simply the context for the text you are reading. Thank you to series editors Robert Lecker and Lorraine York whose support has been constant and steadfast throughout this process. It is a gift to be supported by colleagues in this way.

I could not have done this work without students—past, present, and future—and the hope that perhaps I would write something that would be useful for them. Kaarina Mikalson, Katrina Sellinger, Jacob Sandler, Sunjay Mathuria, Haylan Jackson, Tarini Fernando, Jane Boyes, Ella Ratz, Adrien Robertson, Marina Young, Paisley Coppieters, Trynne Delaney, Krysta Sero, Maya Schwartz, and Brennan McCracken: thanks to you, and to all the students. Special thanks to Katie Clarke and Jessica Hawkes for their invaluable RA work.

Thank you to colleagues and mentors near and far. Your work inspires me.

Thank goodness for the poets.

Thank you to Karen Smith of the Killam Library Special Collections who got me books even when the library was closed. Thank you to Peter Dykhuis and Sym Corrigan at the Dalhousie Art Gallery for making art magic, and thank you to Marlene Creates and her "Fire and Water, Nova Scotia (1985)," which makes the cover of this book.

Thank you to our record player and radio, and to Nina Simone, Ornette Coleman, Julia Nesrallah, and Tom Allen for sonic companionship.

Thank you to the humans of Espresso 46 who were my main source of social interaction for much of 2020–21.

Immeasurable, boundless, galactic thanks to my family. E for patience and learning why word count matters and always reminding me what matters more. Cricket the dog for showing up right on time. And B, for everything, always.

Notes

1 Turtle Island is the name many Algonquin and Iroquois peoples gave to North America. Many Indigenous Peoples have stories of the creation of Turtle Island, each with their own specificity and variation. Many of these stories are stories of creation. We are beginning this book by recognizing that what is now called Canada has been Turtle Island for millennia (*The Canadian Encyclopaedia*). There are many writers who talk about Turtle Island. See, for example, Leanne Betasamosake Simpson, *Dancing on Our Turtle's Back*.

2 The dates denote significant key moments of arrival and exploration.

Works Cited

Arnold, Matthew. *Essays in Criticism*. 1888. Ed. C.D. Warner. London: Kessinger, 2007.

Lighthall, William Douw. *Old Measures: Collected Verse*. Toronto: A.T. Chapman, 1922.

Logan, J.D., and Donald G. French. *Highways of Canadian Literature: a Synoptic Introduction to the Literary History of Canada (English) from 1760 to 1924*. Toronto: McClelland & Stewart, 1924.

Maracle, Lee. *Talking to the Diaspora*. Winnipeg: ARP, 2015.

Simpson, Leanne Betasamosake. *Dancing on Our Turtle's Back: Stories of Nishnaabeg Re-Creation, Resurgence, and a New Emergence*. Winnipeg: Arbiter Ring, 2011.

Sylliboy, Michelle. *Kiskajeyi — I am Ready: A Hermeneutic Exploration of Mi'kmaq Komqwejwi'kaskil Poetry*. Rebel Mountain Press, 2019.

The Canadian Encyclopedia. "Turtle Island." www.thecanadianencyclopedia.ca/en/article/turtle-island

Truth and Reconciliation Commission of Canada Interim Report. Winnipeg: Truth and Reconciliation Commission of Canada, 2012.

Younging, Gregory. *Elements of Indigenous Style*. Edmonton: Brush, 2018.

1 Emergent Patterns and Wandering Trajectories

In *A History of Canadian Literature*, W.H. New underscores how uniform descriptions of Canada and literatures called "Canadian" are both inaccurate and damaging. "Snow, North, Wilderness: these stereotypes of Canada suggest a fierce uniformity—but even from earliest times, such generalizations have been inaccurate. To read Canadian literature attentively," New cautions, "is to realize how diverse Canadian culture is" (1). New suggests that there is illusion everywhere in Canadian history, and those "images of continuity" are misleading (ibid.). Not only does the denotation of "literature in Canada" pose an issue—who gets to be a Canadian writer? What characteristics make a literature Canadian?—even the name of the country eludes definitive translations.[1] Thus, as the diverse and sometimes contradictory epigraphs that opened the Preface suggest, poetry in these lands now called Canada is bound to specific histories, cultures, and communities that deserve our attentiveness. Contextualizing the work of poets writing in and about Canada requires dexterity on the part of the reader. As readers and scholars, we would do well to trace intersecting histories, while at the same time, attending to the specific conditions of each lineage. Poetry is a complex and lush place from which to do this work.

There has been a tendency in anthologies and critical accounts of Canadian poetry for the editor or critic to turn to landscape metaphors or weather in an attempt to organize and categorize poetic production. This tendency emerges in the twentieth century with works such as *Headwaters of Canadian Literature* by Archibald MacMechan and *Highways of Canadian Literature* by J.D. Logan and Donald G. French, both published in 1924. Prior to this Romantic focus on nature, editors and critics categorized poetry in Canada in relation to the nation. In other words, it was Canadian poetry because poets were "building" a nation while "settling" and "setting" the cultural languages of that imaginary nation in metonymic ways onto a "new" geography.[2] Gone were the sixteenth- to eighteenth-century mercantile narratives of travel and exploration. These gave way to collecting and anthologizing the writing of emigrants and settlers. Stylistically, this signals a shift from translating the strange into the familiar, or the embellishment of documentary notes of adventure writing into something quite different. A.J.M. Smith plots the evolution of Canadian

DOI: 10.4324/9780429352966-1

poetry thus in the introduction to his 1960 edition of *The Oxford Book of Canadian Verse in English and French*:

> Canadian poetry .... Arose about a century and a quarter ago—after the hard work of hacking a new home out of the wilderness had been accomplished, and there was time to catch one's breath before the task of consolidation and unification began.
>
> (xxiii)

In addition to observing the tactics of settler colonialism—namely, the erasure of Indigenous presence that Younging and others flag—Smith outlines a caricature of the poet in transition. Poetry written in Canada prior to 1884 is, in the main, regarded by Smith and others as emergent at best. Critics describe early Canadian poets in terms of lack. Take, for example, the descriptors from George Woodcock, who describes the poets "to be at their best—which was often not very good—in larger poetic forms" (*Northern Spring*, 196). Critics note a kind of derivative quality of the poetry preceding Confederation; with few exceptions, poets of this period are seen as poorly attempting to reproduce the lyrical modes of Europe and the United Kingdom. In her *New Oxford Book of Canadian Verse in English* (1982), Margaret Atwood describes the poetic work of the early immigrant writers as "displaced persons who brought their language and preoccupations with them" (19). In Atwood's estimation,

> these poets, very early on, sound two notes that have sunk deeply into the Canadian poetic tradition; the elegiac, a mourning of homes left and things lost; and the satiric, a bitter account of dismal surrounding, both social and geographical.
>
> (ibid.)

Atwood, whose own *Journals of Susanna Moodie* renders her critique into historically engaged poetics, exemplifies and reproduces the prevailing critical opinion of the earliest settler poetry. Put another way, we might consider whether the critics themselves demonstrate an investment in a residual European form and, in turn, a resistance to that form's encounter with utterly new circumstances.

"Good Poetry": Poetic Circulation

The first poem that critics tend to agree is a "good" poem was written by a woman: 1884 marks the publication of Isabella Valancy Crawford's narrative long poem "Malcolm's Katie." Consistently recognized by critics as a significant shift in poetic production in the newly confederated Canada, "Malcolm's Katie" is both a love story and a nuanced perspective of nation-building that introduces the influence of expanding economic shifts. The poem's content maps nicely onto D.M.R. Bentley's perception of the ways that economic developments tell us something about the literary developments of the same period. He periodizes literature in Canada alongside economic development and offers the following "provisional economic coherences":

1 1659–1846: Foundation of the Hudson's Bay Company to the Repeal of the Corn Laws: Mercantilism/Imperialism Preferences.
2 1846–1936: Repeal of the Corn Laws to Reciprocal Trade Agreement (RTA) with United States Comes into Effect: Nationalism/Protectionism.
3 1936–1985: RTA in Effect to *Final Report* of the Macdonald Royal Commission Recommending Bilateral Free-Trade Agreement with the US: Increasing Canada-US Free Trade.
4 1985–present: Macdonald Royal Commission *Final Report* on North American Free-Trade Agreement (FTA, 1989), North American Free-Trade Agreement (NAFTA, 1993), World Trade Organization (WTO, 1995): Increasing Free-Trade with the US and Others/Internationalism.

(Bentley, "Reflections on the Situation" 23–4)

In each of these economic coherences, Bentley neatly demarcates significant shifts in Canada's relationship with global capital. The effect on literary development is evident. Note for example, as Bentley does, where Crawford's poem falls: "Malcolm's Katie" lands in "Coherence Two," where economic change suggests a corresponding attention to both commerce and the nation—a shift from "outside" mercantile forces to supposed "internal" economic forces. But these "internal" economic forces weren't "internal" at all. Rather, they were increasingly mobile and representative of an "open market." Of additional note is the tension between the opening up to a global market and the development of a national economic structure. The contradictions between internal and external forces are fascinating. Consider the following lines that introduce "smooth-coated men" into Crawford's narrative verse:

Then came smooth-coated men with eager eyes
And talked of steamers on the cliff-bound lakes,
And iron tracks across the prairie lands
And mills to crush the quartz of wealthy hills,
And mills to saw the great wide-armed trees,
And mills to grind the singing stream of grain
And with such busy clamour mingled still
The throbbing music of the bold, bright axe—
The steel tongue of the present and the wail
Of falling forests—voices of the past. (237–38)

Published less than two decades after Confederation, Crawford's poem describes a significant shift from subsistence and survival into development predicated on resource extraction and deforestation. Six lines in the excerpt above begin with an anaphoric conjunction—"And." This additive structure shifts the rhythm towards the loud and laborious work of industry. The contrast here is among the "wealthy hills," the "wide-armed" trees, the "singing stream," and the mills which crush, saw, and grind. Crawford piles descriptions of extractions on top of the wailing voices of falling forests. Past and present are personified through this human work of development for capital. Described by Carole Gerson as "our Emily Dickinson" ("Anthologies" 62), and as "politically progressive, even radical" by Katherine Sutherland (125), Crawford herself flags an important moment in poetic culture in Canada. So, rather than reproducing a retroactive aesthetic evaluation of Crawford's poems as the first "good" poem, I take it as important to the critical history of Canadian poetry, but want to shift the discourse of literary-critical assessment away from notions of the foundational or "first" *as well as* away from evaluative projections of quality. Crawford's poems, like the many I'll highlight throughout this book, are important precisely because they help signal shifts—from one thing to another—rather than origins or signposting of predetermined though ever-shifting markers of poetic excellence.

These shifts are important because, despite the work of Crawford and her contemporaries, Canadian poetry was not met with the same international enthusiasm as was the exploration and travel writing of the pre-Confederation period. This is perhaps not as simple as suggesting that the poetry itself did not circulate. Instead, recall Matthew Arnold's distain that opened the Preface. Here again "Canadianness" is a cultural marker that fails to circulate in literary culture. Indeed, the suggestion that there was national literary production from Canada was met with shock and derision by readers outside the new country. We see this in the incredulity of English poet Matthew Arnold's reaction to the publication of the *Primer of American Literature*: "Are we to have a Primer of Canadian Literature, and a Primer of Australian? … [T]hese things are not only absurd; they are also retarding." Here, what post-colonial theorists identify as the tension between the metropole and the colony is in sharp relief: a significant writer from the metropole—Arnold—is both derisive and expressing a multifaceted anxiety about literary production from the colony. Arnold cannot fathom the possibility of literary production that is specifically American, much less Canadian or Australian; he indicates real concern that such literature—should it exist at all—is bound to be detrimental. The suggestion he implies is that literature from a colony rather than the centre of Empire will always be lacking. And yet, two decades earlier in his introduction to one of the first anthologies of poetry from the newly confederated Canada, Reverend Dewart states the necessity of literature in validating the state, at least at an affective level. Dewart was hardly alone. In 1857, a decade before Confederation, Thomas D'Arcy McGee passionately argued for the role of literature in establishing a sense of national identity: "Come! Let us construct a national literature for Canada, neither British nor French nor Yankeeish, but the offspring and heir of the soil, borrowing lessons from all lands, but asserting its own title throughout all!" ("A National Literature for Canada," 1857). McGee, who historian Richard Gwyn has called "Canada's first nationalist," was passionately committed to the idea that a country needs a literary culture of its own to be recognized as such. In McGee's assertion, we encounter an early and abiding set of competing assumptions: primarily that "Canada" needed claiming and taming through literary production. Literary culture is yoked with a colonial project of settlement whose central goal is cultivating cultural legitimacy for the settlers and emigrants. McGee's exhortation has become naturalized into cultural policy in Canada in complex ways that continue to have a hand in how culture is supported, produced, and circulated. Scholars such as D.M.R. Bentley, Carole Gerson, Nick Mount, Daniel Coleman, Phanuel Antwi, Jennifer Blair, and Jade Ferguson have demonstrated the fallacy of a singular narrative of national identity tied to a linear understanding of literary production in Canada. And yet, as the words of Dewart and McGee suggest, and countless introductions to anthologies of Canadian literature confirm, there is both an impulse and a practice of doing just that: invoking such singular narratives. It would do us all a service to recognize this is a critical collation under the national heading and not a literary or poetic move. In other words, the projection of singularity is largely an impulse of critics, not an assertion generally made by poetic practitioners.

Contexts for Critical Consideration

With some literary-critical interrogations of an impulse towards the marking of "beginnings," let us think about how to encounter Canadian poetry in context. For the purposes of this book, "context" is a portmanteau that indicates both historical period and the cultural, regional, and material conditions from which the poet works. This text contends that there is use in contextualizing poetry in its time and place of production. Happily, there are some discernible patterns of continuity in poetic production in Canada that can be read through historical events. I outline them here and then develop them more fully below. What matters about these patterns, spread across different historical conditions, is that they continue to shape and influence the field of Canadian poetry. First, I want to focus on the pattern of non-Indigenous writers inventing pernicious tropes of Indigenous Peoples. Second, I want to outline a pattern aligned more closely with the project of settlement (as opposed to mercantile projects). Third, I employ two case studies to outline a pattern of "Wandering Trajectories" that shows the conditions of Canadian poetry outside the geographic space of Canada. Fourth, I end the chapter with a discussion of a pattern of consolidation best represented through anthologization.

Pattern One: Inventing Tropes of Indigenous Peoples

Gregory Younging points to the pernicious way in which non-Indigenous writers wrote about Indigenous Peoples. Moreover, as noted above, writings by explorers, missionaries, and early settlers about these lands are difficult to encounter *as literature*. The result, in many cases, is documentary writing that was revised for a general readership. As Cynthia Sugars and Laura Moss put it, much of the earliest exploration writing took the form of accounting lists that were then heavily edited for a European reading public. Readers in Europe were hungry for stories of travel and exploration. While explorers such as Jacques Cartier (1491–1557), Samuel de Champlain (1567?–1635), and Samuel Hearne (1745–92) were initially writing to document their explorations for their employers, they saw the opportunity to publish their writing. Usually, these wildly popular travel narratives were heavily edited for style and narrative arc. Sugars and Moss note that, often, these tactics of revision were undertaken in collaboration with the publishers who had a keen knowledge of the expectations and tastes of their literary markets (20). For example, book historian I.S. McLaren demonstrates that, in some of James Cook's stories about his engagements with the Nootka People, a ghost writer inserted fallacious passages about cannibalism that did not exist in Cook's original notes ("English" 36). Similarly, Sugars and Moss observe that, in the published version of Samuel Hearne's "Esquimaux Massacre," there are substantial differences from his journal notes which characterize the event. These differences, they explain, are significant: they introduce melodrama into the event. Indeed, even a short look at the published version demonstrates their claim. The narrative frames the clash between Inuit, Chipewyan, and Esquimaux Peoples as totally unprovoked and unexpected. "In a few seconds the horrible scene commenced; it was shocking beyond description; the poor unhappy victims were surprised in the midst of their sleep, and had neither time nor power to make any resistance," writes Hearne (73). Note the direction of his narrative: there is an assumption of shared feeling in the statement, "shocking beyond description." Here, Hearne suggests he and the reader understand one another. Moreover, the writer positions himself in a place of moral authority: while the "Indian barbarity" plays out around him, he will not lower himself to describe it and thus insult or shock the sensitivities of his reader. And then he goes on to describe in full, excruciating, figurative detail the death of a young woman:

> The shrieks and groans of the poor wretches were truly dreadful; and my horror was much increased at seeing a young girl, seemingly about eighteen years of age, killed so near me, that when the first spear was stuck into her side she fell down at my feet, and twisted found my legs, so that it was with difficulty that I could disengage myself from her dying grasps. As two Indian men pursued this unfortunate victim, I solicited very hard for her life; but the murderers made no reply till they had stuck both their spears through her body, and transfixed her to the ground.
>
> (qtd. in Sugars and Moss 72)

Sugars and Moss describe this scene as Gothic, noting both that it fits the popular literary style of the day and that it is wholly absent from Hearne's journals (72). I would add that, in addition to the Gothic qualities of this literary addition to a text claiming to be documentary, there are clear elements of Christian iconography. The young woman is stabbed in the side, as was the crucified Christ. Hearne's use of the term "wretch" underscores the religiously inflected prose: used to imply exile and misery, the term shows up often in relation to those needing salvation (*OED*). When I have brought this text to students, they have routinely noted the ways in which perspective and elevation tell a story too: the young woman wraps herself around Hearne, hoping to be granted refuge. Hearne positions himself as postulate, begging for her life and, while he is unsuccessful, the trope of the White Saviour is difficult to ignore. As Younging reminds us, writing such as Hearne's fundamentally contributed to the pernicious tropes of Indigenous Peoples that persist well into the twenty-first century. In the twenty-first century, after the findings of the Truth and Reconciliation Commission, it is imperative that scholars are attentive to the ways in which these representations emerge, circulate, and persist. For, while these examples are clearly not poetic *per se*, they do the work of developing what we refer to as *lyric perspective*. Crucially, these early writers develop lyric perspective that privileges the viewpoints, tastes, and expectations of a European readership.

Pattern Two: Projects of Settlement

The second pattern of poetic production hinges on the first: early poetic work by explorers and mercantile agents is, on the whole, concerned with arrival and what has been left behind. The second pattern is more concerned with settlement: a shift in colonial development *and* international attention to this place and the work of the people in it. It is, in other words, poetry bound up in the project of settlement. This is especially evident and exemplary in the work of Oliver Goldsmith in his poem "The Rising Village" (1834). Goldsmith, who was born in St. Andrews, New Brunswick, sets his optimistic account of settlement, the clearing and "taming" of the natural world, and the rise of industry in heroic couplets. The poem celebrates the successes of settlement in the Maritimes and is in direct response to the melancholic lament of rural towns in England in "The Deserted Village," which was written in 1770 by the poet's granduncle and namesake, the Anglo-Irish Oliver Goldsmith. Whereas Goldsmith senior's poem ends with the dispossession and forced migration of rural dwellers in the United Kingdom, Goldsmith junior pens a veritable "the kids are alright" poem that mimics both form and content, albeit inverted to celebrate progress. Consider these lines from the end of the poem:

> Then blest Acadia! Ever may thy name,
> Like hers, be graven on the rolls of fame
> ...
> So may thy years increase, thy glories rise,
> To be the wonder of the Western skies;
> And bliss and peace encircle all they shore,
> Till empires rise and sink, on earth, no more.
> (Goldsmith, lines 547–8, 557–60)

After plotting the agrarian and then mercantile development of the village, Goldsmith closes the poem with a reference to "Happy Britannia" (line 529) and settles on the future of the new colonial village, "blest Acadia" (547). Britannia may fade, but Acadia's "glories rise" well beyond the "rise and sink" of empires. Even in this brief excerpt, we see what Daniel Coleman refers to as evidence of muscular Protestantism, a component of *white civility* by which narratives of capitalist progress are imbued with elements of Christian doctrine and methodology.

Pattern Three: Wandering Trajectories

The third pattern of poetic production is where the poetry under examination in this volume begins in earnest: where poets of the long Confederation period develop what I call wandering trajectories. At the beginning of the long period of Confederation in 1867, the make-up of Canada was limited to the British colonies of Upper and Lower Canada (present-day Ontario and Quebec), Nova Scotia, and New Brunswick. Confederation was not so much an event as a longer process that relied on expanding conceptualization of affinity through the swaying of political allegiances as well as of emotions. After exploration, after colonial settlement and expansion, there were genuine concerns about the development and expansion of a uniquely "Canadian" culture alongside the expansion of the newly formed state. As Gina Starblanket and Dallas Hunt point out, the desire for a Canadian culture is coded as an expansionist white culture that overwrites the existing myriad of Indigenous cultures on these lands. So, while political personalities such as McGee were championing the need for a national literature through expansionist rhetoric, they were also however tacitly (and more often than not, deliberately) championing a narrow and restrictive view of what counts as literature, and whose work—poetic or otherwise—was or *is* valuable. Indeed, as poet, historian, and pedagogue Afua Cooper has shown, the development of a Canadian narrative of Confederation is also built on anti-Black racism.[3] Canonical literary histories of Canada and the inheritors of those traditions thus rarely acknowledge the poetic production of Black writers in Canada.

The descriptor of "wandering trajectories" works on several levels at once, then. It marks a departure from the prevailing stories told about the poets who tend to be grouped together as the "Poets of Confederation." These poets have been hailed by literary critics and historians as writing *place*—namely, writing the idea of Canada generally and rural specificities of the eastern provinces more particularly. In other words, these poets have come to stand in as signifiers of an emergent sense of "Canadianness" while projecting tropes of Romantic "return" to spaces only newly incorporated into a "national" vision. In canonical poems such as "Low Tide at Grand Pré" and "Tantramar Revisited," there is an attentiveness to regional specificity in which the return gets retroactively read as a return to a *Canadian* space, when the poetic time is that of a pre-Confederation geopolitics that, when coupled with lyric soundness, forges an international readership. Ironically, the claims made by early anthologists and writers working in a mode similar to that of Sir Philip Sidney's in his *Defense of Poesy* (1578) such as Dewart and McGee do not always take into account the material conditions of the writers.[4] The irony at work in the critical amnesia is this: much of the poetry that has been hailed for signalling a mature national literature in Canada through site-specific "return" poetry required, first, that the poets go elsewhere. Poets such as Bliss Carman, Charles G.D. Roberts, and a host of others left Canada for the United States and the United Kingdom in order to both write and, crucially, be paid enough to write again. Specifically, taking cues from the work of scholars such as Nick Mount in *When Canadian Literature Moved to New York*, we consider the work of these poets in dislocation from the retro-active constructions of "the nation."

Case Study: Sir Charles G.D. Roberts, Bliss Carman, and Wandering Trajectories

One of the earliest critical accounts of Canadian literature that attempts to differentiate what is happening in Canada from what is being produced *elsewhere*—namely the United States and England—is Archibald MacMechan's *The Headwaters of Canadian Literature*. Published in Toronto in 1924, it exemplifies the Romantic focus on nature as an organizing principle for literary critics and anthologists at a time when, outside of Canada, such organizing principles are abandoned in favour of engagements with emergent modernist practices. Indeed, as the title suggests, he selects an aquatic descriptor for his anthology; *headwaters* are the source of a river, the place from which all water for the river begins. Water, specifically the source for a river's power and flow, is central to MacMechan's retrospective characterization of the peoples of Canada. He describes Canadians as "forest-felling, railway-building, plowing, sowing, reaping, butter-and-cheese making people" who care about laws, church, and debt repayment. Here, in this description, we see MacMechan's focus on the shift from what Bentley identified as a mercantile era of non-settlers to the emergence of a domestic capitalism as an organizing force. In MacMechan's hands, when fused with his veneration of the natural world, we see an early example of how a critic can retroactively *forge* an image of a nation and the literatures being written in it that stands in tension with what the writers, and indeed peoples, may actually be doing, feeling, and creating. The poets are doing what they will do, but the critics may well be working to create an image of the nation that is homogenous and deeply invested in a Romantic relationship to the natural world.

With this tension in mind, let us turn, with MacMechan, to Sir Charles G.D. Roberts. Born and educated in New Brunswick, Roberts became known as the "Father of Canadian Poetry."[5] Yet, as he himself wrote, "I did my literary work in New York, where my market was."[6] How does the Father of Canadian poetry hold this title while spending most of his life, including his writing career, elsewhere? And, importantly for our purposes here, how does his poetry fit with Bentley's coherences? In other words, is it possible to read the "Father of Canadian Poetry" *and* his poems onto the developing critical narratives of nation? Let us see.

"Tantramar Revisited" is perhaps Roberts's most infamous poem, and thus as good a place as any to begin our consideration. Written when he was 23 years old, the poem was reprinted and anthologized multiple times in Roberts's life.[7] The poem is composed in elegiac stanzas, as the poem's speaker reflects on the views of the Tantramar Marshes of his youth. For readers unfamiliar with the marshland that stretches on either side of the border of Nova Scotia and New Brunswick, the imagery is rich and evocative. Indeed, Roberts erases the provincial borders in favour of vivid description of the slant of light at golden hour, reaching across red mud and golden and brown grasses; Roberts renders the landscape clearly. The poem is laden with descriptive language that is surprisingly musical; this is part of the function of the elegiac stanza. Comprised of quatrains in alternating iambic pentameter, the traditional elegiac stanza aims to elevate, mourn, and memorialize a lost person. Roberts instead memorializes his own youth and does so in a setting that would be unfamiliar to all but a handful of readers who may or may not know of the waves of colonial history in the place from which the speaker sits and reflects. In "Tantramar Revisited," Roberts draws on a formula that a literary predecessor, Oliver Goldsmith, employs nearly a half century prior: he uses a poetic form imported from the "Old World" to write about the land and cultures in Canada. The differences between Goldsmith's and Roberts's poems are important. First, Roberts's poem is technically stronger. It not only uses the elegiac stanza, but it also innovates upon it introducing hexameter and pentameter lines—and to good effect. Elise Pomeroy writes of Roberts's technical success based on his metrical skill, noting that "rarely has this elegiac measure so popular with Ovid, been used in English" (406). The intense emotion recollected in a moment of tranquillity, that hallmark of the Romantic lyric advocated by Wordsworth in the *Preface* of the *Lyrical Ballads*, is central to the poem's nostalgic weight. Roberts's literary education was steeped in the works of "Shelley, Keats, and Tennyson," as critics such as MacMechan observe. It is both unsurprising and perhaps even expected that a young writer such as Roberts would aim to emulate the works he was reading in his own writing. As Fred Cogswell notes, in his introduction to *The Collected Works of Sir Charles G.D. Roberts*, his rise to recognition in both Canada and abroad were due in part to the quality of his work and, significantly, to the "fact that influences akin to those which shaped his work were abroad in society and reinforced one another" (xix). Put simply, Roberts's poetry was *recognizably* good; it emulated the formal conventions of European and American poetry, and these two things taken alongside his willingness to relocate at different times to a different literary scene with more opportunity and more readers helped create the "Father of Canadian Poetry." What is surprising, then, is the way in which anthologists and later critics frame Roberts's career and influence through the prism of a handful of poems written in a particular span of time and covering a few key themes. This trend of critical focus can be seen in the work of Roberts's contemporary and cousin, Bliss Carman.

"They laid Bliss Carman in his grave, and Canadian Literature began almost immediately" (Mount 1). So begins Nick Mount's overview of the late-nineteenth and early-twentieth centuries in Canadian literary and cultural development. Mount's evocative claim is less tongue in cheek than one might expect. As he goes on to demonstrate in great detail, the period directly following Confederation in Canada was a paradoxical one shaped, in no small part, by a mass exodus of people. This exodus was significant in both numbers and effects. Mount observes that more than a million people left Canada for the United States during this period, making it the largest emigration in Canadian history to date (6). Among those million people leaving was a significant number of writers. They left Canada because, despite promises of a good life and prosperous future, there were virtually no domestic publication venues and a seemingly equal dearth in domestic readership. Jackson Lears explains the predicament for writers in Canada as a problem of both demand and taste (30). There were, however, many bookstores which, in his estimation, suggest a prevailing desire for writers and reading material from elsewhere. "Post-Confederation Canada was a consumer culture," he notes, "and American culture was mostly what it consumed" (30). Though you wouldn't know it from the consistent anthologizing of a few poems, the working lives of these early poets were focused elsewhere.

In 1867, the same year of Confederation, Thomas D'Arcy McGee lamented that intellectuals in Canada were being influenced predominantly by "Boston books and Boston utterances" (30). While it was New Canaan, Connecticut, and not ultimately Boston where Bliss Carman made his long-time home, McGee's complaint is telling. This period in history was a moment of looking elsewhere. People in Europe had their eyes on Canada as a kind of promised land for starting life anew. For example, reading political cartoons of the period from outside of Canada can be incredibly informative about the competing narratives that rationalize settlement on lands of Indigenous Peoples, the emergent and trenchant modes of racism being imported, and the hopes versus the realities in this new place for many settlers. Just as peoples outside of Canada were looking to Canada as a place of opportunity, so too were people in Canada looking elsewhere, Bliss Carman among them.

Bliss Carman was born in Fredericton, New Brunswick in 1861. After attending the University of New Brunswick, spending time at both Oxford and the University of Edinburgh, and attending Harvard University where he met American poet and his long-time collaborator Richard Hovey, Carman remained in America for the whole of his literary career. The logic behind this decision was in great part economic. Carman was not able to secure stable employment in Boston, so he moved to New York City, where he worked for a time as the literary editor of the *New York Independent* and freelanced for various other publications. While his debut poetry collection was not a commercial success—there was no publisher in Canada that would take it, and the American publisher went bankrupt—Carman's lyricism was hailed as a significant contribution. Indeed, critic Desmond Pacey suggests that "Low Tide on Grand Pré" is the "most nearly perfect single poem to come out of Canada" (65), while Tracy Ware sees the eponymous collection as progressive and demonstrative of Carman's "striking variety of lyric stances" (38). Tom Marshall suggests that "Low Tide on Grand Pré" is a fine example of a return poem working in the style of William Wordsworth's "Tintern Abbey," as well as his cousin Roberts's "The Tantramar Revisited," and that these two return poems develop a modern tradition of the return that can be found in works such as John Glassco's "Luce's Notch" and Al Purdy's "The Country North of Belleville" (21). There's no doubt that "Low Tide on Grand Pré" has contributed to a growing tradition of the return poem, nor is there much room to criticize the poem formally. Like Roberts, Carman is adept with lineation and figurative language. What is worth noting, especially as we trace the tensions between what the poets are doing and the ways in which critics and anthologists categorize what they are doing, is that "Low Tide on Grand Pré" has little to do with nation-building.

The poem opens with the speaker reflecting on the setting sun and the tidal flows of the Bay of Fundy. The land itself, cut through by "a grievous stream," activates a sense of homesickness. The speaker personifies the stream, which "goes wandering, as if to know/Why one beloved face should be/So long from home and Acadie." There is a shift from the solitary reflection of the lyric subject, and the singular reflection expands to include another: "Was it a year or lives ago/We took the grasses in our hands," the speaker wonders. From this point, the poem centres on memory that is grounded in a specific landscape. Days, years, near-lifetimes are hinged to the speaker's nostalgia that is deeply rooted in place. So deeply connected is the poem to place that the speaker ties time to tides. In the final stanza, time and tides are anchored by the stanzaic repetition of "home":

> The night has fallen, and the tide ...
> Now and again comes drifting home,
> Across these aching barrens wide,
> A sigh like driven wind or foam:
> In grief the flood is bursting home. (46–50)

The interlocking rhyme scheme of the stanzas creates a feedback loop—a kind of Mobius strip of reflection—in which time, place, and experience are aquatic and in flux. Written in 1886 during his tenure at Harvard University and published a year later in the American *Atlantic Monthly*, "Low Tide on Grand Pré" may well be the product of an expatriate reflection on home. It is difficult, however, to see this poem as central to a nation-building project, especially when the poet had just begun what would be a peripatetic period of his life in America.

While anthologists have tended to group Carman and Roberts into the categorization of "Poets of the Confederation," it is important to underscore that this demarcation was retroactive. As D.M.R. Bentley notes in *The Confederation Group of Poets, 1880–1897*, the origin of the term came from William Douw Lighthall. In *Old Measures: Collected Verse*, published in 1922, Lighthall dedicated the book "To the Poets of the Confederation, My Friends and Companions." Bentley observes that, "at the heart, the idea of the long Confederation period is an argument for a greater sense of continuity in Canadian literary studies than has frequently been the case" (27).

While Carman is now hailed as a lyric poet whose innovations are more clearly evident in his later works, such as his collected *Poems* (1904, 2 vols.) and *Sappho* (1905), it has not always been thus. In his lifetime, Carman's first collection of poetry, which contained the poem of the same name, *Low Tide on Grand Pré* was a commercial flop, while his enthusiastic verses written in collaboration with Hovey under variations on the *Vagabondia* title were enormously popular. It is curious (and perhaps indicative of a developing tension between poetic production and critical anthologizing and framing in the Canadian context) that Carman's poetic development as a lyric poet focused on musicality, evocation, and voice continued over the course of his career. Critics sketch a different trajectory. As early as 1924, before Carman's death, Archibald MacMechan describes Carman as the heart of Canadian poetry when "one of his lyrics was included in *The Oxford Book of Verse*." However, in stark contrast with later critical framing of Carman and his work, MacMechan writes, "frankly, his later work became vague and affected. His tendency to be formless became confirmed; and much of his later verse seems purely experimental" (126–7). In plotting the developments and trends of Canadian poetry, Carman may stand not only as a performing effigy, but also as a signal of emergent critical fissures between traditional and experimental poetic productions.

Pattern Four: The Work of Poetry Anthologies

With Roberts and Carman, we begin to see that the work of retrospective critical accounts and anthologizing continues to play a significant role in narratives of Canadian poetry. The book you are reading is decidedly not an anthology of twentieth- and twenty-first-century Canadian poetry. You can't encounter much actual poetry here, in this book. But the vast majority of contemporary readers' encounters with historical poetry *do* occur through reading anthologies and therefore anthologies have much to tell us about the history of how poetry in Canada gets framed and distributed. Indeed, it may seem strange at first to give time and space to the work of anthologies and anthologists rather than keep a focus on poetry and poets. But anthologies have much to teach us about the ways in which poetry circulates in scholarly and public life. What choices are made? What stories are told? What stories are continually *re*-told? What selections turn into mythologies? Examining anthologies, as critics such as Robert Lecker and Carol Gerson have shown, goes some way in offering answers to these questions among others.[8] It is worth, then, looking at the way one anthologist (and poet) produced a critical assessment of anthologies of Canadian poetry available in the mid-twentieth century.

In 1942, A.J.M. Smith wrote an article for the *University of Toronto Quarterly* entitled "Canadian Anthologies, New and Old." Precipitated by Ralph Gustafson's *Anthology of Canadian Poetry (English)* published by Penguin Books in 1942, Smith's survey review is a fantastic historical site from which to consider the role of critics and editors in cultivating what gets circulated and who gets highlighted as a Canadian poet of note. In the review, Smith sets out not only to assess anthologies of Canadian Poetry, but also to evaluate them in terms of scope and focus. His often wry and regularly acerbic assessment is this: the anthologies published prior to the 1940s have played a central role in the creation and circulation of ideas about poetry in Canada and—perhaps more significantly—of what count as Canadian values. Smith is referring here not just to poetic values of craft, but also quite literally to what and who counts as Canadian. What represent Canada to Canadian readers? And, how is this best represented in verse? What's interesting here, for our purposes, is Smith's focus on the tension between the poetry in many of these anthologies (not much of it is "good" poetry in his opinion), and the anthologists' desires to construct specific images, representations, and values of Canada *as a nation*.

Smith's range in his survey is from 1864 to 1942, and while the central focus of this book is on the twentieth and twenty-first centuries, it is vital to pay attention to this preceding era, because here is where the notion of aesthetic value and nation are firmly yoked together. Smith notes that the majority of anthologies are aimed at educational purposes and school curriculums, noting "one of the most useful functions of an anthology is to introduce the work of young or unknown writers or to present new developments in technique and feeling" (458). The problem is, for Smith, not with these smaller more focused anthologies. Rather, Smith is concerned with "big general anthologies" (ibid.). The first of these "big general anthologies" that Smith considers is Dewart's, which acts as a kind of litmus for the issues that concern Smith. Specifically, Smith looks for instances where anthologists reflect on tensions between the developing nation and the circulation and reception of poetry written by Canadian poets. Dewart's anthology presents a student reader with biographical and critical information about the literature of the early-nineteenth century as well as offering an insightful assessment of problems "faced by the Canadian poet—problems that do not seem to have been solved, but to have been intensified by the development of the nation" (460). Dewart posits that while the soon-to-be new nation was unparalleled in "making equal pretensions to intelligence and progress," the poetry written by poets in Canada is met with equally unparalleled indifference. Fast forward to 1942, writes Smith, and we are met with the same issue. Turning to E.K. Brown's editorial introduction to the (1941) issue of the American journal *Poetry* which focused on Canadian work, Smith recapitulates Brown's suggestion that "even within the national borders the impact of Canadian literature has been relatively superficial"

(460). This sentiment will be echoed in 1972 by Margaret Atwood in *Survival: A Thematic Guide to Canadian Literature*. But we are getting ahead of ourselves. Referring to Dewart's assertion that opens this chapter, Smith notes Dewart's fundamental belief that "a national literature is fundamental to the formation of a national character" (459). Recalling that the Canadian nation is one built on settler colonialism should give us serious pause when reading this statement. For, what Dewart's claim underscores is the foundational connection between bringing discrete texts together under the heading of "a national literature" and the formation of a prevailing idea of "the nation." Again, we should be asking some serious questions about how those discrete texts are brought together.

With the publication of Lighthall's *Songs of the Great Dominion*, Smith clocks a marked shift. In this collection, the anthologist notes that confidence and enthusiasm are central to the poetry collected, and that these two feelings are connected to nationalism and imperialism (462). Lighthall goes so far as to personify Canada as the perfect Daughter of Empire, "she is full-grown of the family—the first one to come of age and gone into life as a nation" (462). The shift here is important: between the pre- and post-Confederation period, anthologists and editors begin to frame, evaluate, and *gather* poetry in Canada in relation to its adherence to and representation of an emergent and strident sense of national identity. This trend continues with Rand's *A Treasury of Canadian Verse* (1900), wherein he describes tendencies in Canadian poetry towards exhibiting "a glowing devotion to native land and a loyal and loving reverence for our gracious Sovereign" (465). Rand, Smith reminds us, makes a point to tell readers that he was "a Canadian by birth as were my father and his father, my mother and her mother" (465). For readers in the twenty-first century, an increased sense of clarity should emerge: in developing a "national literature," many editors and anthologists imposed not only their subjective literary analysis but also worked to develop a homogenous sense of "Canadianness." Take, for example, this claim made by William Wilfred Campbell's *Oxford Book of Canadian Verse* (1913): "only he who has been closely associated with a country from early childhood, and has spent all the years of his youth and maturity within its borders, can fitly interpret its life and dramatize its problems" (467). It would be extremely interesting to hear what Lee Maracle's Halkomelem speaker would have to say in response to Campbell's claims.

If the work of anthologies is, ideally, to present both craft and context, and if all anthologies bear the complicated tensions of those two things, then where is the ideal anthology? Who is the ideal anthologist? Smith draws his assessment to the following conclusion—the ideal anthologist does not exist:

> The ideal anthologist is a paragon of tact and learning. In him an impeccable taste is combined with a completeness and accuracy of information that is colossal. To an understanding of historical development and social upheaval he adds a sensitiveness to the finest nuances of poetic feeling. He is unprejudiced, impersonable, humble, self-confident,

> catholic, fastidious, original, traditional, adventurous, sympathetic, and ruthless. He has no special ax to grind. He is afraid of mediocrity and the verses of his friends. He does not exist. (474)

Smith's assessment is reasonable, especially when the reader labours to open the limitations in his language. The use of an anthology, for our purposes, is significant and will be worth returning to and thinking about in the context of each chapter's focus: how have the intersecting contexts of history, subjectivity, and colonialism shaped how and who is read as a "Canadian poet"?

In his significant introduction to his own (1960) edition of *The Oxford Book of Canadian Verse*, A.J.M. Smith differentiated between what he terms "native" and "cosmopolitan" writers. Poets grouped in the "native" category, sometimes also referred to as "national," are those who "sought to discover something distinctly and essentially 'Canadian' and thus come to terms with what was new in the natural, social, and political environment in which they found themselves, or which they helped to create" (xxiv). The second group of writers, the "cosmopolitans," were making efforts to "escape the limits of provincialism of colonialism by entering into the universal civilizing culture of ideas" (xxv). To a reader of the twenty-first century, the problems with these categories are, I suspect, stark. What is "essentially Canadian" but settler colonialism? And what is unsurprising—or even negative—about poets working to locate themselves in the landscapes and politics of the colonial project, if for no other reason than to locate and mark their experiences, observations, and imaginings in verse? What does it mean to "escape colonialism" and who is able to do this? In Smith's estimation, as we have already seen, the shift from the "backwoods poet" whose lot is to deal in a realist fashion with what is right at hand occurs with the so-called Confederation poets. And, as we have also seen, at least two of these poets—Carmen and Roberts—were retroactively harnessed in the service of building a consolidated projection of literary nationalism. As we shall see, critics were less able (or willing) to make attempts at consolidating poetic production of the interwar years into literary nationalism in the same way that they did with the grouping of the Confederation Poets.

Key Terms for Preface and Introduction

Anthology: A collection of literary texts that have been selected and organized by an editor.

Confederation: In Canada, Confederation is the process of federal union in which the British North American colonies Nova Scotia, New Brunswick, and Quebec and Ontario joined together forming the Dominion of Canada. This occurred on July 1, 1867.

Lyric poetry: At its most fundamental, lyric poetry refers to a poem that has a speaker and can express emotions and feelings. The form has roots in Ancient Greece, where lines were set to the music of a lyre. In the Romantic period, lyric poetry was revolutionized by poets such as William Wordsworth who, in his 'Preface' to the *Lyrical Ballads*, reflected that lyric poetry can draw on common experiences and use common language.

Poets of the Confederation: A portmanteau which refers to Sir Charles G.D. Roberts, Bliss Carman, Archibald Lampman, and Duncan Campbell Scott, among others.

Settler/settler colonialism: Settler colonialism is an ongoing system of power that oppresses Indigenous Peoples through violence that get normalized such as the dispossession of lands, genocidal practices, and the normalization of ongoing repression or destruction of Indigenous Peoples and cultures. Scholars differentiate settler colonialism from colonialism insofar as settler colonials come to stay, whereas colonials come to exploit peoples and resources for a period of time. See for example Cox, Wolfe, Veracini.

Turtle Island: For some Indigenous Peoples, this refers to the continent of North America. Though each individual story is unique, the general common thread is that of a turtle who holds the world on its back.

Truth and Reconciliation Commission: As a part of the Indian Residential Schools Settlement Agreement (2007) the Truth and Reconciliation Commission of Canada was established to facilitate reconciliation among survivors, their families, and Canadians. The TRC travelled across Canada for six years and heard from more than 6500 witnesses, hosted seven national events to engage and educate people about the history and legacy of the residential school system. In June of 2015, the TRC presented its report on the findings as well as 94 calls to action for reconciliation between Canadians and Indigenous Peoples (Truth and Reconciliation Commission of Canada, npag).

Notes

1 New's catalogue is as follows:

> Canada … has variously been taken as the Spanish word for "nothing here" *(a ca nada)*, the Portuguese word for "narrow road," the Montagnais Cree for "clean land," the Mohawk work for "castle" *(canadaghi)* and a word meaning "the mouth of the country" or "hunting land" or "province." The people of the North Shore of the St Lawrence, wrote François de Belleforest (1530-83) in 1575 were "Canadeen." The most common contemporary view accepts the early observation of Jacques Cartier (1491–1557): that the Iroquois referred to their "village" as *ka-na-ta*, the Hurons as *an-da-ta*. Some of these interpretations indicate guesswork and simple ignorance; a few reflect the strange cringe that betrays an embarrassment at colonial origins. Some hint at determination to locate European connections; some suggest a desire for a romantic history or a desperate need to fix a certainty. Some seem ironic. Some are undoubtedly wrong.
>
> (2–3)

2 There are notable exceptions to this statement. In *The Book of Canadian Poetry*, A.J.M. Smith posits a dichotomy between those Canadian poets who "concentrated on what is individual and unique in Canadian life," and those who have commented on "what it has in common with life everywhere" (1943). More recently, critics such as Carmine Starnino claim, "any poetry intending to make a case for its importance beyond its own borders needs to show some ability to

travel" (*A Lover's Quarrel*, 2004). Nick Mount's *When Canadian Literature Moved to New York* details the fallaciousness of the claim that Canadian writers wrote about or, for that matter, in Canada.

3 See Cooper in both *The Hanging of Angelique* (2007) and *Report on Lord Dalhousie's History on Slavery and Race* (2019).

4 Sir Philip Sidney (1554–86) was an English courtier, soldier, diplomat and writer. He is, among other things, the author of *The Defense of Poesy* which is a spirited and thorough treatise arguing for the necessity of poetry as a means of drawing readers "to as high as a perfection as our degenerate soul, made worse by their clayey lodgings, can be capable of" (n.pag).

5 References to Roberts as the "Father of Canadian Poetry" abound. See D.M.R. Bentley.

6 Qtd. in Mount (136).

7 Published first as "Westmoreland Revisited" in *The Week* (December 1883), the poem was republished in *In Divers Tones*, 1886; *Songs of the Great Dominion*, 1889; *Canadian Poems and Lays*, 1893; *Poems*, 1901/17; *Oxford Book of Canadian Verse*, 1913; *Our Canadian Literature*, 1934; *Selected Poems*, 1936; *Telegraph Journal*, July 1937; *A Book of Canadian Poetry*, 1943/48 to list but a few in Roberts's own lifetime. (*The Collected Works of Sir Charles G.D. Roberts*, 406.)

8 See the work of Lecker's *Keepers of the Code: English-Canadian Literary Anthologies and the Representation of Nation*; Gerson's "Anthologies and the Canon of Early Canadian Women Writers," *History of the Book in Canada* and *Canadian Women in Print, 1750–1918*; Kamboureli and Irvine's *Editing as Cultural Practice in Canada*; Lent, Vautour, and Irvine's *Making Canada New: Editing, Modernism, and New Media.*

Works Cited

Antwi, Phanuel. *Hidden Signs, Haunting Shadows: Literary Currencies of Blackness in Upper Canadian Texts*. Phd dissertation. McMaster University, 2011.

Arnold, Matthew. *Essays in Criticism*. 1888. Ed. C.D. Warner. London: Kessinger, 2007.

Atwood, Margaret. *Journals of Susanna Moodie*. Toronto: OUP, 1970.

———. *Survival: A Thematic Guide to Canadian Literature*. Toronto: Anansi, 1972.

———. *The New Oxford Book of Canadian Verse in English*. Toronto: OUP, 1982.

Bentley, D.M.R. *The Confederation Group of Poets, 1880–1897*. Toronto: UTP, 2004.

———. "Reflections on the Situation and Study of Early Canadian Literature in the Long Confederation Period." *Home Ground and Foreign Territory: Essays on Early Canadian Literature*. Ed. Janice Fiamengo. Ottawa: UOP, 2014. 17–45.

Blair, Jennifer, Daniel Coleman, Kate Higginson, and Lorraine York, eds. *ReCalling Early Canada: Reading the Political in Literary and Cultural Production*. Waterloo: WLUP, 2005.

Brown, E.K. "The Development of Poetry in Canada, 1880–1940." *Poetry: A Magazine of Verse* (April 1941): 34–47.

Campbell, William Wilfred. *Oxford Book of Canadian Verse*. Oxford: Oxford UP, 1913.

Carman, Bliss. "The Mother of Poets." *More Songs from Vagabondia. Bliss Carman and Richard Hovey*. Boston, MA: Small, Maynard, & Co., 1896. 12–14.

———. *Sappho: One Hundred Lyrics*. Boston, MA: L.C. Page, 1904.

Cogswell, Fred. "Introduction." *The Collected Works of Sir Charles G.D. Roberts*. Eds. Desmond Pacey and Graham Clevearn Adams. Ann Arbour, MI: Wombat Press, 1985. xix–xxxii.

Coleman, Daniel. *White Civility: The Literary Project of English Canada.* Toronto: UTP, 2006.

Cooper, Afua. 2007. *The Hanging of Angélique: The Untold Story of Canadian Slavery and the Burning of Old Montréal.* Athens: University of Georgia Press.

——— et al. *Report on Lord Dalhousie's History on Slavery and Race.* September 2019. https://cdn.dal.ca/content/dam/dalhousie/pdf/dept/ldp/Lord%20Dal%20Panel%20Final%20Report_web.pdf

Cox, Alicia. "Settler Colonialism." *Oxford Bibliographies.* Online. www.oxfordbibliographies.com, Last modified: July 26, 2017. DOI:10.1093/OBO/97801902219911-0029

Crawford, Isabella Valancy. *Malcolm's Katie: A Love Story.* 1884. Ed. D.M.R. Bentley. London: Canadian Poetry Press, 1987.

Dewart, Edward Hartley. *Selections from Canadian Poets.* Montreal: J Lovall, 1867.

Ferguson, Jade. *From Dixie to the Dominion: Violence, Race, and the Time of Capital.* Phd dissertation. Cornell University, 2009.

Gerson, Carole. "Anthologies and the Canon of Early Canadian Women Writers." *Re(Dis)covering Our Foremothers.* Ed. Lorraine McMullen. Ottawa: UOP, 1989. 55–76.

———. *Canadian Women in Print, 1750–1918.* Waterloo: WLUP, 2010.

———, and Jacques Michan, Eds. *History of the Book in Canada: Volume Three 1918–1980.* Toronto: UTP, 2007.

———, and Veronica Strong-Boag. *Paddling Her Own Canoe: The Times and Texts of E. Pauline Johnson, Tekahionwake.* Toronto: UTP, 2000.

Goldsmith, Oliver. *The Deserted Village.* London: J.B. Lippincott, 1770.

———. *The Rising Village.* 1834. Ed. Gerald Lynch. London: Canadian Poetry Press, 1989.

Goldsmith, Oliver. *The Rising Village.* St. John, NB: John McMillan, 1834.

Gustafson, Ralph. *Anthology of Canadian Poetry (English).* Toronto: Penguin Books, 1942.

Gwyn, Richard. *The Northern Magus.* Toronto: M&S, 1980.

Hearne, Samuel. "Esquimaux Massacre." *A Journey from Prince of Wales's Fort in Hudson's Bay to the Northern Ocean.* 1769, 1770, 1771, 1772. Ed. Richard Glover. Toronto: Macmillan, 1958. 32–47

Irvine, Dean and Smaro Kamboreli. *Editing as Cultural Practice in Canada.* Ontario: Wilfrid Laurier University Press, 2016.

Lears, Jackson. *No Place of Grace: Antimodernism and the Transformation of American Culture 1880–1920.* 1981. Chicago, IL: Chicago UP, 1994.

Lecker, Robert. *Keepers of the Code: English-Canadian Literary Anthologies and the Representation of Nation.* Toronto: UTP, 2013.

Lent, Vanessa, Bart Vautour, and Dean Irvine, Eds. *Making Canada New: Editing, Modernism, and New Media.* Toronto: UTP, 2017.

Lighthall, William Douw. *Songs of the Great Dominion.* Toronto: A.T. Chapman, 1922.

Lighthall, William Douw. *Old Measures: Collected Verse.* Toronto: A.T. Chapman, 1922.

Logan, J.D., and Donald G. French. *Highways of Canadian Literature: a Synoptic Introduction to the Literary History of Canada (English) from 1760 to 1924.* Toronto: McClelland & Stewart, 1924.

MacMechan, Archibald. *Headwaters of Canadian Literature.* Toronto: McClelland & Stewart, 1924.

Marshall, Tom. "Mountaineers and Swimmers." *Canadian Literature*, 72 (Spring 1977): 21.
McGee, Thomas D'Arcy. "A National Literature for Canada." *The New Era* (June 17, 1857): 2.
McLaren, I.S. "English Writings about the New World." *History of the Book in Canada, Vol. 1: Beginnings to 1840*. Eds. Patricia Lockhart Fleming, Gilles Gallichan, and Yves Lamonde. Toronto and Montréal: UTP, 2004. 33–44.
Mount, Nick. *When Canadian Literature Moved to New York*. Toronto: UTP, 2005.
New, W.H. *A History of Canadian Literature*. 1989. Montreal: MQUP, 2003.
Pacey, Desmond. *Ten Canadian Poets: A Group of Biographical and Critical Essays*. 1958. Toronto: Ryerson, 1969.
———. *The Collected Works of Sir Charles G.D. Roberts*. Eds. Desmond Pacey and Graham Clevearn Adams. Ann Arbour, MI: Wombat Press, 1985.
Pomeroy, E.M. *Sir Charles G. D. Roberts: A Biography*. Toronto: Ryerson, 1943.
Rand, Theodore Harding. *A Treasury of Canadian Verse*. New York: E.P. Dutton & Co., 1900.
Roberts, Sir Charles G.D. *The Collected Works of Sir Charles G.D. Roberts*. Eds. Desmond Pacey and Graham Clevearn Adams. Ann Arbour, MI: Wombat Press, 1985.
Sidney, Sir Philip. *The Defense of Poesy*. *Critical Theory since Plato*. Ed. Hazard Adams. 3rd ed. Belmont: Wadsworth, 2004. 186–206.
Smith, A.J.M. "Canadian Anthologies, New and Old." *University of Toronto Quarterly*, 11.4 (1942): 457–74.
———, Ed. *The Book of Canadian Poetry*. Toronto: Gage, 1943.
———, Ed. *The Oxford Book of Canadian Verse in English and French*. Toronto: Oxford, 1960.
Starblanket, Gina, and Dallas Hunt. *Storying Violence: Unravelling Colonial Narratives in the Stanley Trial*. Winnipeg: ARP, 2020.
Starnino, Carmine. *A Lover's Quarrel*. Erin Mills: The Porcupines Quill, 2004.
Sugars, Cynthia, and Laura Moss. *Canadian Literature: Texts and Contexts*. Vol. 1 and 2. Toronto: Nelson, 2008.
Sutherland, Katherine. "Re-evaluating the Literary Reputation of Isabella Valancy Crawford." *Diversity and Change in Early Canadian Women's Writing*. Ed. Jennifer Chambers. Newcastle: Cambridge Scholars, 2008. 120–38.
The Canadian Encyclopedia. "Turtle Island," 2018. www.thecanadianencyclopedia.ca/en/article/turtle-island
Truth and Reconciliation Commission of Canada Interim Report. Winnipeg: Truth and Reconciliation Commission of Canada, 2012.
Veracini, Lorenzo. *Settler Colonialism: A Theoretical Overview*. New York: Palgrave Macmillan, 2010. DOI: 10.1057/9780230299191
———. "Introducing Settler Colonial Studies." *Special Issue: A Global Phenomenon. Settler Colonial Studies*, 1.1 (2011): 1–12. DOI:10.1080/2201473X.2011.10648799
Ware, Tracey. "The Integrity of Carman's *Low Tide on Grand Pré*." *Canadian Poetry*, 14 (1984): 38–52.
Wolfe, Patrick. *Settler Colonialism and the Transformation of Anthropology: The Politics and Poetics of an Ethnographic Event. Writing Past Colonialism*. London: Cassell, 1998.
———. "Settler Colonialism and the Elimination of the Native." *Journal of Genocide Research*, 8.4 (2006): 387–409.
Woodcock, George. *Northern Spring: The Flowering of Canadian Literature*. Toronto: Douglas MacIntyre, 1987.
Younging, Gregory. *Elements of Indigenous Style*. Edmonton: Brush, 2018.

2 Poetry of Critique, Engagement, and Transnationalism

A word would have dulled the exquisite edge of the feeling,
An oath would have flawed the crystallization of the hate.
For only such culture could grow a climate of silence, —

(E.J. Pratt, "Silences," 1936)

What solace, outlet, or call-to-action can poetry excite in us, especially amid the most extreme or abstract experiences and events? Can poetry, for which language is its very material, *do* anything? I think *yes*, poetry can and does *do things*. The work of literary critics and casual readers of poetry alike is to explore the question of how and what poetry does, as well as to consider the ways people were thinking about these questions in the decades following Confederation, when technological, economic, and political change came at a then-unimaginable speed. For, while these abstract questions about poetry are rooted in language itself, they are also questions that underlie much of the poetry written in the decades between Confederation and the end of the Great Depression.

The question is worth posing again: what solace, outlet, or call-to-action can poetry excite in us, especially amid the most extreme or abstract experiences or events? Can poetry, whose material is language, *do* anything? Scholars working in the field of linguistics have long asked these questions, so too anyone observing children at play. In children's wild and kinetic imaginations, language can make worlds appear and walls turn into magical portals. *Let's pretend*, a child says, and just like that they are off. As adults, we are often taught to eschew the magic and whimsy that is bound up in the very stuff of language. Depending on the field in which you find yourself working or studying, language tends to be understood as the tenuous relationship between sounds, the things they reference, and the meaning a group of language speakers understand them to refer. Why? Language is one system humans use to make meaning, and meaning can often call for action.

A theoretical perspective that was prominent through the twentieth century about how language can indicate a change in relationships comes from Ferdinand de Saussure's famous *Course in General Linguistics* (1913).

DOI: 10.4324/9780429352966-2

Saussure, who was recognized as a compelling teacher, introduces the concept of signification. Language, he explained, is a kind of equation between the signifier and the signified.[1] His observations had a profound effect on the ways we understand language to work. To this set of ideas we can add J.L. Austin's notion of language's performative speech acts—those utterances in human speech that, when undertaken in the right conditions, change material circumstances. *I do*, for example, carries particular weight when uttered in a civil union service. *It's a girl* carries another kind of weight when pronounced by a midwife. In both cases, the utterance makes a claim and a change for reality. In both cases, the frailty of language as well as its power is on display. For *is* it a girl? Only the child can say, and it won't have access to speech for years yet, but the utterance of the attending midwife or doctor will most likely shape the child's experience of the world for years to come, if not a lifetime.[2] Taken together, language becomes an agent capable of change, while at the same time maintaining a tenuous relationship to referentiality. Language makes things happen, and yet it does so based on the shared understanding that it can only ever stand in for the people, places, and things it aims to represent.

Franco Berardi, an Italian-Marxist theorist, has offered another compelling metric for understanding the material and movement of language. Looking back at the global financial crisis of 2008, Berardi surmises that poetry and money are similar. This strikes me as an evocative suggestion—one that makes me sit up and think *what? Say more*. In Berardi's estimation, finance is at a remove from referential value now that it is no longer connected to the gold standard. Likewise, prose is always somewhat illusory because it is by necessity separated from direct referentiality, yet it is tied to the logics of poetic grammar. Language, in this view, can only ever be representational. But, Berardi writes, though money and language have commonalities, they are not identical, because language "exceeds economic exchange." Poetry offers possibility—a way out—because it is the language of "nonexchangeability." Berardi explains: "I'm talking about poetry here as an excess of language, a hidden resource which enables us to shift from one paradigm to another" (140). Poetry, in other words, cannot be reduced to an exchange value. Poetry is a mode of engagement, of relationality.

Whether or not these are compelling theories for you, the questions—what can poetry do, and how does it do it—form some of the key concerns of the generations of poets who follow Confederation. Whether it directly describes, lyrically imagines, or conceptually creates, poetry works with language, and language does not exist in a vacuum. It is a communicative and relational medium that exists in historical context. The power of poetic language to engage and grapple with its own historical context is not a new concept. Poetry need not directly engage in social context, indeed, as we will see in later chapters, there are many opinions about poetry of social engagement. Nonetheless, it remains that language emerges from contextualized grounds. The poetry of the period spanning from post-Confederation to 1950 exemplifies the variegated contexts of its own production.

Take, for example, the excerpt that opens this chapter. The poem is not the most famous of this long period, to be sure. What it offers us is this: in it, the poet addresses speaking and silence. What can language do? In asking this question in verse form, and in placing the poem in a deep oceanic setting, the poet moves language out of a solely anthropomorphized context and into an aquatic one. Newfoundland poet E.J. Pratt offers the following reflections on "Silences." He writes,

> This bit of verse is based on the idea that speech, whether it is the speech of language or just inarticulate utterance, is meant not only to convey thought but to express emotion, and that expression in itself has a social value independent of both the thought and the emotion. It is a matter of common observation that any feeling which is pent-up is apt to fret and fray the heart. I suppose that is the reason why engines, whether organic or mechanical, must have valves. We often remark to one another or to ourselves—"Say it, say it, or write it, write it. Get it out of your system … . You'll feel better."
>
> (*On His Life and Poetry*, 108–9)

Language, when moved into the space of poetry, becomes a means by which to navigate pressures for Pratt. In "Silences," which was published in 1933, Pratt uses the foil of undersea violence to reflect on human violence. The poem, which will be examined in depth later in the chapter, is one of his few recognizably modernist works. In the excerpt that serves as an epigraph to this chapter, the speaker imagines the ways in which silence cultivates hate and other violent feelings. In his explanatory notes, Pratt observes that his interest in undersea violence comes from the "impression that all of the everlasting conflict which goes on in marine life under the sea is perfectly silent" (108–9). While Pratt's knowledge of the sonic qualities of submarine life are not accurate, his concerns are relevant for framing this significant period. How, in a period of rapid social and political change and technological development, can poetry attend and attune itself to growing tensions? How, and indeed, *can* poetry "say it," and in so saying, release the pent up "repressions" (*On His Life and Poetry*, 106)?

I have elected to open this chapter with Pratt's "Silences" because it offers a textual site from which to think about how conceptions of what poetry can do shifts in the period under study in this chapter. Between 1914 and 1930 we see, as critics such as J.A. Weingarten observe, both the beginnings of Canadian modernism, as well as "a growing discontent among Canadians with conventional poetic forms and styles" (108). "Silences" marks an important evolution in Pratt's writing and is an example of why he is understood as a hinge figure between the poetic concerns of the previous chapter, and those that emerge in this one. And, while it is folly to suggest a single poem—certainly not this one—can encapsulate all components of its era, I have nonetheless also began with "Silences" for the tensions, violence, and human indecency that Pratt explores. If language can show the "exquisite edge of feeling," it can also interrupt the "crystallization of hate." What, then, is Pratt probing when the stanza lands on the dangers of a "culture of silence"?

The changes that took place in Canadian society and culture between the early- and mid-twentieth centuries are, frankly, so significant that a detailed study of each is well beyond the scope of this volume. The post-Confederation period saw the development of aggressive policies of cultural assimilation and annihilation that were codified with the Indian Act (1876), the Chinese Head Tax (1885), the development and deployment of the amendment that ratified the Residential School System (1894), the Komagata Maru Incident (1914), and the Chinese Exclusion Act (1923). The twentieth century saw the further development of transportation and communications systems, a national broadcasting corporation, and a national film board. And, significantly for both the country and its literary cultures, Canadian people participated in the First World War and then, a generation later, the Second World War. The ends of each of these wars saw additional sea changes. Waves of immigration occurred, and with them the development of a complex and often xenophobic set of immigration policies.

It is challenging to adequately sketch even the peaks of the waves of change that occurred between the post-Confederation period and the post-war cultural shifts that roughly coincide with the publication of the Royal Commission on National Developments in Arts, Letters, and Sciences better known as the Massey Report.[3] However, there are some clear patterns that emerge in cultural, political, and poetic contexts. There are tensions—some productive, others whose deep violence we reckon with well into the twenty-first century—that emerge with the increased and increasingly diverse population. While this is overly simplistic, I will begin in this chapter by continuing to think about the tensions between Indigenous and settler identities and add to this a consideration of what critics refer to as cultural nationalism. Generally understood as an organizing principle, cultural nationalism refers to a feeling of connection and definition for people within a nation where that feeling of connection and identification is based on a set of shared cultural values. If, as Raymond Williams suggests, "culture is ordinary"—meaning that what gets called "culture" is predicated on everyday rather than extraordinary things—then cultural nationalism is especially tricky in countries built on the foundations of settler colonialism and constantly evolving through subsequent waves of immigration.

Thus, the second set of tensions we will trace in this chapter is connected to, but different from cultural nationalism. Cosmopolitanism is not a new concept in the period under study in this chapter. Indeed, cosmopolitanism has its roots in Ancient Greek, where it translates literally to "citizen of the world." In the context of the Canada of this period, critics such as D.M.R. Bentley have identified a "cosmopolitan nationalism" defined as "[an] enabling combination of the international and the local, the classical and the Canadian" (*Confederation*, 62). Philosopher Will Kymlicka offers a nuance, suggesting that "instead of nationalism cosmopolitanism should be defined by contrast with its real enemies—xenophobia, intolerance, chauvinism, militarism, colonialism, etc." (32). Between these two definitions lie some of the key developments and trends in poetry written in Canada between the post-Confederation period and the publication of the Massey Report.

Canada and the First World War: Effects and Poetics

In 1931, Sir Charles G.D. Roberts observed that there was an intergenerational camaraderie between the poets of his generation and the new modernist generation: "all lie down together very amicably, the lions and the lambs; and no one is quite sure which one is which" (23). Indeed, J.A. Weingarten refers to the intermingling of generations of poets—from meeting in person, to being published together in little magazines—as a phenomenon. For Weingarten, the continued popularity of the Confederation poets can be attributed in large part to the "surging cultural nationalism" brought on by Canada's involvement in the First World War (315).

The First World War (1914–18) had a significant effect on people in Canada. Despite Confederation and the British North American Act, Canada was and is still very much a part of the British Empire and joined the fighting as soon as Britain declared war on Germany. What is perhaps more surprising is the home-front enthusiasm with which Canadians met the war effort, especially given the enormous losses incurred by Canadian troops. More than 60,000 Canadians were killed abroad and another 117,000 were wounded. These are staggering numbers, considering that the population at the time was slightly less than eight million people. Perhaps more incredible still is the fact that 4000 service people were Indigenous, which is remarkable given the concurrent aggressive policies of genocide and assimilation that the government was undertaking during this time. It was felt that Canada's significant contribution, along with the staggering losses of Canadian soldiers at battles such as Ypres and Vimy Ridge, gave the country recognition on an international stage. In a few short years, Canada was no longer viewed as an infantilized colonial outpost, but as a country that could hold its own in global affairs. This affective shift—from inferiority complex to emergence—influenced everything from policies to cultural productions, and poetry was no exception.

In the previous chapter, we considered some of the ways in which narratives of arrival and emergence informed poetic production and literary cultures more broadly. This is not to say that all writers were writing in identical ways with identical aesthetic concerns and experiments, but as is still the case, trends were often tied to broader socio-political developments. Thus, it makes sense that the endurance of soldiers, the effort at home, and attempts to navigate both grief and horror resulted in an explosion of new writing, much of which took poetic form. And while John McCrae's "In Flanders Fields," which was first published in the British magazine *Punch* in 1915, is still recited in many public schools in Canada and internationally, it is hardly the only piece of writing to emerge during this time. As Joel Baetz demonstrates, many people in Canada published poems during this period and poetry, whether public or private, became a particularly apt medium through which to navigate the tumult of global warfare (1–2). A year prior to Armistice, University of British Columbia librarian John Ridington observed that:

> confronted by Armageddon, with personal, social, national, racial ideals of liberty imperiled, men think deeply, feel acutely, react powerfully. It would be unthinkable that this reaction should not find vent in poetry, the most permanent of all the great avenues of human expression.
>
> (4)

Ridington observes the relevance of form as a container for navigating complex emotions. As we will encounter in future chapters, the root of this claim still has traction in the twenty-first century.

The war effort on Canada's "home front" was met with a kind of mania and excitement that is worth considering; why were people so taken with the war effort? Was it a sense of responsibility and connection to Britain? A desire to be part of world events? For many people in Canada, the response to Britain's declaration of war was immediate and decisive. Baetz notes, for example, the reaction of poet and Anglican priest Frederick George Scott who, in the summer of 1914 upon hearing the pledge to send thousands of troops, feels a sense of both thrill and responsibility:

> One after another the reports were given, and at last there flashed upon the boards the words, "General Hughes offers a force of twenty thousand men to England in case war is declared against Germany." I turned to a friend and said, "That means I have got to go to the war."
>
> (15)

Scott's reaction is not singular, and this decisiveness had a variety of consequences, including a shift in poetic production.[4]

In his presidential address to the Royal Society of Canada, W.D. Lighthall explained his view of the war's effect on the country and its culture proclaiming, "The Great War is vastly more stirring as an era than Confederation was and must be regarded as a new starting point" (qtd. in Baetz, 16). But what kinds of poems were being produced? In addition to functioning as a kind of archive of ideas and emotions, the poetry of this period is a curious storehouse of thoughts and feelings on a variety of topics including strength, race, community, obligation, gender, vulnerability, truth, obscurity, trauma, and death. As Baetz suggests, drawing on the work of historian Jonathan Vance, the War was framed as a kind of "progenitor of good in Canada," but what we can find in the poetry itself is "nothing less than a culturally informed archive of ideas" (5). Baetz identifies key trends in the poetry of this period as first and foremost focusing on *collective action*. Baetz differentiates between the collective power and resolve of a "we" and the relative despair of an "I," most often embodied in the persona of a soldier: "the celebration of strong and unified communities usually takes one of two forms: the dramatization of the assembly or successful effort of a military group, or the insistence that a single soldier embodies an entire nation" (7). The poetry of the First World War manages to shrink the distances and differences between communities in Canada by unifying lyric speakers against a common enemy, challenge, or call-to-action. In work such as Albert William Drummond's "The Colonial's Challenge," Baetz observes the trend of presenting the gathering together or group action of members of the military, while in work such as Douglas Leader Durkin's "The Men Who Stood" readers encounter the trend of having a single soldier stand in as synecdoche for the nation. In each case, the poet enacts an idealized image of the nation as exhibiting idealized qualities of masculinity. Daniel Coleman has described the idealized national ethos of this period as "white civility," which, while extending beyond the specific event of the First World War, conveys important information. For Coleman, searching to answer the question of why and how white Anglo Canada came to be understood as normative in a country built on settler colonialism led him to recognize a genealogy of white supremacy he calls "white civility." For Coleman, "White Canada is obsessed with its own civility … and the central organizing problematic of this endeavor has been the formulation and elaboration of a specific form of whiteness based on a British model of civility" (5). Poetry produced during the First World War performs this model of "white civility" that is indebted to hegemonic forms of heteronormativity. In short, as Baetz writes, while the war afforded some social movement for women, the poetry of this period reifies a woman's role as conduit for mourning and a man's role as courageous and brave, and there is little room for any deviation.

The participation of Canadians in the First World War marked a shift, for Canadians, in the country's global reputation. Canada was described by politicians and businesspeople in terms ascribed to youth: strong, virile, filled with the possibility of the future. But a future for whom, and under what conditions? These are but a few of the questions the post-war writers of the modernist period grappled with through experimentation in poetic form as well as content.

Tracking Modernist Shifts

Modernism is habitually characterized as a rupture. A break with what came before. One of the most cited adages used to describe the global shift comes from American expatriate writer Ezra Pound who demanded that writers and artists of the age "make it new."[5] And, while Pound himself borrowed the adage from Confucian philosophy, the slogan remains sutured to understandings of modernist ethos and aesthetics. Canadian modernism has been described by various critics and writers as belated, long, and utterly absent, but these claims are not entirely accurate. Rather, as Adrian Fowler points out, the difficulty in describing the aesthetic post-war shift is perhaps better read as a continuation of English writers and critics of settler descent continuing the struggle to forge a literary history that both acknowledged lineage and, in a kind of cognitive dissonance, existed in a state of exceptionalism. Fowler points to two introductions in significant anthologies of the period as emblematic of this shuffle. The first, *The Oxford Book of Canadian Verse* (1913) edited by Wilfred Campbell, begins with five standards for defining Canadian poetry and then writes "the true British-Canadian verse, if it has any real root and lasting influence, must necessarily be but an offshoot of the great tree of British literature, as the American school also is, though less obviously" (viii).

A mere three years later, John W. Garvin offers the following analysis of the past and future of Canadian poetry as part of the editorial forward to *Canadian Poets* (1916):

> Love of Nature has been their chief source of inspiration; but themes based on love of humanity and man's kinship with the Infinite Life, have steadily gained of late in number and potency, and the Great War must necessarily arouse a more intense interest in human and divine relationships.
>
> (5–6)

With these two examples, Fowler observes the utter lack of evidence that these writers are aware of the changes afoot in both literary and social spheres and asks, "was this Canada at the advent of the modern age?" (273). The answer, for Fowler, is that yes, on the whole this was indeed the landscape of Canadian poetics, though there were some notable examples to the contrary. In 1914, Arthur Stringer observes that traditional forms are no longer adequate to convey contemporary concerns, and J.M. Gibbon advocated for poetry that reflected the times more accurately: "The times are moving. Dynasties are falling, are caste. The voice of today is the voice of the people" (qtd. in Dudek and Gnarowski, 5, 20).

What can we make of these characterizations of poetry during this period? Literary critics and producers in English Canada remained focused on developing a literary history of the nation, they were increasingly looking abroad both for overt aesthetic connection and for differentiation between home and away. They were not yet focused on the asymmetrical social structures that form the bedrock of the nation, but that was to change, at least somewhat, with the shifts that were to come with the next generation.

Case Study: E.J. Pratt and the Long Poem

E.J. Pratt might be best understood in the context of poetic history as a hinge figure. Born and raised in Newfoundland, Pratt made his way to Toronto where he remained, after taking his degree at the University of Toronto. While perhaps not an obviously example of a modernist poet, Pratt's work was recognized by his contemporaries as marking something new and different.

Whether this aesthetic and poetic difference is due to Pratt's childhood experiences in the landscape and cultures of Newfoundland, which was not to officially join Canada until 1949, is unclear. What is certain is this: the publication of Pratt's *Newfoundland Verse* in 1923 signalled a shift at the level of both form and content. Northrop Frye, in 1958, describes it as a break from the prevailing lyric mode. In his editorial introduction to *The Collected poems of E.J. Pratt* he posits "the noises that exploded in *Newfoundland Verse*, the pounding of surf, the screaming of wind, the crash of ships on rocks, rudely shattered" the mood of the Romantic lyric (xxvi).

What is the mood of the Romantic lyric? In Wordsworth's *Preface* (1802) he describes the lyric as a collection of intense emotions *re*collected in moments of tranquillity. The Romantic lyric tends to elevate the authority, or at least affective authority of the speaker, and it demarcates a distance between speaker and subject. That is in part the reflection: lyric time condenses experience, makes it present to the reader, but is in this framework backward-looking. Equally important in the Romantic lyric is the elevation of Nature into the realm of the sublime. What is key to recall here is that in elevating Nature there is also an inherent and underscored division—humans are separate from rather than a small part of the world. For the Romantics, however, deep in the throes of rising Industrialism, the French Revolution, and the impending shift from mercantile imperialism to capitalism, the elevation of the natural world both reified it and separated humans and non-humans. What is particularly important for a study of poetry written in Canada is this: in the Romantic lyric, nature and humans are separate, and this division is extended to a perceived separation between "civilized" and "savage." Romantic primitivism is a genre of aesthetics that idealizes and, sometimes, seeks to embody perceptions of "primitiveness." Most visible in the characterization of cultures and communities other than white European ones, Romantic primitivism is an ideological and aesthetic approach integrated into art, literature, philosophy, and social and political organization. Otherness is either framed as a remnant of an ideal but inaccessible past, out of which tropes such as "the dying race" emerge, or otherness is framed as dangerous, and here policies based on fear of miscegenation such as cultural genocide are justified. In Canada, Romantic primitivism forms the bedrock of the Indian Act, for example.[6]

E.J. Pratt's poetry exemplifies both the ongoing struggle of settler writers to grapple with the coexistence of settler and Indigenous cultures, as well as with a changing aesthetic relationship to poetics. Trained first to follow his father into religious work, Pratt experiences a crisis of faith and did not become a minister. Instead, he studied emergent fields such as evolutionary theory and psychoanalysis at the University of Toronto. This, coupled with his familiarity with life in Newfoundland has led critics such as Fowler to suggest that Pratt's poetry marks a significant shift from the previous generation because he is incapable of maintaining a view of nature that is comparable to the Romantic vision proffered by Wordsworth and so many others. In a similar vein, Barker Fairley, in review of *The Titans* in *Canadian Forum*, applauded Pratt for "seeing with primal freshness" and "avoiding the weary vision of older cultures" (149). Pratt signals a change with his altered focus on both form and content.

Encounters with the work of E.J. Pratt in classrooms in recent years are most likely through his book-length poem *Towards the Last Spike* (1952). This poem works between the documentary and the epic long poem traditions, elevating successes and capitalist visions of "progress" while employing his expertise in psychology to imaginatively interrogate the key figures of westward expansion and settlement. And while "Towards the Last Spike" is indeed an important poem, I want to focus on an earlier epic to think through Pratt's aesthetic and ideological effects on English Canadian poetics specifically.

The epic is an ancient and global form that pre-exists writing and has several conventions including the elevation of past events to near-mythic status. We might think of the epic as a form of myth-making, memory-keeping, and documenting. Pratt wrote in many forms, including writing several epics. *Brébeuf and His Brethren* (1940) is an epic poem written in blank verse which returns to and imagines the Jesuit priest's mission to New France in the seventeenth century. Sent from France with the mission to convert the Huron-Wendat, Brébeuf and others were killed by the Haudenosaunee people in an event that has been elevated to martyrdom. Pratt's epic illustrates some of the central social concerns of settlers while offering some evidence of his discomfort with these Romantic primitivist assumptions and tactics.

Sandra Djwa ("The Civil Polish of His Horn") compares *Brébeuf and His Brethren* to T.S. Eliot's *Murder in the Cathedral* (1935) where Pratt has likewise "invoked a hero from the national past whose actions are an example of the troubled present." While Djwa aligns this with the emergent drama and trauma of the Second World War, there are key connections to the violent settler-colonial past, and present of the nation. First, she notes, Pratt was influenced by University of Toronto colleague Pelham Edgar, author of *The Romance of Canadian History* (1902), who suggested to Pratt that the story of Brébeuf would make an important contribution to Canadian poetry. Interestingly, Djwa also notes that it is Pelham who encouraged Pratt to make the shift from teaching psychology at the university to teaching in the Department of English. Pratt's interest was further piqued, Djwa finds, by the work of Francis Parkman who was a Victorian author of *The Jesuits in North America*. In his epic poem, Pratt adopts Parkman's stance, Djwa suggests. Building on his extant interests in theology, evolutionary theory, and psychology, Pratt uses the Brébeuf story to explore his own theory of humanity. In the poem, we see Bretheren's work as misguided, though ultimately Pratt frames Brébeuf as an epic hero if not a muscular Christian hero in Daniel Coleman's sense of the term. *Brébeuf and His Brethren* might best be understood as a marker in Pratt's career-long focus on evolutionary theory and psychology as he saw it playing out in his own time.[7] However, taken as a standalone epic, Pratt's poem emblematizes an ongoing problem in both literary history in Canada as it is yoked in service of the nation, and in prevailing systems of oppression. Dwja puts it this way,

> even if we do go back to read a second time and perceive that Pratt is pointing out similarities between will and *hubris*, between priest and Indian [sic] and between religious sacrifice and fertility myth [sic] we are still conscious that the religious justification is always dominant.
>
> (99)

An utterance made by Pratt's Brébeuf is telling: "I shall be broken before I break them," reflects the Jesuit. While the lyric reflection breaks somewhat with Romantic lyricism, and especially with Romantic Primitivism, the violent intent is impossible to ignore. In it, Pratt both anticipates the oppressive policies of cultural genocide that would come more than a century after Brébeuf's martyrdom and reflects the intent in the policies which were in full motion by the time he is writing the epic. By focusing on Pratt, who is a hinge between the post-Confederation poets and the modernist poets, we can give attention to the ways in which poetry can function as a site of struggle, storytelling, and reckoning. And, when calcified and considered outside of its social and cultural context, it can have lasting and significant consequences.

Of course, this is not the whole, or even the partial account of Pratt's influence and contribution to poetic production in Canada during this period. Tensions between old forms and new content can have lasting effect. So too can the role of teachers, editors, and mentors. In both cases, those effects can be generative or they can be damaging. They are rarely neutral, though there are often attempts to cast them as such. In addition to being a three-time Governor General's Award winner for poetry and called "the foremost Canadian poet of the first half of the [twentieth] century," Pratt was also an editor and a professor (Pitt, 1962[1958]).

In 1920, Pelham Edgar encouraged Pratt to move from the Department of Psychology to the Department of English where he himself was Head. Edgar was also the driving force behind the establishment of the Canadian Writers' Federation, and close friends with Duncan Campbell Scott.[8] He was also the mentor and teacher of Northrop Frye, and an early recipient of the Royal Society's Lorne Pierce Medal for distinguished service to Canadian literature, a co-founder of the Canadian Author's Association, and initiator of the Governor General's Awards. Indeed, as E.K. Brown wrote, "no academic figure has done more to foster Canadian literature than Pelham Edgar" (Harrington, 82). Thus, Edgar's invitation to Pratt to join the Department of English as a professor is both significant and an example of the ways in which a single person can have significant and lasting effect on institutions.

Pratt was the founding editor of *Canadian Poetry Magazine* (1936) and held the role until 1943. As Susan Gingell notes, Pratt's legacy is rooted in his long narrative poetry—the epics—which tend to show him as "a mythologizer of the Canadian male experience" (npag). Yet, as Gingell observes, in both the epics and the shorter philosophically engaged poems, Pratt's tension between form and content tells a more nuanced story. While the forms he worked in, and even the choice of metre ended up being "conservative for his time," his diction was experimental and charged with his belief in "the poetic power of the accurate and concrete ... and the poet's task to be a bridge" between science and aesthetics (ibid.). It is curious to note, as David Pitt does, that Pratt is unique in both his poetic and editorial influence, and his positioning in literary history: he is clearly an influential poet, and yet belonged "to no school or movement." Looking to his poetics and his editorial work though, it seems clear that he is a hinge figure between two distinct zeitgeists in Canadian poetry: aesthetics and social engagement. He is one of the few who was actually able to embody Robert's 1931 claim that modernists and Romantics in Canadian poetry "all lie down together very amicably." Pratt managed to move between so-called groups, but the development of modernist aesthetics amongst a younger generation of poets was to be built, in part, on making clear divisions between the Romantics and the modernists. Those divisions often find their textual materialization in the pages of periodicals.

Case Study: Little Magazines and Aesthetic Developments in Poetry

One watershed moment in the development of modernist poetry in Canada was on the campus of McGill University in Montreal. The Montreal Group formed at the university with the express aim of bringing Modernist aesthetics and concerns to Canadian poetry. Comprised of A.J.M. Smith, F.R. Scott, Leo Kennedy, John Glassco, and Leon Edel, the group focused on the new developments in Modernist poetics which were, for them, happening most obviously in the United States and Britain. The Montreal Group first organized their efforts in the publication of the short-lived but influential little magazine *McGill Fortnightly Review* (1925–27). Critics have noted that the initial issue does not immediately betray the group's aims, but rather arose from frustration with institutional decisions.[9] In the first issue, there are critiques of the student union decisions, as well as the observation and celebration of Bliss Carman, who had recently been appointed as a visiting professor to give lectures on Canadian literature. However, the tone and content of the *McGill Fortnightly Review* quickly narrowed its sights on a critique of the previous generation of poets. As Fowler and others note, the *McGill Fortnightly Review* was a student production including an announcement "in glowing terms" of the appointment of Bliss Carman to give lectures on Canadian literature alongside a "censure of undergraduates who booed the decision of the referee in recent McGill Varsity game." The second issue gets more serious as it takes up the "authoritarianism that seemed to pervade the McGill campus from the top down" in which the journal editors "confront this climate of oppression and claim the right to voice dissenting opinions"

(276).[10] There is an impatience that is perceptible in the little magazine; the editors—especially Smith and Scott—are clearly frustrated with what they see as a "stifling authoritarianism" that permeated the entire institutional structure (ibid.). How they each dealt with it will, as we see, lay the further groundwork for developments in modernist aesthetics and social engagement. Indeed, as we will consider in future chapters, pronounced authoritarianism and misogyny remain at the backbone of literary and educational institutions in Canada well into the twenty-first century.

For the Montreal Group, the *McGill Fortnightly Review* became a platform for stating as well as circulating their critiques and their views. These critiques were often addressed through satiric poetry that was published under pseudonyms as well as in unsigned editorials and asides that oscillate between wit and snark. An example of the latter is the critique of *Canadian Book Week*, which was lambasted because it "boosts second-rate Canadian books, doing considerable harm to good literature," while the McGill debate team was met with similar ire when compared to the team from Cambridge who were able to "sweep aside" all positions "with a single thrust, a brilliant epigram." At first glance, at least, the editors of the *McGill Fortnightly Review* appeared to be disenchanted with where they were and deeply invested in anything that was happening anywhere else—ideally outside the borders of Canada. There are some clear reasons for this intellectual wanderlust: both Smith and Scott had recently returned to Canada from Britain where Scott had begun to write poetry seriously. However, critics have also noted that these editors did not root their disdain in studied experience. Sandra Djwa, for example, observes that Smith and Scott "had actually read little Canadian poetry, but they were predisposed to believe that it was not of a high quality" (*Politics of Imagination*, 90–1). The "looking elsewhere" was not a new trend in Canadian literature or poetry, but with the poets of the Montreal Group it was developing new qualities. With their focus on America and Europe, the Montreal Group were developing both an internationalism with potent levels of cosmopolitanism that were to be further explored and expounded by Smith. It is perhaps ironic that in their focus on bettering poetry in Canada they were engaging with a kind of slantwise cultural nationalism of the previous generation, albeit with tongues often firmly in cheeks. Despite the sometimes-searing critiques written by the editors and contributors, the work published in the *McGill Fortnightly Review* betrays their complex and variegated influences. For example, the work of both Smith and Scott was not appearing without aesthetic precedence. As Brian Trehearne has pointed out, there is evidence of both aestheticism and decadence in the work, and that for at least Smith these dual influences continued well beyond his early work (Trehearne, *Aestheticism and Canadian Modernists*). Further, Bart Vautour identifies a growing sense of social responsibility and institutional critique in the work of Scott (*Writing Left*). In short, despite the purported focus on new modernist aesthetics, there was much more going on in the work of this early little magazine.

When Smith left to undertake a PhD in Scotland, the little magazine ceased to publish. And while the *McGill Fortnightly Review* may have had a short life, its aims and claims made an impact that reverberated beyond the McGill campus. After its dissolution, a new little magazine emerged in short order. In December of 1928, *The Canadian Mercury* published its first issue. Described as a "monthly Journal of literature and public opinion," it aimed to have a readership that extended beyond campus. There were several familiar names listed as its editorial board as well as some new ones: F.R. Scott, Leo Kennedy, Jean Burton, and Felix Walker were editors, while A.J.M. Smith was documented as a contributor. While the aim was at a broader readership, there remained some of the tone of the previous publication. For example, in the initial issue the editors explained that the aim of the new publication was to "contribute ... to the consummation of that graceful ideal, the emancipation of Canadian literature from the state of amicable mediocrity and insipidity in which it now languishes" (3). The *Mercury* did not have a long life either, though in a short period of time it drew a line under some of the emergent concerns demonstrated in the *McGill Fortnightly Review*. These included a focus on the paucity of "good" literature in Canada,[11] a veneration of youth,[12] and an emergent and pervasive misogyny.[13] In an essay entitled "The National Literature Problem in Canada," satirist Stephen Leacock claimed that there "is no such thing as a Canadian way of writing" and argued that instead of delineating a style that was distinctive like those to be found in Scotland, England, or even America, Canadian writers instead produce an amalgam of those other influences. From our current juncture in history, this might seem a rather obvious statement: for surely a country settled initially by people from Western Europe who share a border with America would be influenced by those intersecting histories. The influence and indeed integration into American literary culture seems especially comprehensible, given the work done by scholars such as Nick Mount who demonstrates the clear and pressing need for writers in Canada to go to the United States to build a career. Indeed, there were the experiences of writers such as Carman and Roberts who were still alive. Yet rather than acknowledge the settler-colonial and transnational development of Canada and its literatures, and rather than look to the oral and story-telling traditions rooted in Indigenous nations across the land, the young men of the Montreal Group looked elsewhere and lamented.

Case Study: F.R. Scott, Aesthetics, and Poetics that "Do" Things

Born in Quebec in the last year of the nineteenth century, Francis Reginald Scott dedicated his life to *doing*. Whether in his poetic production, his political organization, or his study, practice, and pedagogy of constitutional law, he was committed to action. While Scott was a poet and editor, he was also a law professor at McGill University for the whole of his career and was a founding member of the Cooperative Commonwealth Federation (CCF), a socialist-democratic political party. Scott embodies some of the opening questions of this chapter: what can poetry do, and how does it do it? If, as we saw in the previous section, poetry of the First World War was focused generally on articulating a single-minded nation, and the poetry of the early part of the modernist period was engaged with aesthetic and formal changes, then we might say of Scott's long and significant oeuvre that he was committed to action. In his academic, activist, and literary life, Scott maintained a focus on critiquing the institutions that structure our lives—language and the law—from within those institutions.

Scott's life was fully imbricated in art, literature, and the law.[14] He married Marian Dale, a painter, muralist, art teacher, and commercial artist in 1928, and together they filled their Westmount sitting room with the artistic and literary figures of the day. We know from the previous section in this chapter that Scott was central to the development of little magazine culture in both Quebec and Canada. Here, we will take a closer look at the ways in which Scott focused his literary as well as social production on critique. Whereas some writers of this period, like Dorothy Livesay and Leo Kennedy, cast their poetic and political attentions on developing transnational solidarities, others, such as Scott, had a slightly different focus. These differences can be seen in the complementary but distinctive poetics and poetry each wrote.

First, let us consider the ways in which Scott's poetic and political attentions developed after the heady days of the *McGill Fortnightly Review* and *The Canadian Mercury*. In the 1930s, with the founding of the CCF, Scott's work in both poetic and political organizing came together. In the 1930s, alternative political parties emerged to challenge the long-held two-party political system in Canada. The Communist Party of Canada (CPC), which was founded in 1921, gained wider support in the 1930s, while the CCF was founded in 1932 and held seats in the Parliament of Canada until 1961, at which point it transitioned into the New Democrat Party.[15] Scott was himself a Democratic Socialist, and with Frank Underhill and others he helped to form both the League for Social Reconstruction and the CCF. Both the CCF and the CPC boasted membership and support from key literary figures, and periodicals played a central role in each party's organization.

While Scott did not publish a poetic monograph until *Overture* (1941), he was actively writing as well as editing, teaching, organizing, and practicing law. He understood political organization and poetic production to be convivial work and wrote that:

> the modernist poet, like the socialist, has thought through present forms to a new and more suitable order. He is not concerned with destroying, but with creating, and being a creator, he strikes terror into the hearts of the old and decrepit who cannot adjust themselves to that which is to be.
>
> (ibid.)

Laura Moss characterizes Scott as a critic of institutional structures as well as a poet engaged with public modes of building a socially-just Canada. She notes that within his poetry, readers can discern tensions between legacies of "loss and the fragility of both humanity and the environment" (xi).

Vautour has written that the beginnings of Scott's mode of institutional critique can be located in his earliest publications and cites both his early poems critiquing universities and national organizations of artistic productions such as the Canadian Authors Association as evidence. Trehearne suggests that Scott's poetic work commenced when he was a Rhodes Scholar at Oxford where he wrote lyric works that drew on Romantic poetics. While this work is evident in poems such as "Lament after Reading the Results of Schools" which nods to Keats's "On First Looking into Chapman's Homer" (1816), it shifts the sonnet's focus to the speaker's dismay at his scholastic rankings. Vautour reminds readers that Scott had been incorporating Romantic poetics into institutional critiques as early as 1918.[16] This use of existing poetic forms to critique shifting social ills remains constant in Scott's career.[17] In poems such as "Sweeney Comes to McGill (With apologies to Mr. Eliot)" and "Sweeney Graduates (With all necessary apologies)" Scott continued his practice of using extant forms, but shifts his focus from the Romantic lyric to the new poetics of modernism by inhabiting and parodying T.S. Eliot.[18] This mode of poetic critique is further developed when, in 1927, Scott published "The Canadian Authors Meet" in the *McGill Fortnightly Review*. Here is the final stanza:

> Far in corner sits (though none would know it)
> The very picture of disconsolation,
> A rather lewd and most ungodly poet
> Writing these verses for his soul's salvation.
> (25–8)

This poem both satirizes and critiques the function of the Canadian Authors Association. In this regularly anthologized poem, Scott teases the middle-brow women who "percolate self-unction" over the flag waving poets of the previous generation ("Lampman, Roberts, Carman, Campbell, Scott") and one can almost hear the inferred *blah blah blah.*[19] And, while it is impossible to deny the critical tone Scott's speaker employs in this poem, there are also a few key evolutions in Scott's poetics of critique. In addition to his ongoing frustration with conservatism and tradition, there is also a developing critique of the larger institution of colonialism itself. Here, as Vautour observes, is a poem that implores resistance to the colonial mentality and policies of the Victorians and the Georgians:

> Scott confronts Canada's residual imperialist ties as he gestures toward the poets who are "puppets" to the waning myth of imperial order, positioned "Beneath a portrait of the Prince of Wales" (1–2). Indeed, Scott would write in "New Poems for Old: I. The Decline of Poesy" that poetry in Canada "in a word, was cut and trimmed to suit a

> particular body politic with a revered constitutional monarch and wide Imperial interests ... and it fitted like a frock coat on an M.P." (297). Scott recognized that there was already an institutional connection between poetry and politics in Canada, but importantly, he did not see the development of a new vision for an institutional and national poetics as something coming out of formal literary criticism but out of critical poetic practice.
>
> (108)

For Scott, poetry was a viable method of both critiquing structural and institutional problems, as well as developing a modernist aesthetic. We might even consider that Scott's institutional critique—his poetics of critique as Vautour calls it—is his response to Pound's dictum "make it new." Likewise, Moss points to one of Scott's earlier poems, "Overture," as evidence of Scott's urgent mandate of change. "Overture" was first published in 1934 in *Canadian Forum*, the periodical most closely associated with the CCF, and later the poem appeared in Scott's 1941 full-length collection of the same title. Moss focuses her attention on the following stanza, and we will follow her cues:

> But how shall I hear old music? This is an hour
> Of new beginnings, concepts warring for power,
> Decay of systems—the tissue of art is torn
> With overtures of an era being born.
>
> (23)

The stanza begins with a rhetorical question: *But how shall I hear old music?* The conjunction "but" is a signal: the speaker is mid-conversation. Whether that conversation is real or imagined is less important than the indication that the reader has been dropped into its epicentre. After the enjambment—This is an hour/Of new beginnings,—we realize that "old music" is figuratively referring to a previous generation of thought, convention, and policy. The third line of the stanza repeats the enjambment, which reinforces the speaker's frustration and urgency. While systems "decay," the "tissue of art is torn/With overtures of an era bring born." An overture is a suggestion, a kind of opening move. It is also an orchestral piece at the beginning of a longer musical composition. The implication of an overture is that there is more to come. Here, Scott's inference is clear: the overture does not lead to more significant action, but rather tears apart art and in so doing damages the future. The tension in the stanza is thickened by the rhyming couplets: power is tied to a measurable unit of time, suggesting both the possibility of change, and the frustration of watching minutes tick by. Meanwhile, "torn" and "born" together underscore the violence of inaction in this context. Taken together, the poem, as well as its placement in the periodical of the CCF, is a clear example of what Moss describes as Scott's advocacy for rethinking "structures of poetry, of law, and of government" (xvi).

Scott's poetry demonstrates a zeal for action and a readiness to address inaction directly. Not one to ever revere his elders, certainly not his poetic elders, Scott wielded pith and satire as tools. Take, for example, his response to E.J. Pratt's documentary epic *Towards the Last Spike*. The poem narrativizes political tensions between Sir John A. MacDonald's drive to complete the trans-Canada railway system and those who disagreed with his vision. It also sets up a dichotomy between human labour and ingenuity and a magnificent personified natural world. Published in 1952, the blank verse epic long poem earned Pratt the Governor General's Award for Poetry. Three years later, F.R. Scott wrote "All Spikes But the Last." In the ten-line unrhymed poem, Scott undermines both the form and content of Pratt's epic and calls into question both his accuracy and his choice of subject matter and form:

> Where are the coolies in your poem, Ned?
> Where are the thousands from China who swung
> Their picks with bare hands at forty below?
> Between the first and the million other spikes
> They drove, and the dressed-up act of
> Donald Smith, who has sung their story?
> Did they fare so well in the land they helped to
> Unite? Did they get one of the 25,000,000 CPR acres?
> Is all Canada has to say to them written in the Chinese
> Immigration Act?
>
> (*Selected Poems*, 64)

"All Spikes But the Last" refuses the "old music" of traditional form. Two lines short of a sonnet, the poem is a quick and stinging response to Pratt's long laudatory poem. The intimacy of the first line—"... in your poem, Ned"—draws a line under the relationship between Pratt and Scott. This is both a call out and a call in; call out because it takes place in a public-facing format, a call in because the cascade of interrogatives suggests room for a response. Recall that Scott and Pratt were well known to one another. Indeed, when Scott and A.J.M. Smith were working to publish *New Provinces: Poems of Several Authors* in 1936, they included the iconoclastic Pratt in great part because he was popular and an influential teacher and editor (Fowler, 282). But it is also worthy of note that tensions emerged when Pratt and others took issue with Smith's draft Preface to the anthology (Fowler, 284). Whether or not these tensions extended to Scott's own relationship with Pratt, the textual fact remains that Pratt's work became a key site for another of Scott's poetic critiques.

Scott returns to the pithy response poem in 1957 when he *again* calls Pratt's work in epic form into question. This time his critique is of Pratt's *Brébeuf and his Brethren*. In this poem, Scott repeats Pratt's title, which functions again as a kind of flag or topic heading. Instead of the interrogatives of "All Spikes But the Last," Scott employs a kind of inhabitation of form to levy his critique:

> When Lalemant and de Brébeuf, brave souls,
> Were dying by the slow and dreadful coals
> Their brother Jesuits in France and Spain
> Were burning heretics with equal pain.
> For both the human torture made a feast:
> Then is priest savage, or Red Indian priest?
> (*The Eye of the Needle*, 18)

Here, in an even shorter retort, Scott again uses rhymed couplets to create both mood and criticism. The rhymed coupling of "souls" and "coals" moves the martyrdom of Jesuit priests out of the sacred and into near-nursery verse. The true rhyme slows the enjambed second line from moving swiftly to the focus on the European Order, causing the reading to rest on the similarities. As the two missionaries die a slow and torturous death, Scott aligns their suffering with the suffering, death, and murder of so-called heretics at the hands of the very same Jesuit Order. The final couplet functions as a volta, though here rather than offer a solution or settlement in the final two lines Scott instead raises a rhetorical question. Strategically parroting the language of Romantic primitivism and settler colonialism, Scott draws a connection between both events and in so doing clearly undermines the dominant ideology of white supremacy.

In later work, such as *Trouvailles: Poems from Prose* (1967), critics identify in Scott's work a redoubled focus on critiquing the institution of settler colonialism in Canada. *Trouvailles*, or "finds" in English, is a collection of works built around found or readymade materials, much of which Scott encountered in the display at the "Indians of Canada" Pavilion at *Expo '67*. Christina Alt suggests that in his later work, exemplified in *Trouvailles*, Scott aims to "reinscribe Indigenous presence into his readership's consciousness" (2–3). Alt suggests that this project of reinscription was not a radical shift from Scott's history of critique, but rather a progression of his own development of social consciousness. Indeed, as she points out, Scott himself offers support for this hypothesis:

> I in my innocence was feeling that we could start afresh in Canada. I was newly arrived from Oxford, and deeply impressed by the northland … and its sense of something waiting to be made. I forgot we had already imported from Europe our languages, our laws, our religion, and most of the factors that make up a social community.
> ("Three Documents," 92)

Scott's description of his own shifting consciousness maps onto his shifting poetics of critique. From his early satirical work as a student, to his response critiques, to the work in *Trouvailles* and "The Robinson Treaties," which use modernist methods[20] to focus readerly attentions on the presentness of Indigenous Peoples and the failures of colonial governments, Scott's work documents a commitment to social change.[21] And, while there are well-documented failures, Scott's influence on poetry in Canada extends well beyond the modernist period.

Case Study: Dorothy Livesay, Leo Kennedy, and Poetics of Engagement and Transnationalism

Shifting focus from Scott's poetics of action to another, related mode, in the works of Dorothy Livesay and Leo Kennedy we encounter poets who looked both to their own local contexts and, perhaps even more so, to transnational and global contexts. And while Livesay and Kennedy are perhaps not always held at the forefront of literary history as is Scott, they were recognized in their own periods as poets with something dynamic to offer.

Livesay was very much a part of the modernist generation, but she differs from the poets we have considered thus far in some fascinating ways. While she had a short story "Heat" published in the short-lived *Canadian Mercury*, she was not included by Smith and Scott in *New Provinces*. And while she was a student at the University of Toronto, where Pratt worked, and aware of the Montreal Group by at least 1928, she is not clearly associated with the Group. Her poetic skill was clear, however. F.R. Scholl in a 1944 review of Livesay's "Day and Night" for *First Statement* describes her work as that of "a contemporary of the growing number of Canadian poets on whom the impact of the present age is direct and not derivative" (23). In correspondence identified by Gnarowski in his introduction to the reprint of *New Provinces*, Smith attempts twice to encourage Scott to include Livesay. Scott, eager to get the much-delayed anthology in print, refuses, suggesting her politically engaged poetry would be better suited to a second volume. That second volume never emerged.

Livesay was, by her own account, raised in a household that valued the written word and held the opinion that women were capable of producing excellent writing.[22] Born in Winnipeg a decade prior to the General Strike of 1919, Livesay moved with her family to Toronto where she studied social work and received a diploma in the emergent field in 1934. She published her first collection of poetry in 1928. *Green Pitcher* was a collection of Imagist poems influenced by Livesay's reading.[23] Despite the collection's reception, Livesay later expressed disappointment with *Green Pitcher* explicitly for the poems' failure to engage in social issues (Davey, npag).

Livesay's commitment to socially engaged praxis in both life and poetics shaped the entirety of her career. It may also have shaped her reception and her recognition and acceptance by her poetic contemporaries. By 1931, while studying at the Sorbonne in Paris, Livesay became dedicated to Communism. In 1933, she joined the Communist Party of Canada and became very active in many organizations including the Canadian Labour Defense League, the Canadian League against War and Fascism, Friends of the Soviet Union, and the Workers' Unity League.[24] In the poetry that followed *Green Pitcher*, Livesay's poetics demonstrated an aesthetic as well as a content-driven commitment to the policies and focus of the Communist Party. Her poetic focus evolves with the Party focus. As Bart Vautour notes, the 1936 formation of a Popular Front policy in the Party is visible in the evolution of Livesay's own poetic form. With a poem such as "Day and Night," she considers aesthetics at the level of form and focus on the ways in which poetry has the capacity to model instances of solidarity across national and cultural borders. She was joined in this mode of the long poem by Anne Marriott and Kenneth Leslie, whose *The Wind Our Enemy* and "The Censored Editor" model similar aims. But before Livesay adopted a popular-front aesthetics, she developed and articulated a more hardline, revolutionary poetics of engagement during a short period of time in which she left Canada for the United State. Jade Ferguson locates Livesay's development as an activist and a socially engaged poet as constellating around the Canadian publication of *Masses*.[25] *Masses* had a focused Canadian addressee, and the editors were aiming to bring an international proletarian culture to Canada with the hopes of fostering its development.[26] Livesay's poetry that appeared in *Masses* evidences her attempt at articulating a proletarian aesthetics. It was with her publication of the documentary poem "Day and Night," which appeared as the first poem in the first issue of Pratt's *Canadian Poetry*, that we see a significant development that marks a shift in the history of Canadian poetry.[27] "Day and Night" is a modernist poem that works in a different aesthetic and political idiom from that emerging out of the Montreal Group. Rather than using satire to conduct institutional critique, Livesay was deeply affected by her time in the United States, during which her political engagement with the Communist Party deepened. Ferguson explains that her work of this period, exemplified in "Day and Night," engaged with the poetics of documentary modernism that were employed by American poets of the Left such as Sol Funaroff, Kenneth Fearing, and Muriel Rukeyser (117). Michael Denning describes the Popular Front period of the Communist Party's politics as "a radical social-democratic movement forged around anti-fascism, anti-lynching, and the industrial unionism" (xviii). Livesay's use of both the poetics of documentary modernism, and more specifically what Ferguson identifies as a critique of anti-Black racial violence, and specifically lynching, in relation to bigger imbroglios with capitalism are pathbreaking (144). In "Day and Night," as Ferguson writes, Livesay uses multiple contemporary modes, idioms, and cultural practices including Leninist diction, blues refrains, and African American spiritualisms together with a Marxist analysis that allows her to both critique the intersecting violence of racism and capitalism as well as call for transnational modes of solidarity. Ferguson observes in Livesay's work a significant shift that is also grounded in an evolving intersectional feminist analysis:

> Rather than voyeuristic indulgences, the proliferation of lynching images in Livesay's *Day and Night* produce an experience of shame. Livesay's representations of lynching serve not only to condemn the

> "unrestrained barbarity" in the South ... but also forces Canadians to recognize and understand their own complicity and participation in these acts of racial terror and violence.
>
> (145)

Between her activist and poetic engagement with the Popular Front in the United States, as well as her work as both contributor and editor for *Masses*, Livesay was developing a poetics of engagement that made her stand out in Canada.

In 1971, Livesay published an article entitled "The Documentary Poem: A Canadian Genre." In it, Livesay retrospectively outlines her poetic and political theory. Building on an essay published in *Masses* in 1933 entitled "Brief History of Canadian Art," in which the development of her theory of documentation as the responsible artist's role to both reveal and bring to life the experience of workers, Livesay further articulates the aesthetic praxis of many in her generation of writers. She writes that the characteristics of documentary poetry focus on the visual and aural, and that by attending to these things documentary poems have the capacity to bear witness to histories and to do so in affecting and emotionally forceful language. Preceding Berardi's suggestion that poetry offers other possibilities, Livesay's poetics of engagement reminds us that poetry has the power to move us to action.

Livesay, with her shift from the Imagist work of *Green Pitcher* to politically forceful poetry, wasn't alone in adopting a new poetics in the 1930s. She was joined in her radical shift by Leo Kennedy, who was born in England and emigrated to Canada in 1912. Connected with the Montreal Group, Kennedy is now recognized as a significant and influential figure in Canadian poetry in this period. Kennedy's *The Shrouding* was published in 1933, predating his inclusion in *New Provinces* by three years. *The Shrouding* exemplifies modernist tenets and was hailed by A.M. Klein as "incomparably done," and exemplifying the "resurrection of Canadian poetry" ("Mortal Coils," 8). The collection was well received in its day, though Kennedy never followed up with a second full collection of poetry. Rather, as Robert May notes, Kennedy instead wrote and published single poems throughout his life, though most of his writing is uncollected and therefore quite challenging to access. Nonetheless, Kennedy's work as a literary producer and social and cultural commentator is vital to an understanding of this period.

One site of Kennedy's ongoing publication in the 1930s was *New Frontier*, and while short-lived, like so many magazines, it too holds important literary and cultural import for the period. Both Kennedy and Livesay wrote and edited for *New Frontier*, and each was deeply invested in raising awareness about global injustices. In addition to Livesay's focus on civil rights in the United States, for example, both Kennedy and Livesay were deeply invested in the fight against fascism in Spain. The pages of *New Frontier* were a shared site of poetic activism.

New Frontier: a Monthly Magazine of Literature and Social Criticism was left of its contemporaries such as *Canadian Forum*. In the introductory volume editor William Lawson described the mandate of the magazine this way:

> The aims of *New Frontier* are twofold: to acquaint the Canadian public with the work of those writers and artists who are expressing a positive reaction to the social scene; and to serve as an open forum for all shades of political opinion. [...] Though technically adequate, so many interpretations of the Canadian scene in creative writing, criticism, and art, have been singularly disregardful of or unfaithful to the social realities of our time .... On the other hand, certain individual creative artists and groups who are becoming more interested in the social implications of Canadian life, are turning out work which has both social and artistic value. *New Frontier* is anxious to make the best of this work available to a wide circle of Canadian readers.
>
> (3)

Note the attention paid to context as well as creative production. This socially engaged connection between art, culture, and responsibility is important, because while some of the Montreal Group such as Scott would go on to dedicate both career and creative production to a praxis of institutional critique, the work undertaken by *New Frontier* is slightly different. Using Kennedy's work as an example, critics such as May observe that *New Frontier* was critical for "contributi[ng] to socially conscious Canadian writing of the 1930s because, over the course of the eight poems, five essays, and one book review (of W.H. Auden's "Spain"), Kennedy develops an explicit link between domestic and international politics" (10). Specifically, Kennedy connects emergent fascist tendencies of the Duplessis government in Quebec with the attempted fascist coup that led to the Spanish Civil War. Like his co-editor Livesay, Kennedy saw the role of the poet as vitally connected to social change. Unlike Livesay, whose poetics of engagement employs documentary and modernist methods, Kennedy is not quite as direct.

In a careful study of Kennedy's essays and poetry published in *New Frontier*, Vautour discerns a calculated shift. As a standalone, "Directions for Canadian Poets" is programmatic and focused on what must change in Canada. Published prior to the outbreak of war in Spain, Kennedy's focus in the essay is backward-looking; covering the failures of the post-Confederation generation as well as the narrow scope of the Canadian Authors' Association and its *Canadian Poetry Magazine* edited by E.J. Pratt, as well as their *Poetry Year Books* series (Vautour, "From Transnational Politics" 49). Kennedy's critique, while rooted in Canada, shows an awareness of the need for global connection:

> In this time of impending war and incipient fascism, when the mode and standard of living of great numbers of middle class persons (from whose ranks Canadian poets hail) are being violently disrupted ... the

> function of poetry is to interpret the contemporary scene faithfully; to interpret especially the progressive forces in modern life which alone stand for cultural survival ....
>
> (21)

Kennedy lands on this sentiment:

> We need poetry that reflects the lives of our people, working, loving, fighting, groping for clarity. We need satire,—fierce, scorching, aimed at the abuses which are destroying our culture and which threaten life itself. Our poets have lacked direction for their talents and energies in the past—I suggest today that it lies right before them.
>
> (24)

Vautour speculates that Kennedy's focus on "poetry that reflects the lives of our people" was about to be realized in the growing poetic production focused on Spain, albeit with a more global focus and suggests that a suite of poems published in *New Frontier* are particularly salient for understanding the emergent new poetics.

Like so many other writers, poets, and artists around the world, Kennedy's sights were set on the war being waged against fascism in Spain. While it may be difficult to imagine from this juncture in history, the Spanish Civil War caught the imagination and the consciences of a generation. Similar, perhaps, to the effect of the French Revolution on the Romantics, the Spanish Civil War has been and continues to be a flashpoint in poetic production in Canada and around the world. While readers may be familiar with Pablo Picasso's *Guernica*, Martha Gellhorn's searing reportage, or even the work of Federico García Lorca who was murdered at the beginning of the war by the fascists, there has been less attention paid to the transnational solidarity that emerged between Canada and Spain.[28] For Kennedy, as with Livesay and other Canadian writers and artists who went to or wrote about Spain in the 1930s, the fight against fascism abroad was necessarily tied to fighting the emergent fascism in Canada. Indeed, as May points out, before Kennedy's focus turned to Spain, much of his concern was aimed at the French-language presses and the Roman Catholic Church in Quebec: "It is the duty of every Canadian man, woman and child to help keep Fascism out of Quebec, for that is the first measure towards keeping Fascism out of Canada," he wrote in 1936 ("Meet Quebec's Fascists!" 8).

The war in Spain galvanized Kennedy's focus, and as Vautour, Vulpe, and Rifkind each observe, this is evident most clearly in his poem "Calling Eagles." Vulpe and Rifkind focus on the ways in which "Calling Eagles" uses modernist free verse to address other writers. Rifkind attends to the ways in which Kennedy's mode of poetic address is in keeping with the "majority of Popular Front verse about the Spanish Civil War" (*Comrades* 94), and Vulpe reads the poem as a poetic version of "Direction for Canadian Poets" (41). Vautour extends these arguments and triangulates them with Kennedy's poetic publications in *New Frontier*. What he sees in "Calling Eagles" is an evolution and extension of Kennedy's argument in "Direction for Canadian Poets." The manifesto lands on industrial relations in Canada, while the poem focuses on the crucial import of a transnational fight against fascism (Vautour, Spring 2010, 51). "Calling Eagles," one of the few poems Kennedy published under his own name in the periodical, eschews traditional form for enjambed free verse:

> Come down to life, Eagles, where iron grinds bone, hands falter
> And brave men perish for a tyrant's peace;
> Come where Spain strangles in blood, Ethiopia
> Groans at the ironcased heel, Vienna
> Numbers the dead, remembers Weissel and Wallisch;
> Scream for Brazilian dungeons where Prestes rots
> And fascist madmen rattle gaoler's keys.
>
> (9–15)

The eagles to whom the call is issued are other poets who, in writing, have the capacity to address "life" where "iron grinds bone" and real people are killed in the fight for equality and peace. The speaker is situated on the ground—in the midst of "life"—and brings together those murdered in the fight to keep Austria free from fascism[29] with one of the leading Communists in Brazil[30] and the Italian invasion of Ethiopia.[31] Each of these events located across multiple continents are yoked together under the growing threat of global fascism. The enjambed lines stack people and places atop one another, as though piling up the victims of fascism, until landing on the words of the final two lines. The madness of fascism piles bodies atop one another, both living and dead. The key held by the "fascist madmen" who buries revolutionaries and dissenters in prison may be rattled, but the implication is that the key could be taken and the door unlocked and opened if only the poets rally together in common cause.

Kennedy's poetry is concerned with action, and it focuses on the future generations doing better than the ones that came before. Themes of inheritance, such as an early line from *The Shrouding* ("may he inherit the earth") are echoed in the remainder of his socially engaged poems about Spain, Canada, and the need for poets to be engaged in the social struggles of their day, and their world.

Conclusion

By reading Pratt, Scott, Livesay, and Kennedy across the early-twentieth century, I aim to show not only touchstone moments and works, but to show the range of ways poetry made inroads into the social and political life of the country. From Pratt's epic attempts at writing Canadian history, to Scott's mode of poetic critique of Canadian institutions, and to Livesay and Kennedy's building transnational solidarities between poetry and people, the poetry of the post-Confederation period through the 1930s demonstrates shifts in aesthetics, poetics, and literary circulation. Forms changed, groups shifted alliances, and poetic attention again moved not only locally, but also transnationally as well. By the 1940s, Canadian poetry had "caught up" with international modernism and was expanding in a variety of directions whose influences can still be discerned well into the twenty-first century. If Canadians thought they had gained some global influence at the end of the First World War, by the end of the 1930s Canadian poetry had fully joined a global chorus of poetic production.

Key Terms

Cosmopolitanism: Deriving from the Ancient Greek term for "world" or "universe," this is the notion that humans share commonalities and as such are joined as a global or world community.

Cultural nationalism: Collective practices that form modern political communities. Nationalism in this context is defined by a set of shared or purportedly shared cultural values and languages.

Little magazines: Small periodicals dedicated to literary writing, often of the non-commercial or avant-garde varieties.

Massey Report: Colloquial reference for the *Royal Commission on National Development in the Arts, Letters, and Sciences.* So-called for the Commission's Chair, Vincent Massey. The Report examined Canada's cultural needs, interviewed Canadians in a series of town hall meetings across the country, and made recommendations that led to infrastructural support for arts and culture in Canada.

Modernism: Broadly, an international movement in culture and society that begins in the early part of the twentieth century and is marked by attempts to align society and culture with the experiences and values of modernity.

Romanticism: Spirit, intellectual alignment, or attitude that was associated with many works of literature, art, music, architecture, criticism, and history in the late-eighteenth to mid-nineteenth centuries.

Transnationalism: The extension of economic, social, and political processes both in between and beyond the boundaries of individual states.

Notes

1 Saussure named these parts the signifier (thing that gives meaning; word/image), the signified (the thought created in the mind by the signifier), and together they make the sign.
2 See for example the work of J.L. Austin and John Searle. See also Judith Butler's foundational work on gender and performance.
3 So-called for Vincent Massey, a co-chair of the commission.
4 It is notable that Scott is the father of F.R. Scott, discussed at length later in this chapter.

5 As Vanessa Lent, Bart Vautour, and Dean Irvine explain, Pound's statement is taken out of context often. See Lent et al (2017).
6 See, for example, Theodore Binnema and Kevin Hutching's work on colonial administrator Sir Francis Bond Head, who employed aesthetic theories of Romantic primitivism to write colonial policies for relocating Indigenous Peoples in Upper Canada between 1836 and 1838.
7 Indeed, in this vein Djwa notes a similarity in framing the human condition as one that is fraught and often turns to brutality. The focus on humanity's capacity to hurt one another is redoubled in a poem that focuses on the brutality of the Second World War entitled "Autopsy On a Sadist (After Lidice)" in which, as Djwa muses, "Pratt sees man's [sic] movement towards torture and murder as the civilized perversion of reason, a taint or 'toxin' in the blood" (98).
8 Scott, who was a poet and is grouped with the Confederation poets, was employed by the Department of Indian Affairs (now Crown-Indigenous Relations Canada and Indigenous Services Canada) for the entirety of his career. As an employee, he implemented the repressive policies including the forcible removal of children from their families into residential schools. Renowned and respected as a poet in his day, Scott is both a regularly anthologized and deeply contentious figure in the twenty-first century. Some critics suggest he should not be vilified or read for his work (see, for example Fiamengo in *Home Ground*), while others suggest it is impossible and irresponsible to read Scott and his work separately from his full participation in racist and genocidal policies (Ruffo et al.). I mention him here because his friendship with Edgar, his prolific production as a poet, and his proximity to educators is a nuance that is important to track in the development of poetics, policies, and indeed pedagogies in Canada.
9 See Fowler, Vautour.
10 Fowler goes on to describe the *McGill Fortnightly Review* as a "programmatic attempt to advance modernism as an aesthetics" (Fowler, 275).
11

> With rare exceptions the best prose and poetry hitherto produced in Canada compares unfavorably even with the eyewash poured annually from third rate British and United States Presses … young men are inclined, and wisely, to look abroad for that which will influence them.
>
> (*The Canadian Mercury*, 8)

12 "The editors are all well under thirty and intend to remain so" (ibid.).
13 Writes Fowler, "it is characteristic of the McGill Group to assume, despite evidence to the contrary, that the prospective poets would be young men" (278).
14 An example: Scott managed to not just work but excel in both his literary and legal careers, winning the Governor General's Award for Non-Fiction for *Essays on the Constitution*, as well as the Governor General's Award Poetry with his *Collected Poems of F.R. Scott*.
15 Vautour 2011: 94. See also Avakumovic (1974), Purdy (1998), Rodney (1968), and Penner's *Canadian Communists* (1988), and see Azoulay (1997), and Penner's *From Protest to Power* (1992).
16 In a co-written poem in Bishops' University's *Mitre* entitled "The Girls Are Too Much With Us Late and Soon": Vautour notes that in addition to the obvious misogyny over the dismay and disdain of admitting women to the university, there is also evidence of Scott's awareness of using extant form to critique contemporary social shifts. See Vautour, *Writing Left*, 101.

17 Ibid., 105.

18 This continues in the *McGill Fortnightly Review* and includes a prose work that adopts Gertrude Stein's poetics, entitled "Gertrude Stein Has Tea at the Union" (Vautour 2011: 105).

19 The citations are from lines 1 and 10 of "The Canadian Authors Meet." Published in 1927 and then again in 1936 in *New Provinces* Sugars and Moss note that Scott made a few edits changing "lily" for maple (Sugars and Moss, 85).

20 Dudek equates the found poem with modernist methods, citing Eliot's use of fragments in "The Waste Land," Pound's use of quotation, and Joyce's documentation in *Ulysses.* See "Introduction." *Trouvailles: Poems from Prose*, 1–3.

21 Manina Jones points to the readymades of the Dadaists as well as Yeats's recontextualizations.

22 Her mother, Frances Randal Livesay, was a poet and a journalist. Her father, J.F.B. Livesay, was the General Manager of the Canadian Press. See Lever.

23 Her parents subscribed her to little magazines from the United States and Britain such as *Dial* and *Poetry*, and she read the work of H.D., T.S. Eliot, and William Carlos Williams, all of which influenced her experimentation with form. She reflected in conversation with Lever that, "the Imagist movement was very close to me. I liked particularly their ideas about breaking away from set forms, so that in my teens I was writing quite free verse" (Davey 2021).

24 She also continued as a social worker, and in 1937 married Duncan McNair and relocated to Vancouver, British Columbia, where she had two children.

25 Ferguson writes

> During its short publication run (1931–1934), Canada's *Masses*, published by the Progressive Arts Clubs of Canada (PAC), printed reports on lynching and racial terrorism in the US South. Canada's *Masses* took at least its name form one of its US predecessors, the *Masses* (1911–1917) or *New Masses* (1926–1948).
>
> (142)

26 Livesay served as both an editor and a contributor to *Masses* during the time that she wrote the poem "Day and Night" (1935) and later published it under E.J. Pratt's editorship at *Canadian Forum* (1936). See Irvine.

27 Of the poem Livesay writes that "this documentary is dominated by themes of struggle: class against class, race against race. The sound of Negro spirituals mingled in my mind with Cole Porter's 'Night and Day'" (see Sugars and Moss, 164).

28 There is no formal recognition of service from Canadian volunteers by the Federal Government, for example. There are, however, a few scholarly exceptions to this claim, specifically the work done by Vautour, Sharpe, et al.

29 Austrofascism (1934–38) saw the rise of Adolf Hitler's National Socialism as well as its predecessor Ständestaat (1933–38). Georg Weissel and Koloman Wallisch were two of the first victims who led the failed February Uprising.

30 Luís Carlos Prestes was a politician and Brazilian revolutionary. He served as the General Secretary of the Brazilian Communist Party between 1943 and 1980, was a leader of the 1924 Tenete Revolt, and imprisoned until after the Second World War.

31 In October of 1935, 200,000 Italian soldiers under the leadership of Marshal Emilio De Bono attacked Eritrea without a declaration of war. Simultaneous attacks were led in Italian Somalia, Adwa, and Aksum. The aim was to create an Axis-expansion prior to the Second World War.

Works Cited

Ahmed, Sara. *The Cultural Politics of Emotion*. 2nd ed. London: Routledge, 2014.
Alt, Christina. "'Recreating What Is Generally Forgotten' F.R. Scott and Native History." *ESC*, 81 (2004): 1–16.
Anderson, Patrick. "Editorial." *Preview No. 1* (March 1942): 1.
Austin, J.L. *How to Do Things with Words*. 2nd ed. Cambridge, MA: Harvard UP, 1975.
Avakumovic, Ivan. *The Communist Party in Canada: A History*. Toronto: M&S, 1975.
Azoulay, Dan. *Keeping the Dream Alive: The Survival of the Ontario CCF/NDP, 1950–1963*. Montreal: McGill-Queen's UP, 1997.
Baetz, Joel. "Beyond Flanders Fields." *Canadian Poetry from World War 1: An Anthology*. Ed. Joel Baetz. Toronto: Oxford, 2009. 1–18.
Baetz, Joel, ed. *Canadian Poetry from World War 1*. Toronto: OUP, 2009.
Bentley, D.M.R. *The Confederation Group of Canadian Poets, 1880–1897*. Toronto: U Toronto P, 2013.
———. "Reflections on the Situation and Study of Early Canadian Literature in the Long Confederation Period." *Home Ground and Foreign Territory: Essays on Early Canadian Literature*. Ed. Janice Fiamengo. Ottawa: UTP, 2014. 17–44.
Berardi, Franco "Bifo." *The Uprising: On Poetry and Finance*. Los Angeles, CA: Semiotext(e), 2012.
Betcherman, Lita-Rose. *The Swastika and the Maple Leaf Fascist Movements in Canada in the Thirties*. Toronto: Fitzhenry & Whiteside, 1975.
Binnema, Theodore, and Kevin Hutching. "The Emigrant and the Noble Savage: Sir Francis Bond Head's Romantic Approach to Aboriginal Policy in Upper Canada, 1836–1838." *University of Toronto Quarterly*, 39.1 (Winter 2004): 115–38.
Campbell, William Wilfred. "Preface." *The Oxford Book of Canadian Verse*. Toronto: OUP, 1913. i–xvi.
Coleman, Daniel. *White Civility: The Literary Project of English Canada*. Toronto: UTP, 2008.
Davey, Frank. "Dorothy Livesay Biography." *Encyclopedia of Literature*, JRank.org. Web (June 9, 2021).
Denning, Michael. *The Cultural Front: The Laboring of American Culture in the Twentieth Century*. London: Verso, 2011.
Djwa, Sandra. "The Civil Polish of His Horn: E.J. Pratt's *Brebeuf and his Brethren*." *ARIEL: A Review of International English Literature*, 4.3 (1973): 82–102.
———. *The Politics of Imagination: A Life of F.R. Scott*. Toronto: M&S, 1987.
Dudek, Louis. "Geography, Politics, and Poetry." *First Statement*, I.15 (2021): 2–3.
Dudek, Louis, and Michael Gnarowki, Eds. *The Making of Modern Poetry in Canada: Essential Articles on Contemporary Canadian Poetry in English*. 1967. Toronto: Ryerson Press, 1970.
Edgar, Pelham. *The Romance of Canadian History*. Toronto: Macmillan, 1902.
Fairley, Barker. "Rev. of 'The Titans'." *The Canadian Forum* (February 1927): 148–9.
Ferguson, Jade. *From Dixie to Dominion: Violence, Race, and the Time of Capital*. PhD dissertation. Cornell University, 2009. https://hdl.handle.net/1813/14012
Fiamengo, Janice, Ed. *Home Ground and Foreign Territory: Essays on Early Canadian Literature*. Ottawa: UTP, 2014.
Fowler, Adrian. "E.J. Pratt and the McGill Poets." *The Cambridge History of Canadian Literature*. Eds. Eva Marie Kroller et al. Cambridge: Cambridge UP. 272–88.
Frye, Northrop. "Editor's Introduction." In *The Collected Poems of E.J. Pratt. 1958*. Toronto: Macmillan, 1962. 8.

———. "Letters in Canada—1954." *The Bush Garden*. Toronto: Anansi, 1971. i–xiv.

Garvin, John W. "Editor's Foreword." *Canadian Poets*. Toronto: McClelland, Goodchild and Stewart, 1916: np.

Gingell, Susan. "E.J. Pratt Biography (1882–1964)." *Encyclopedia of Literature*, 8534. JRank.org, Web (March 2, 2022).

Harrington, Lyn. *Syllables of Recorded Time: The Story of the Canadian Authors Association, 1921–1981*. Toronto: Dundurn, 1981.

Irvine, Dean, ed. *The Canadian Modernists Meet*. Ottawa: U Ottawa P, 2005.

Jones, Manina. *That Art of Difference: "Documentary Collage" and English-Canadian Writing*. Toronto: UTP, 1993.

Kennedy, Leo. *The Shrouding*. Toronto: Macmillan, 1933.

———. "'Meet Quebec's Fascists!' Peter Quinn, pseud." *New Frontier*, 1.5 (1936): 5–8.

———. "Direction for Canadian Poets." *New Frontier* 1.2 (1936): 21-24. Print.

Klein, A.M. "Mortal Coils." *Canadian Jewish Chronicle* January 5. 1934. 8.

———. *The Collected Poems of A.M. Klein*. Ed. Miriam Waddington. Toronto: McGraw-Hill Ryerson, 1974.

Kymlicka, Will. *Politics in the Vernacular: Nationalism, Multiculturalism, and Citizenship*. Toronto: OUP, 2003.

Leacock, Stephen. *The Greatest Pages of American Humour*. London: Methune, 1937.

Lent, Vanessa, Bart Vautour, and Dean Irvine, Eds. *Making Canada New: Editing, Modernism, and New Media*. Toronto: UTP, 2017.

Leslie, Kenneth. "The Censored Editor." *New Frontier*, 2.3 (1937): 10–1.

Lever, Bernice. "Interview with Dorothy Livesay." *Canadian Forum* (September 1975). https://bcbooklook.com/interview-dorothy-livesay/

Lighthall, W.D. *Canadian Poets of the Great War: Presidential Address*. Ottawa: Royal Society of Canada, 1918.

Marriott, Anne. *The Wind Our Enemy*. Toronto: Ryerson Press, 1939.

Massey, Vincent. *Report: The Royal Commission on National Development in the Arts, Letters, and Sciences, 1949–1951*. Ottawa: King's Printer, 1951.

May, Robert G. "The Socially Conscious Poet from Canada to Spain: Leo Kennedy and *New Frontier*." *Canadian Poetry*, 77 (2015): 9–29.

McCrae, John. "In Flander's Fields." *Punch* (1915): np.

Moss, Laura, Ed. *Leaving the Shade of the Middle Ground: Selected Poems of F.R. Scott*. Waterloo: LPS, 2016.

Parkman, Francis. *The Jesuits in North America*. Boston, MA: Courthope, 1963.

Penner, Norman. *Canadian Communists: the Stalin Years and Beyond*. Toronto: Methune, 1988.

———. *From Protest to Power: Social Democracy in Canada 1900-Present*. Toronto: James Lorimer & Co.

Pitt, David G. "Pratt, Edwin John." *Canadian Encyclopedia*. Edmonton: Hurtig, 1962[1958]. 341–5.

Pratt, E.J. "'Silences'. 1936." *E.J. Pratt: Complete Poems*. Eds. Sandra Djwa and R.G. Moyles. Toronto: University of Toronto Press, 1989. 252.

———. "Box 9, No. 68.3." *On His Life and Poetry*. Victoria: University of Victoria Special Collections, 1940. 108–9.

Precosky, Don. "Editor's Introduction." *Preview*, 8 (1942): 8–9.

———. "*Preview*: An Introduction and Index." *Canadian Poetry*, 8 (Spring/Summer 1981), https://canadianpoetry.org/volumes/vol8/precosky.html

Purdy, Sean. *Radicals and Revolutionaries: The History of Canadian Communism from the Robert S. Kenny Collection*. Toronto: UTP, 1998.

Ridington, John. "The Poetry of the War: An Address Delivered before the Pacific Northwest Library Association at the Public Library, Portland Oregon." *UBC Archived* (1918): np.

Rifkind, Candida. *Comrades and Critics: Women, Literature, and the Left in 1930s Canada*. Toronto: UTP, 2009.

Rodney, William. *Soldiers of the International: A History of the Communist Party in Canada, 1919–1929*. Toronto: UTP, 1968.

Ruffo, Armand Garnet. *Grey Owl: The Mystery of Archie Belaney*. 1996. Hamilton: Wolsak & Wynn, 2021.

Saussure, Ferdinand. *Course in General Linguistics*. Eds. Charles Bally and Albert Sechehaye with Albert Reidlinger. Trans. Wade Baskin. Toronto: McGraw-Hill, 1959. 341–5.

Scott, Frederick George. *The Great War As I Saw It*. Toronto: Goodchild, 1922.

Scott, F.R. *Overture*. Toronto: Ryerson, 1945.

———. *The Eye of the Needle: Satire, Sorties, and Sundries*. Toronto: Contact Press, 1957.

———. *Selected Poems*. Toronto: Oxford, 1966.

———. *Trouvailles: Poems from Prose*. Montreal: Delta Canada, 1967.

———. *Essays on the Constitution: Aspects of Canadian Law and Politics*. Toronto: UTP, 1977.

———. "Three Documents from F.R. Scott's Personal Papers. Ed. D.M.R. Bentley and Michael Gnarowski. *Canadian Poetry*, 4 (1979): 73–119.

———. *Collected Poems of F.R. Scott*. Toronto: M&S, 1981.

Smith, A.J.M. "Editorial." *The Canadian Mercury*, 1.1 (1928): 3–8.

Sullivan, Rosemary. "A Size Larger Than Seeing: The Poetry of P.K. Page." *Canadian Literature*, 79 (1978): 32–42.

Sugars, Cynthia, and Laura Moss. "Making It New in Canada." *Canadian Literature: Texts and Contexts*. Vol. 2. Toronto: Pearson, 2009. 1–26.

Trehearne, Brian. *Aestheticism and Canadian Modernists: Aspects of a Poetic Influence*. Montreal: McGill-Queen's UP, 1989.

Vautour, Bart. "From Transnational Politics to National Modernist Poetics: Spanish Civil War Poetry in *New Frontier*." *Canadian Literature*, 204 (Spring 2010): 44–60.

———. "F.R. Scott and the Emergence of a Poetics of Institutional Critique." *Canadian Poetry: Studies, Documents, Reviews*, 66 (2010): 68–86.

———. *Writing Left: The Emergence of Modernism in English Canada*. Dissertation. Dalhousie University, 2011.

Vautour, Bart, and Emily Robbins Sharpe. *Canada and the Spanish Civil War: A Virtual Research Environment*. https://spanishcivilwar.ca/introduction

Vautour, Bart and Emily Robins Sharpe, eds. "Introduction." *Meet Me on the Barricades*. 1938. Charles Yale Harrison. Ottawa: Ottawa UP, 2016.

Weingarten, J.A. "Modernist Poetry in Canada, 1920–1960." *The Oxford Handbook of Canadian Literature*. Ed. Cynthia Sugars. Toronto: OUP, 2016. 315.

Williams, Raymond. "Culture Is Ordinary." *Resources of Hope: Culture, Democracy, Socialism*. Ed. Robin Gable. London: Verso, 1989. 5–6.

3 Poetic Witness and the 1940s

If the poetics of the 1930s were focused on critique and call to action, what follows in the 1940s offers yet another opportunity to think about how and what poetry does, especially when taken in the context of its production. In the rapid shift from the Great Depression to the wartime economy that accompanied the Second World War, a tumultuous era continued, albeit in a different and changed context. The country had officially (though belatedly) joined the anti-fascist cause when war was declared against Nazi Germany and its allies. Canada had remained neutral in global warfare in the 1930s, refusing to officially aid in the fight against fascism in Spain and elsewhere, and instead focusing on social and economic strife in the country. This was not the case within the next decade. Like the Great War of the previous generation, Canadians went *en masse* to fight abroad. The 1940s saw more than a million Canadians fight in the Second World War. It was a time of tremendous upheaval and the fate of the world was uncertain.

Lest we become too comfortable with the image of Canada as a helping nation, it is important to note that the decade also bears the shameful record of having enacted Japanese internment when, in 1942, the government succumbed to pressure to intern more than 22,000 Japanese Canadians, Canadians of Japanese descent, and naturalized Japanese citizens. Unlike the internment camps in the United States, Canadian internment camps separated men from women and children, sending many of the men to sugar beet plantations in the prairies, while many of the women and children were sent to camps in the interior of British Columbia. The conditions were so horrific that people in wartime Japan sent aid to the camps.[1] A similarly horrifying fact is that due to rising anti-Semitism in the country, as well as an utter failure to intervene in both social and structural racism, Canada had one of the worst records for accepting Jewish refugees in the world. In 1939, the *MS St. Louis* sailed first to Havana, Cuba, and then after being denied visas, it sailed first to the United States and then to Canada. All three countries denied the passengers entry. The ship returned to Europe where 254 of the passengers died in Nazi concentration camps.[2] Amidst the horrors of war, the Holocaust, increased class stratification, restricted borders, the internment of Japanese Canadians, and its own domestic genocide of Indigenous Peoples, the 1940s were complex to say the least.

DOI: 10.4324/9780429352966-3

What role does poetry have to play in this context? Who were the poets, and what were they doing? Indeed, what was the poetry doing? In 1931, Charles G.D. Roberts published "A Note on Modernism." In it, he updates his thesis that the new and old poets work well together and observes that while it is a "strictly relative term," which has gone under different terms, "it has always been, and is, a reaction of the younger creators against too long domination of their older predecessors" (*Selected*, 296). His essay acknowledges the generational tensions that almost inevitably arise as one generation works to demarcate their work from the previous one, but he does not address the extraordinary influence of international poetic as well as artistic movements on the newer generations. As Cynthia Sugars and Laura Moss demonstrate, experiments in representation in both the literary and fine arts were flourishing.[3] If the self-conscious development of modernist aesthetics took root in Canada in the 1930s, there is little doubt of their further flourishing in the ensuing decades. By 1943, recall, we see A.J.M. Smith demarcating what he saw as two dominant trends in Canadian poetry of the period. "Native" poets were those who focused on that which is "individual and unique in Canadian life." The second category was what he termed "cosmopolitan." The poetry and poets who he categorized as cosmopolitan he saw as undertaking a "heroic effort to transcend colonialism by entering into the universal, civilizing culture of ideas" (5). These attempts to galvanize trends were met with varied responses. For example, poet John Sutherland edited *Other Canadians: An Anthology of the New Poetry in Canada 1940–1946* which both expands on Smith's anthologizing by adding additional poets and critiques Smith's claims.[4] Less than a hundred years after Confederation, critical poetic discourse in Canada remained focused on questions of here and there, but again with a difference.

Case Study: *Preview* (1942–45), *First Statement* (1942–45), and *Northern Review* (1945–56)

One of the major issues in Canadian poetry of the first half of the twentieth century was a material issue: there were not many places to actually publish poetry in Canada. The Depression had devastated many sectors, and while there were some literary magazines as well as commercial and trade publications, the publishing industry in Canada was in dire need of support, a fact identified by the 1951 release of the *Massey Report*. While the publishing industry floundered, the poets of this era were committed to the production of poetry and to the fostering of poetic discourse in public spaces.[5] As Sugars and Moss point out, this commitment to making poetry as well as talking about poetry in public initiated a tradition of the poet-critic and poet-editor creating magazines and small presses that continues well into the twenty-first century.

While the emergence of poet-critic and poet-editor did much for the production and circulation of poetry, it has also created some interesting complications. The new "little magazines" of the 1940s offer a context from which to consider these complications. Indeed, Trehearne opens his study, *The Montreal Forties*, with an intervention: rather than add to the general critical consensus and focus on the war and post-war poetics through the lens of little magazines, he argues instead that critics … read the actual poetry. While his focus is narrow in that he attends solely to Montreal in the 1940s, his suggestion to read the poetry itself is fundamental.[6] Contra to arguments made by poet-critics who enter the academy and the arena of public opinion in the later part of this period, Trehearne suggests readers focus their attentions less on the differing aesthetics of the little magazines *Preview* and *First Statement* and more on the ways in which a different iteration of modernist aesthetics in Canada was emerging. Indeed, it is crucial to attempt to do both, first, examining the magazines as the context in which ideologies and aesthetics were circulating, and then turning to focus on some of the poetry itself.

Founded in 1942 and largely edited by Patrick Anderson, *Preview* aimed to create a coterie and give that coterie space for experimentation and discourse. In his first editorial, Anderson puts it thus: "Montreal writers who recently formed themselves into a group for the purpose of mutual discussion and criticism ... hope, through speculations, to try out their work before a somewhat larger public" ("Editorial," 1). Notice the emphasis Anderson places on "mutual discussion and criticism." There is a discernible hope for community, for conversation, and, perhaps, for the much-storied literary salons of Stein's Paris or Woolf's London. Anderson, who arrived in Montreal by way of Oxford, was invested in and influenced by the modernist modes of that side of the Atlantic including Imagism. Imagism is perhaps most readily connected with the early work of Ezra Pound, he of many dictums, but the mode was taken up by many influential poets including but not limited to H.D., William Carlos Williams, and, in Anderson's own circle some decades later, P.K. Page. The work in *Preview* was indebted to and engaged with a late-modernist cosmopolitan aesthetic, and this was for a time a source of some tension, namely, between Anderson and John Sutherland, the editor of *First Statement*. While an important part of literary history, as Trehearne (1954) emphasizes, the tensions between these two editors, while significant, cannot be the source of all our understanding of poetic developments at the time.

The aesthetic focus of *Preview* aimed to bring together like-minded poets who were interested in a similar aesthetic influence by cosmopolitan modes. In addition to a late-modernist Imagism, which reached Canada via Pound and Amy Lowell to be taken up in the work of Page and Irving Layton, so too did other forms arrive indirectly via Eliot, Auden, and Spender, both English and French Surrealism, as well as Mass Observation.[7] Practically speaking, *Preview* was an example of the do-it-yourself culture of little magazines. Anderson describes the process this way:

> The first six issues which were monthly were all mimeographed in foolscap form with only a printed title which alternated between blue and red. The meetings of the group [included] …. Mrs. Phillip Surrey who wrote as Margaret Day and who really only participated (although

> she was always a friend of the magazine) for about two issues; Bruce Ruddick who, as I remember was about to become a young medical student; Neufville Shaw; Frank Scott; and myself; and after about one issue, very valuably P.K. Page. The group met very often in my apartment behind Dorchester Street (for which I paid $17 a month—three almost unheated rooms over an unheated garage), sometimes at Neufville's who was then living in Notre Dame de Grace, occasionally at Frank's. We were supposed to have two meetings a month. The first was to read new work and discuss it, and the second meeting was a practical one of getting the magazine stapled and arranged for distribution to its subscribers. It always had subscribers; it was never on sale to the general public.
>
> (Mayne, 53)

Again, note the emphasis here on a group of writers getting together to read, write, and consider one another's work. Unlike the exuberant intervention of the *McGill Fortnightly Review* where the editors declaim a wholesale poetic revolution, the emphasis of *Preview* was to work with and for the group to hone a sense of shared poetic discourse. Theirs aimed to be a generative poetics.

The poets associated with *Preview* were invested in leftist political beliefs, predominantly democratic socialism (Precosky, "*Preview*"). In addition to working to bring social issues into poetic context—a continuation of the early work of Scott—the group also aimed to create a "fusion between the lyric and the didactic elements in modern verse, a combination of vivid, arresting imagery and the capacity to 'sing' with social content and criticism."[8] And while the work in *Preview* was focused on cosmopolitan issues and modes, and while there was come recognition and uptake by international poetry journals, the group's main discursive engagement was with *First Statement*.[9]

First Statement began the same year as *Preview*. At the helm was poet and editor John Sutherland, and other writers associated with the magazine included R.G. Simpson, Mary Margaret Miller, and Audrey Aikman. Described in a tagline first as "A Magazine for Young Canadian Writers" (later changed to "A Canadian Literary Magazine"), *First Statement* did not have the same specific focus that was the heart of *Preview*. One much-discussed focus of *First Statement* was Sutherland's ire for *Preview*, and specifically Anderson himself. Indeed, this "rivalry" or difference of opinions is integral to much of the critical discourse of the era, perhaps most notably in Sutherland's own scathing critiques of *Preview* that were central to many of his early editorials. The magazine shifts its focus, however, by the ninth issue which included poems by an emergent set of writers including Irving Layton, Louis Dudek, Miriam Waddington, and Raymond Souster. If the focus of *Preview* was on cosmopolitan aesthetics and socialist politics, that of *First Statement* was more on American rather than British late-modernism.

In 1945, despite real and amplified tensions and rivalries between them, *Preview* and *First Statement* merged to form a new little magazine called *Northern Review*. Here, the relationship between finance and poetry was simply the need to have the former to create and circulate the latter. Initially, the editorial board appeared to be a smooth combination of both magazines; it included Sutherland as the managing editor, as well as F.R. Scott, A.M. Klein, Irving Layton, Patrick Anderson, A.J.M. Smith, Audrey Aikman, R.G. Simpson, and Neufville Shaw on the editorial board. P.K. Page, Dorothy Livesay, James Wreford, and Ralph Gustafson served as regional editors. Two years later, after a controversial review of Robert Finch's collection, *Poems*, which had recently been granted the Governor General's Award for Poetry, a number of editors resigned from the board. Ultimately, the magazine was edited by Sutherland and Aikman until Sutherland's death in 1956.

In the shifting background of culture in Canada in the 1940s, poetry and little magazines were sites from which culture, community, and commentary could function. The general consensus of poetic criticism focused on this period underscores the tension between *Preview* and *First Statement* and, as Trehearne writes, "depends largely on the little magazine polemics of the *First Statement* editors Sutherland and Louis Dudek as they worked to distance themselves from the (to them) dominant *Preview* poetics characterized in the work of Anderson and Page" (25). But does this tension overwrite what was happening in the poetry itself? How much gets lost in the focus on editors sparring with one another in print? Undoubtedly, the fiery relationship between the two little magazines did much to create an atmosphere of energy and excitement around poetry and poetic discourse in Canada in the 1940s. While the discursive tensions between the little magazines are useful for context, it is vital that we look to the poetry itself to develop a more fulsome understanding of how and what the poets were doing in the midst of ongoing global upheaval and crisis.

Case Study: P.K. Page

P.K. Page had an incredible poetic career that spanned seven decades. Indeed, when her literary executor Zailig Pollock began cataloguing her papers after her death in 2010, he discovered a poem written in fridge magnets suggesting Page never ceased poetic production.[10] Born in 1916 in England, Page's peripatetic transnational and global life was emblematic of the period. From England she moved with her parents to Alberta and later to Manitoba. She spent a year in England as a teenager, lived in New Brunswick in the 1930s, and, significantly for Canadian poetry, moved to Montreal in 1941. It was upon arrival in Montreal that she became a member of the *Preview* coterie, and it was in this decade that she wrote critical essays[11] and poetry, including "The Stenographers," which has become one of the most anthologized poems in Canadian literature. With her husband, Canadian ambassador Arthur Irwin, Page lived in Australia, Brazil, Mexico, and Guatemala. In each place, her writing and her visual art practice evolved. Always, her work attended to visual qualities.

"The Stenographers" (1942) is a visual and psychological study of young women in the wartime workforce. Stenography, or the work of typing, copying, and taking dictation, was a career opening for women during the war, and at first glance Page's poem operates as a cinematic shot of these young women's days. Driven by visuality, simile, and metaphor, the poem walks the tightrope of impossible gendered options and limited opportunities. The focus is on the stenographers—a faceless group of undifferentiated young women whose entrance into the workforce has bound them as much as it has offered them so-called freedom and agency. What at first glance appears to be filled with movement and possibility shifts quickly to a kind of trap. Consider the opening stanza:

> After the brief bivouac of Sunday,
> their eyes, in the forced march of Monday to Saturday,
> hoist the white flag, flutter in the snow-storm of paper,
> haul it down and crack in the mid-sun of temper.

The poem begins in medias res, with Sunday a memory of unsheltered encampment. "The forced march" of the week aligns the work of the stenographers with the scores of global displacements and death marches of the present and previous decades. The white flag of surrender is a synecdoche for the endless labour expected of them, as well as the barrage of abuse they are required to endure. Notice the way in which Page separates the subjects of the poem from the action—the stenographers appear as "they" in the second line and are increasingly alienated from the very labour that facilitates their existence. Their labour ceases to be meaningful; like Charlie Chaplin's character in *Modern Life*, they are the cogs that drive the machine, only here Page attributes qualities of battle-worn soldiers to the young women.[12] They are without loft, "no wind for flight"; only the smallest breeze "at most, to tumble them over/ and leave them like rubbish—the boy-friends of blood." Here again the women are flattened, displaced, and stripped of agency. Thingified, they are rubbish, aligned not with upward mobility but with the cannon fodder of bodies that once were boys, now felled and furrowed on fighting fields. It is not until the final lines of the final stanza that the seemingly omniscient speaker is displaced by the lyric I:

> In their eyes I have seen
> the pin men of madness in marathon trim
> race round the track of the stadium pupil.

Who are the "pin men of madness"? On top of the moving parts of their typewriters reflected in their eyes, as the characters fly up to impress ink on paper, there are expanding possibilities. Bosses. Husbands. Businessmen. What is perhaps most arresting is the racetrack: it is the women, the stenographers who are both containers and reflectors of the marathon. Held fast in a double bind of gender and capitalism, the stenographers are caught. But where is the speaker who sees it all? At a distance, protected behind a fortress of poetic syntax and image, perhaps.

Page was widely celebrated in her life, and early in her poetic career, for her crystalline verse. She was also criticized for the same poetics that were the hallmarks of her craft. For example, professor and writer Northrop Frye described *The Metal and the Flower*, which won the Governor General's Award for Poetry in 1954 saying,

> if there is anything such as "pure poetry," this must be it: a lively mind seizing on almost any experience and turning it into witty verse .... Miss Page's work has a competent elegance about it that makes even the undistinguished poems still satisfying to look at.
>
> ("Letters," 49)

Despite this backhanded praise, just a few years prior John Sutherland used Page and "The Stenographers" specifically as an example of the problems of the *Preview* style and of its particular brand of modernist poetics. His contention was that the *Preview* writers had two poetic goals. The first was to "deal with subjects of importance," while the second was to "preserve a lyrical beauty" (7). His central example of the preservation of lyrical beauty is Page's "The Stenographers," which he condemns because Page's work and phrasing is "too overwhelming to be entirely true" (8). Louis Dudek would echo and redouble Sutherland's condemnation (2–3). And, while both Sutherland and Dudek are ostensibly using Page's work as an example of what they saw to be a problematic modernist style—one focused on decadence and not enough on the social realities of the day—it is notable that each uses Page's work around which to hinge their criticism.[13] Indeed in response to her later work, Sutherland continues his critique of Page's visual and figurative prowess writing "each of Miss Page's stanzas is so crowded with new and exciting pictures that ...[each] seems ... to require the attention of a whole poem" (3). More recently, Rosemary Sullivan grapples with Page's image-driven focus and suggests that Page "has such a remarkable verbal gift that the image-making process can become almost too seductive .... The poet is trapped by her remarkable responsiveness to nature," and her openness to nature and "sensual detail, to each 'bright glimpse of beauty', that even the sense of self, of separateness from the world, seems threatened."[14] Page's critics appear to be outraged or at least confounded by her poetic skill as well as the fact that she is a woman poet refusing to stay in her lane. Yet, their critiques are instructive, not so much for the way they spurn Page, but for the way they demonstrate some of the oppressive frameworks in which she—and her stenographers—lived and wrote.

Trehearne has a hypothesis for Page's poetics when he identifies what he calls the 1940s' style. It is poetics of impersonality, where the lyric I—that same position Sutherland identifies as *too present* in Page's work—is muted in favour of the image, of sensuality, and of stylistic innovation. Here is what Trehearne sees at work in Page's poetics of the period:

> She makes plain the surviving of Imagist drift of modernist poetry ... the decades' common tendency to accumulation (with little subordination) of such post-Imagist fragments as the structural basis of longer poems ... lends new vividness to our ideas of modernist impersonality .... Page helps us see that the idea of impersonality was not only powerful, hegemonic, as she began to write poetry, but attractive—the sublimation of personal desires in a "new poetics of objectivity and aesthetic distance."
>
> (320)

That is to say, Page's poetics—her focus on the image, her facility with metaphor—may well be a place from which she found both innovation and relative safety.

Let us close our consideration of Page by looking at "After Rain." Written in 1954, the poem was reprinted in the American journal *Poetry* in 1956. The poem opens with a vivid scene cropped close on the work of snails who have made their way through the cabbage and cauliflowers:

> The snails have made a garden of green lace:
> broderie anglaise from the cabbages,
> Chantilly from the choux-fleurs, tiny veils-
> I see already that I lift the blind
> upon a woman's wardrobe of the mind.
>
> Such female whimsy floats about me like
> a kind of tulle, a flimsy mesh,
> while feet in gumboots pace the rectangles-
> garden abstracted, geometry awash-
> an unknown theorem argued in green ink,
> dropped in the bath.

The speaker interrupts the image to make another observation, and here the reader encounters an "I": to lift the blind on not just a *woman's* mind, but the wardrobe of a woman's mind is curious. The observation moves the action of looking back, displaces it from the speaker, and places it not in the speaker's mind—thereby gendering them—but rather *displaces* it into a container or clothing (or both) of *a* woman's mind. The "female whimsy" of the second stanza elides the work of the snails with the inner life of women—meticulous, expert, diminished—and then zooms out to contrast the tulle work of the snails with the geometric march of human feet in gumboots. What is the hierarchy of knowing, here? The scene widens again to show a man "in soggy denim" who "squelches by my hub." Gardener?

Lover? Foil? Each of these is possible, and the speaker does not settle the reader's questions. Instead, the speaker turns to the birds, imploring them to work on them both. Specifically, the work the speakers ask the birds to "choir" is this:

> To keep my heart a size
> larger than seeing, unseduced by each
> Bright glimpse of beauty striking like a bell,
> so that the whole may toll,
> its meaning shine
> clear of the myriad images that still-
> do what I will-encumber its pure line.

The speaker's focus doubles back to the gendered container of perception and makes it both larger and extends its force beyond the individual. Instead of cabining the image, seeing and perception are rendered other than, and therefore elevated from the seer. This seems to move sharply away from a romantic lyric I whereby the authority of thinking, feeling, and perception is centred squarely in the individual, and towards a kind of interconnection and respect that we see in the later twentieth-century work of feminist writers and philosophers. To keep the heart "larger than seeing" required a poetics that moved without removing the gendered seeing subject. Shortly after writing this poem, Page would turn to artistic endeavours outside of writing poetry. She would, of course, return to poetry. When she did, she continued to work and be engaged with poetry and its contexts well after the period this chapter covers. While her "silent period" marked a shift, even though she moved through her textual silence, one of her contemporaries encountered a silence from which he did not emerge.

Case Study: A.M. Klein

Abraham Moses Klein was born in Ratno, Ukraine, and emigrated to Montreal with his parents when he was still a baby. The Klein family, like so many other European Jewish families, came to Canada in search of a life away from persecution. Their exile and the experience of the Jewish diaspora more broadly remained central to Klein's poetry. After attending a high school immortalized in Mordecai Richler's *The Apprenticeship of Duddy Kravitz*, Klein studied at McGill where he became a member of the McGill Group.

In his study of the decade Trehearne suggests that in Klein's work, as with Page's, there are examples of both the aesthetic and the individual impasses of the time: "that the problem of unifying intense images of the world, to create poems, or of one's self, to achieve identity and authenticity, was broad and deep and *can* help us to understand the complexity of literary culture in the period" (107). A careful focus on the poet's work draws a line between the social and political complexities of the era, as well as the aesthetic attempts in little magazines such as *Preview*, *First Statement*, and even earlier in the *McGill Fortnightly Review* to assert a cohesive group aesthetic which, when under pressure, failed. Klein, who was both integral to and somewhat marginal from these groups working to assert aesthetic cohesion, offers many examples of the complexities, tensions, and strategies poetry offers.

Klein was an active poet whose work began circulating in the 1920s, first with the *McGill Fortnightly Review*, and later with *Preview*, though he also maintained a functional relationship with the poets associated with *First Statement* as well. Indeed, depending on the tone and focus of the poem, he submitted work to both magazines.[15] His work focused on Jewish culture, heritage, and experience; he saw himself as a teacher whose medium was first poetry, then prose, and whose mission was to introduce Jewish experience to a wider readership. His work in the Jewish tradition as well as in modern poetics marks him as a singular and crucial figure of the period. His ability—similar to Page's—to both adhere to the prevailing modernist impulse of impersonality, as well as to attend to his own cultural and community experience is remarkable and is worth an extended focus of our attention.

Like F.R. Scott, Klein trained and worked as a lawyer while maintaining an active role as both critic and producer of poetry. And, while he published numerous poems in the 1920s and 1930s, like many of his peers he did not publish a single-author poetry collection until the next decade. *Hath Not a Jew* was published in 1940 by Behrman, a New York publisher, and its poems focused on the violent anti-Semitism Klein observed both locally and globally. The title of the collection comes from Shylock, the Jewish antagonist of Shakespeare's *The Merchant of Venice*. In Shylock's monologue, he employs rhetorical modes of logic and empathy to humanize both himself and Jewish peoples more broadly. Klein's collection, which contains poems written between 1920 and 1940, marks an increasingly pessimistic view of the future.[16] Note, for example, this excerpt from "Heirloom":

> My father bequeathed me no wide estates;
> No keys and ledgers were my heritage;
> Only some holy books with *yahrzeit* dates
> Writ mournfully upon a blank front page—
>
> Books of the Baal Shem Tov, and of his wonders;
> Pamphlets upon the devil and his crew;
> Prayers against road demons, witches, thunders;
> And sundry other tomes for a good Jew.

The opening stanzas, with their interlocking ABAB rhyme scheme, track an inheritance of cultural knowledge "bequeathed" to the speaker by the father. While the poem alludes to a diasporic heritage—"no wide estates/ no keys and ledgers"—the heirlooms offer connection and community across generations. The poem moves through the speaker's experience of returning to the books, "beautiful: though no pictures on them," and encountering both the textual material they contain *and* the evidence of previous generations who have held them and read their words. "The snuff left on this page, now brown and old" are the speaker's "coat of arms, my noble ancestry" and he adds to the material traces on the pages with his own tears when he turns the page and finds "a white hair fallen from my father's beard" (*The Collected Poems*, 158). The warm, intergenerational connection shifts dramatically in correlation to the devastating rise of fascism both in Quebec and in Europe. Brenner observes that in both his personal journals and in his poetic production, Klein was acutely aware of the coming disasters both in Canada and, of course, in Europe. In Quebec, the rising fascist movement was led by Adrien Arcand and marked a significant rise in anti-Semitism.[17] Across the Atlantic, the escalation of anti-Semitic terror and violence exacerbated for Klein the urgency to articulate, record, and write about Jewish life and culture in Europe and in North America. If the poems of *Hath Not a Jew* track the poet's relationship to the rise of violent anti-Semitism and his own increased attention to the instability and danger faced by Jewish communities in Canada as well as Europe, the collection that follows demonstrates a shift in aesthetics but not in focus. *The Hitleriad*, published in 1944, is a long mock epic that employs satire to address the Holocaust, lambaste and mock Hitler's genocidal regime, and demand a humanistic response to human acts of violence, terror, and hate.

Later in the decade, Klein wrote several notes towards his own theory of aesthetics which are illuminating both for his own poetic production, and for a sense of what, at the end of the 1940s, poetry could *do*. Theodor Adorno, the cultural philosopher oft-quoted for his remarks about the possibilities of poetry after the Holocaust wrote that "to write poetry after Auschwitz is barbarism" (34). This comes from the end of Adorno's essay "Cultural Criticism and Society," in which the German philosopher reflects on the ways in which production of art without a consideration of the culture from which it is produced can only reproduce the staggering defaults and violence of that context. Often misread as a wholesale refusal of poetry, it is perhaps more useful to consider—as we are doing throughout the whole of this text—what poetry does and how it does that work. In the context of genocide, can poetry that does not attend to the cultural and historical contexts that led to genocide *do* anything other than reproduce or tacitly condone the violence? For Adorno, the answer is no. For Klein too the answer is no, but the means by which he produced his own poetry become increasingly difficult. Midway through the 1950s, Klein stopped writing.

The Rocking Chair, which won the Governor General's Award for Poetry in 1948, was comprised of poems that shifted their focus away from global anti-Semitism and onto francophone-Jewish relations in Quebec. The poems, which were first conceived of as *Suite Canadienne*, are marked by absence—specifically, they are marked by the absence of Klein's heretofore consistent focus on Jewish peoples, culture, community, and the atrocities of anti-Semitism. Zalig Pollock points to "Not All the Perfumes of Arabia" (1943) as Klein's last poem to attend to Judaism for several years. The poems of *The Rocking Chair* have a new aesthetic—one that is more in keeping with Klein's affiliation with the modernist poetics of the *Preview* coterie. Trehearne and others suggest that this new aesthetic was a vital part of Klein's process of surviving his own survival.[18] Of the many poems in *The Rocking Chair* worthy of consideration, specifically within the context of tracking Klein's evolving poetics, "Portrait of the Poet as Landscape" is divided into six sections, each of which offers an angle on the poet. Reminiscent of American poet Wallace Stevens's 1917 poem "Thirteen Ways of Looking at a Blackbird," Klein's "Portrait" circles around the possibilities of subjectivity, perspective, and existence. It opens this way:

> Not an editorial-writer, bereaved with bartlett,
> mourns him, the shelved Lycidas.
> No actress squeezes a glycerine tear for him.
> The radio broadcast lets his passing pass.
> And with the police, no record. Nobody, it appears,
> either under his real name or his alias,
> missed him enough to report.

The poem begins with negation upon negation, each with its own intertextual or cultural reference. For example, "the shelved Lycidas" refers to John Milton's classic pastoral elegy, "Lycidas" which elevates, mourns, and memorializes the death by drowning of a school friend. Here, though, Klein has updated the possible ways in which a person of so-called merit might be mourned in a public fashion. The tears of an actress move the context to the Golden Age of Hollywood, while the reference to radio broadcast subtly incorporates the fact that national radio had begun to do that work of creating imagined communities of connection where previously, as cultural critic Benedict Anderson suggests, that work has been done by literature and little magazines. The poet as missing person moves from this first stanza of speculation, to the second in which the poem hones in on a changing cultural relationship. No longer is the poet central to a readerly community's experience of encountering and processing emotion. By the end of the first section, the speaker connects the missing poet with markers from Klein's own writing, referring to "he who unrolled out culture from his scroll," as being

> … if he is at all, a number, an x,
> a Mr. Smith in a hotel register,-
> incognito, lost, lacunal.

Each of these possibilities—a number, an x, an alias, a void—are undermined in the following stanza which reveals the poet is "not dead, but only ignored." The poet "has moods, just like a poet" and "sometimes, depressed to nadir, he will think all lost." The reflections that follow are refracted though syntactical mirrors. The poet remembers and travels back through generations, determined "as a character, with a rehearsed role: / The Count of Monte Cristo, come for his revenges" which hinge on a double entendre of release and the function of language: "the convince of the parole."

The third stanza leads the reader through the poet's reflection of various rooms—in colleges, as "caretakers of art," in offices where his is "alone; yet not completely alone." The various possibilities and paths are laid out as the poet sees them:

> And always for their egos—their outmoded art.
> ...
>
> Some, Patagonian in their own esteem,
> And longing for the multiplying word,
> Join party and wear pins
>
> ...
>
> And some go mystical, and some go mad.

The references here are rife with contextual possibility. Recall that among Klein's generation of poets F.R. Scott and Dorothy Livesay begin or increase their political action. Indeed, Klein too ran for election in 1949 on the CCF ticket. Others, such as the younger Irving Layton and Louis Dudek, break off to form new and exuberant claims of what poetry is and should do. And there, amid it all, is the speaker; not lost, but marginal on the brink of mysticism (like Ginsburg to come?) or madness.

The poem draws to completion by thinking about what, after all that has come before, poetry, and indeed the poet, can do:

> To find a new function for the declassé craft
> archaic like the fletcher's; to make a new thing;
> to say the word that will become sixth sense;
> perhaps by necessity and indirection bring
> new forms to life, anonymously, new creeds-
> O, somehow pay back the daily larcenies of the lung!
>
> These are not mean ambitions. It is already something
> merely to entertain them. Meanwhile, he
> makes of his status as zero a rich garland,
> a halo of his anonymity,
> and lives alone, and in his secret shrines
> like phosphorous. At the bottom of the sea.[19]

Note the references to the modernist imperative to make it new loping alongside Klein's intergenerational and international attentions. Finding "new function for the declassé craft" lands the poet a lone submarine, not in the oceanic violence of Pratt's "Silence," but in a veritable diving bell of otherness. In cataloguing Klein's poetic development, as well as his multiple identifications and experiences—of generative and nurturing childhood, moving between oft-fractious aesthetic coteries, practicing law amid rising and virulent anti-Semitism both at home and abroad, navigating the impossible experience of surviving the Holocaust—critics identify in Klein's work a poetic tension between modernist impersonality and lyric attentiveness. We may add to this an important reckoning: Klein's work offers places to think through what poetry can, and does do in both personal and cultural contexts.

Conclusion

In the previous chapter, the extraordinary set of changes happening in Canada in the lead up to Second World War was the main focus, and it was clear that those changes were reflected in the loud call for poetic action and articulation of what poets ought to do. With the onslaught of the Second World War, the tenor shifts slightly to the work of using poetry as a form of witness and community building, even if at times the animosity of competing visions overshadowed that work. The formation of little magazines in Montreal in the 1940s demonstrates an insistence that poetry must persist amongst terrible and unthinkable conditions. The work of P.K. Page and A.M. Klein serves as examples of this insistence. If poetry of the 1930s was a rallying cry, poetry of the 1940s was a thing around which people could rally. Following the 1940s, that rallying would build the foundations of a state-based recognition that in order for culture to support us, we must support culture.

Key Terms

Coterie: A small group of people bound together by shared interests marked often by a sense of exclusivity.

Imagism: An early twentieth-century movement in poetry that favoured clear and sharp language and a sense of precision of image.

Japanese Canadian Internment: In early 1942, the Canadian government enacted the War Measures Act in order to detain and dispossess more than 90% of Japanese Canadians who lived in British Columbia. More than 21,000 people were dispossessed of their homes and detained at their own cost by the government. In 1988, Prime Minister Brian Mulroney apologized for the government's violence against Japanese Canadians, and made symbolic redress payments.

Notes

1 For an overview of internment to redress and settlement in 1988 see Roy Miki and Cassandra Kobayashi. See also Kerber.
2 See *BBC*. See also Abella and Troper.
3 Sugars and Moss cite the experiments of the Group of Seven painters who were turning away from dominant modes of realist representation. See also Gregory Betts whose *Avant-Garde Canadian Literature* flags the Armory Show in New York City as an early manifestation of avant-garde aesthetics in Canada.
4 See Sugars and Moss who cite Sutherland's essay "Literary Colonialism" in which he takes on Smith directly. Sutherland writes, "Mr. Smith, who apparently sees special virtue in importing other people's ideas and literary forms believes that the future belongs to the cosmopolitan group, because they respond to every change in fashion." He goes on to suggest that "Canadian poetry will be a poetry that has stopped being a parasite on other literatures and has had the courage to decide its own problems in its own way."
5 An earlier example of poetic discourse in public space can be found in the column *At the Mermaid Inn* which ran for a time in *The Globe*. See Wunker and Mason. See also Davies.
6 The narrowness of focus is deliberate and allows an extremely thorough consideration of one particular context. The risk of such studies without attendant considerations of the wider context is that they necessarily omit a larger picture, and in so doing may likewise risk the reification of attention to Canada's largest cities while neglecting other regions. Thus it is important to remember as scholars that we need to look at both specific and broad studies if we want to develop a more fulsome picture.
7 Trehearne (1999) notes John Glassco was directly influenced by André Breton, and the English Surrealist David Gascoyne and that both Page and Layton were also influenced by Mass Observation, a "sociocultural (and briefly literary) experiment" (22).
8 This may well be an interesting antecedent to the lyric and conceptualism debates of the 2010s which are discussed in Chapter 6.
9 Precosky notes that *Poetry* and *Horizon* had "kind words for the magazine" and that James Laughlin asked permission to publish Anderson's work in *New Directions*.
10 See Pollock and Ballantyne.
11 From Precosky:

> P.K. Page notes the improved climate for poetry in Canada by comparing the current situation with that in 1939 and then writes in "Canadian Poetry 1942" that "Anne Marriot wrote 'The Wind Our Enemy'—a long poem of the drought on the prairies—in which she dared to use a modern technique, and more terribly still, to display a consciousness of Canada's social problems. But the annual poetry award that year went to Mr. Arthur Bourinot, who wrote, if I remember rightly, of the first trillium and shadows on the hills. And what hard-bitten judge of Canadian poetry is not won over and softened by the first trillium? I ask you."
>
> (8–9)

12 See critic Medrie Purdham who observes socialist concerns in *As Ten as Twenty*.
13 Some critics see Sutherland's most vociferous and egregious act of critical aggression as not critiquing Page, but outing Patrick Anderson's queerness in

print. Given both the homophobia and the misogyny of the era, it is notable that these critics associated with *First Statement* began building their sense of a modernist poetics on a critical practice rooted in othering and aggression. We will see this trend continue well into the twenty-first century.

14 See Sullivan for a more detailed analysis of this point.

15 Trehearne (1999) notes that Klein sent his "more sardonic and impersonal work" to *Preview* and his "lyrical and explicitly Jewish work" to *First Statement* (108).

16 Rachel Feldhay Brenner describes the collection as displaying a "complex vision of the world at large at a critical historical juncture" and notes that poems in the earlier section such as "Gift," "Wandering Beggar," and "Dwarf" depict a happy childhood. Fusing together Chasidic fairy tales "brought from the Eastern European 'shtetl'," the poems of this section resonate the easy relationship between Jewish people in Quebec and the French community. See also Caplan and Betcherman.

17 Arcand, a journalist in Quebec, was also an ardent fascist who idolized Hitler. An editor of several far-right newspapers, Arcand founded the Ordre patriotique des Goglus (1929) and actively advocated and amplified anti-Semitism. Founder of the Parti national social chrétien (1934), Arcand actively campaigned for the forced removal of Jewish Canadians and called for their relocation to Hudson Bay. See Kaplan.

18 Trehearne (1999) usefully cites Eugéne Lambert here "Genius is a way out that one invents." See also Kertzer.

19 In addition to a kind of sympathetic connection to Pratt's undersea "Silences," which opens this chapter, it will be interesting to note the ways in which Margaret Atwood's "This is a Photograph of Me" (1966) both echoes and innovates some of the subaquatic poetics of both Pratt and Klein. This is not to suggest that the poems of these three generationally, politically, and aesthetically different poets are deliberately connected, but rather to draw some lines of connection between the transferrable influences and connections poems and poets can have on one another.

For Further Reading

Betts, Gregory. *Avant-Garde Canadian Literature: The Early Manifestations*. Toronto: UTP, 2013.

Djwa, Sandra. *Journey with No Maps: A Life of P.K. Page*. Kingston: McGill-Queen's UP, 2012.

Pollock, Zailig. *A.M. Klein: The Story of the Poet*. Toronto: UTP, 1994.

Trehearne, Brian. *The Montreal Forties: Modernist Poetry in Transition*. Toronto: UTP, 1999.

Works Cited

Abella, Irving, and Harold Troper. *None Is Too Many: Canada and the Jews of Europe, 1933–1948*. Toronto: Lester & Orpen Dennys, 1982.

Adorno, Theodor. "Culture, Criticism, and Society." *Prisms*. London: Neville Spearman, 1967. 17–34.

Anderson, Benedict. *Imagined Communities: Reflections on the Origin and Spread of Nationalism*. London: Verso, 1983.

Anderson, Patrick. "Editorial." *Preview No. 1* (March 1942): 1.

Atwood, Margaret. "This is a Photograph of Me." *The Circle Game*. Toronto: Contact Press, 1966.

BBC World News. "Canada Apologizes for Turning Away Jewish Refugee Ship in 1939." November 7, 2018. www.bbc.com/news/world-us-canada-46105488

Berger, Thomas. *Fragile Freedoms: Human Rights and Dissent in Canada*. Toronto: Clarke, Irwin, & Co, 1981.

Betcherman, Lita-Rose. *The Swastika and the Maple Leaf Fascist Movements in Canada in the Thirties*. Toronto: Fitzhenry & Whiteside, 1975.

Betts, Gregory. *Avant-Garde Canadian Literature: The Early Manifestations*. Toronto: UTP, 2013.

Brenner, Rachel Feldhay. "A.M. Klein's *The Rocking Chair:* Toward the Redefinition of the Poet's Function." *Studies in Canadian Literature*, 15.1 (1990), https://journals.lib.unb.ca/index.php/SCL/article/view/8114

Campbell, William Wilfred. "Preface." *The Oxford Book of Canadian Verse*. Toronto: OUP, 1913. ii–xiv.

Caplan, Usher. *Like One that Dreamed: A Portrait of A.M. Klein*. Toronto: McGraw-Hill Ryerson Limited, 1982.

Coleman, Daniel. *White Civility: The Literary Project of English Canada*. Toronto: UTP, 2008.

Davies, Barrie, ed. *At the Mermaid Inn: Wilfrid Campbell, Archibald Lampman, Duncan Campbell Scott in the Globe 1892–93*. Toronto: UTP, 1979.

Djwa, Sandra. "The Canadian Forum: Literary Catalyst." *Studies in Canadian Literature*, 1.1 (1976): 7–25.

Dudek, Louis. "Geography, Politics, and Poetry." *First Statement*, I.15 (1942): 2–3.

Dudek, Louis, and Michael Gnarowki, Eds. *The Making of Modern Poetry in Canada: Essential Articles on Contemporary Canadian Poetry in English*. 1967. Toronto: Ryerson, 1970.

Filewod, Alan. "Why Are the Canadian Authorities Afraid of This Play? Eight Men Speak and Section 98 of the Criminal Code of Canada." *Performances that Changed the Americas*. Ed. Stuart A. Day. New York, NY: Routledge, 2021. 222–41.

Harvey, Jocelyn. "Canada Council for the Arts." *The Canadian Encyclopedia*. 2021. https://thecanadianencyclopedia.ca/en/article/canada-council-for-the-arts

Jones, Manina. *That Art of Difference: "Documentary Collage" and English-Canadian Writing*. Toronto: UTP, 1993.

Kaplan, William Edward. "Adrien Arcand." *The Canadian Encyclopedia*. 2018. www.thecanadianencyclopedia.ca/en/article/adrian-arcand

Kerber, Jenny. "Pulling up Roots; Border-Crossing and Migrancy on Southern 2018Alberta's Irrigation Frontier." *The Dalhousie Review*, 90.1 (2010): 47–60, https://dalspace.library.dal.ca//handle/10222/61907

Kertzer, J.M. "A.M. Klein's Meditation on Life." *Journal of Commonwealth Literature*, 13.1 (1978): 1–19.

Klein, A.M. "Mortal Coils." *Canadian Jewish Chronicle* (1934). Digital publication. 8.

———. *The Hitleriad*. Norfolk, CT: New Directions, 1944.

———. *The Rocking Chair and Other Poems*. Toronto: M&S, 1948.

———. *The Collected Poems of A.M. Klein*. Ed. Miriam Waddington. Toronto: McGraw-Hill Ryerson, 1974.

———. "A Modest Proposal." *Canadian Jewish Chronicle 14 July 1939; rpt. A.M. Klein Beyond Sambation; Selected Essays and Editorials, 1928–1955*. Eds. M.W. Steinburg and Usher Caplan. Toronto: UTP, 1982. 56–7.

Leacock, Stephen. "The National Literature Problem in Canada." *The Canadian Mercury* (1928): 9.

MacLennan, Hugh. "Where Is My Potted Palm." 1952. Reprinted in *The Other Side of Hugh MacLennan*. Ed. Elspeth Cameron. Toronto: Macmillan, 1978. 186–9.

Massey, Vincent. *Report: The Royal Commission on National Development in the Arts, Letters, and Sciences, 1949–1951*. Ottawa: King's Printer, 1951.

Mayne, Seymour. "A Conversation with Patrick Anderson." *Inscape*, 11 (1974): 53.

Miki, Roy, and Cassandra Kobayashi. *Justice in Our Time: The Japanese Canadian Redress Settlement*. Vancouver: Talonbooks, 1991.

Mount, Nick. *When Canadian Literature Moved to New York*. Toronto: UTP, 2005.

Page, P.K. "Canadian Poetry 1942." *Preview*, 8 (1942): 8–9.

———. *As Ten as Twenty*. Toronto: Ryerson, 1946.

———. *P.K. Page: Poems Selected and New*. Toronto: Anansi, 1967.

Pollock, Zaillig, and Emily Ballantyne. "Magnetic Poetry in Page's Kitchen." Library and Archives Canada. AMICUS n/a, 2010, www.flickr.com/photos/lac-bac/13888279091

Precosky, Don. "Preview: An Introduction and Index." *Canadian* Poetry, 8 (Spring/Summer 1981), https://canadianpoetry.org/volumes/vol8/precosky.html

Purdham, Medrie. *The Encyclopedic Imagination in the Canadian Artist Figure*. 2005. PhD dissertation. McGill University.

Roberts, Charles G.D. "A Note on Modernism." *Open House*. Eds. William Arthur Deacon and Wilfred Reeves. Ottawa: Graphic, 1931. 19–25.

———. *Selected Poems*. Toronto: The Ryerson Press, 1936.

Smith, A.J.M. "Editorial." *The Canadian Mercury*, 1.1 (1928): 3–8.

———, Ed. *The Book of Canadian Poetry*. Toronto: Gage, 1943.

Sugars, Cynthia, and Laura Moss. "Making It New in Canada." *Canadian Literature: Texts and Contexts*. Vol. 2. Toronto: Pearson, 2009. 1–26.

Sullivan, Rosemary. "A Size Larger Than Seeing: The Poetry of P.K. Page." *Canadian Literature*, 79 (1978): 32–42.

Sutherland, John. "P.K. Page and *Preview*." *First Statement*, I.6 (1942): 7–8.

Trehearne, Brian. *Aestheticism and the Canadian Modernists: Aspects of a Poetic Influence*. Kingston: McGill-Queen's UP, 1989.

——— *The Montreal Forties: Modernist Poetry in Transition*. Toronto: UTP, 1999.

Vautour, Bart. *Writing Left: The Emergence of Modernism in English Canadian Literature*. 2011. PhD dissertation. Dalhousie University.

Weingarten, J.A. "Modernist Poetry in Canada, 1920–1960." *The Oxford Handbook of Canadian Literature*. Ed. Cynthia Sugars. Toronto: OUP, 2016. 315.

Wunker, Erin and Travis V. Mason. "Introduction: Public Poetics." *Public Poetics: Critical Issues in Canadian Poetry and Poetics*. Eds. Bart Vautour, Erin Wunker, Travis V. Mason, and Christl Verduyn. Waterloo: WLUP, 2015. 1–25.

4 Post-War Poetics and New National Mythologies

Rarely is there a period in history that can genuinely be described as "quiet." The period we will focus on in this chapter—1951–85—is again a tumultuous one. The decade immediately following Canada's involvement in the Second World War was filled with post-war reckoning that took various forms: a new wave of support for artistic and cultural production key for the life of poetry in Canada. While at no point was literary production fallow, there were few infrastructural supports for poets and other cultural producers in Canada. The publication of the Royal Commission on National Development in the Arts, Letters and Sciences, more commonly known as *The Massey Report* for its head Vincent Massey, radically changed the conditions under which literature and the literary arts were produced in Canada. The changes were facilitated by following through on some of the key recommendations of the *Report* and made poetic production—along with other modes of cultural production—more possible.

Struck by Prime Minister Louis St. Laurent in 1949, the Commission was charged with determining how and what people in Canada considered culture, and where their cultural consumption was coming from. The *Report* was issued on June 1, 1951 and made several key recommendations aiming at the preservation and amplification of cultural production in Canada. These recommendations included but were not limited to the founding of the National Library of Canada (now called Libraries and Archives Canada), the creation of the Canada Council for the Arts, and federal financial aid for universities. The *Report* also found that financial and other infrastructural support for arts and culture in Canada was extremely low. There were very few book publishers in Canada and that had been the case for some time. The lack of a viable publishing industry in Canada meant that writers had been leaving for elsewhere—predominantly New York and Boston—since the Confederation era. Add to this the participation by people in Canada in international wars, as well as the pervasive presence of American culture through growing access to literature, music, film, and television. The production *and* consumption of Canadian culture was in need of support.

While the Canadian Broadcasting Corporation (CBC) was founded in 1936, it was struggling to maintain itself and compete with the available programming coming from the United States. In 1936, the Canadian

DOI: 10.4324/9780429352966-4

Broadcasting Act solidified the CBC/Radio-Canada as a crown corporation. Three years later, the government moved to create a National Film Commission (what would become the National Film Board or NFB) to "make and distribute films designed to help Canadians in all parts of Canada to understand the ways of living and problems of Canadians in other parts" (iv). With these two organizations already extant, the recommendations of the *Massey Report* were to provide financial support for the production and circulation of additional cultural work in the country.

The findings of the *Massey Report* were bleak. After years of interviewing people in Canada and gathering data, its authors described the cultural landscape in Canada as "moribund," "meager," lacking, and almost non-existent outside the largest urban centres. English fiction writers were only producing on average 14 publications per annum, and

> No novelist, poet, short story writer, historian, biographer, or other writer of non-technical books can make even a modestly comfortable living by selling his work in Canada. No composer of music can live at all on what Canada pays him for his compositions. Apart from radio drama, no playwright, and only a few actors and producers can live by working in theatre in Canada. Gifted Canadians must be content with a precarious and unrewarding life in Canada or go abroad where their talents are in demand.
>
> (Harvey, npag)

The establishment of the Canada Council for the Arts as an arm's length body of the federal government was meant to specifically and directly address the financial precarity of cultural producers in the country through artistic grants based on the merit of the artist's application. The Council, which has undergone needed revision to address structural barriers to BIPOC and other marginalized applicants, does, nonetheless, offer unprecedented financial support to artists in Canada. In addition to administering some of the most significant cultural awards in the country, such as the Governor General's Awards, the Council also established the Public Lending Right (PLR) programme in 1977. The PLR, which came about after significant labour by members of The Writers' Union of Canada, offers writers financial compensation for readers checking their books out of libraries. Like the granting system of the Canada Council, the PLR was a distinctly different model for supporting writers than existed elsewhere in North America. It should be no surprise that changes in the material conditions of artistic production had significant effect on the development of poetry and other art forms.

One of the prevailing issues with assessing the very real outcomes the *Massey Report* and the subsequent changes to the material conditions of making and publishing poetry in Canada is that the *Massey Report*—and then decades worth of cultural criticism and cultural historiography afterwards—was drenched in the language of cultural nationalism. What is more, that discursive language of cultural nationalism has stuck—has become sticky in the sense that Sara Ahmed uses the word. For Ahmed, a feminist theorist of affect, among other things, sticky concepts are those that shape our modes of relating with the world. For Ahmed, stickiness is "an effect of the histories of contact between bodies, objects, and signs" and is the result of repeated imprints. She offers an example of stickiness in language as when "a word is used in a certain way, again and again, then that 'use' *becomes* intrinsic."[1] Looking back over the periods of poetic production from the first half of the twentieth century and earlier, it is useful to consider the ways in which the *Massey Report* and the literary criticism that arose, in part, because of the results of building greater support for arts in Canada is sticky with nationalist discourse. This stickiness continues across the late-twentieth and into the twenty-first centuries.

As an example of stickiness, consider novelist Hugh MacLennan, who, in looking back to the 1930s, described Canada as "an uncharacterized country, unrealized and unappreciated by Canadians themselves, while the rest of the world had never thought about Canadian art at all, and knew nothing whatever about us" (46). This is a curious statement that is both familiar and worthy of consideration. It is familiar because MacLennan, writing this in 1952, circles back to much of the discourse around literature and the nation that we have encountered already. It is also worthy of consideration because, I think, it offers us an instance of stickiness that reproduces a set of "feelings" about, in this case, poetry. This kind of statement—a confident truth claim that, frankly, bears shaky actual truth—can have a huge influence on how people see themselves. It is a kind of twentieth-century meme that, while catchy, can never capture nuance because nuance is not what a claim—or a meme—aims to do. And, while MacLennan went on to suggest by the late 1950s that "... there is no need any longer to ask whether there can be a Canadian literature. There is one now," this again marks a kind of line in the sand that is a defensive and exclusionary one, rather than a nuanced one. Must poetry be yoked to a sense of national identity? How are poets in a nation supported? What is poetry doing to the "nation"? These are three decidedly different questions with only some periodic overlap, and yet as we have seen and will continue to see, they are often collapsed as though one and the same. And while some working in service of facets or notions of "the nation" may periodically use poetry or other forms of cultural production to animate national projects, poetry itself does not care, but the language or signs of "the nation" continue to be attached to poetic production in a way that was unseen prior to the 1950s.

After the Report

A new surge in cultural nationalism arose during the decades of the 1950s, 1960s (marked the centennial anniversary of Canada's colonial project), and the 1970s. As Cynthia Sugars and Laura Moss write, while nationalist feelings were prevalent at various points of the country's history—Confederation and the First World War to name but two—there was a new quality to debates about Canadian cultural identity in this period.[2] The national celebration of the centenary of Confederation in 1967 marked an apex for this new iteration of cultural nationalism, one quality of which was a virulent anti-Americanism. And while tensions and ambivalences towards America were not new, they reached new heights in this period. Poet Dennis Lee's caution is emblematic of the atmosphere when, in 1973, he cautions against the "American tidal-wave that inundates us, in the cultural sphere as much as in the economic and political" ("Cadence, Country, Silence: Writing in Colonial Space," 47). It is significant to note that alongside a heightened awareness of the influence of the United States there was also a new and deeply violent iteration of the Indian Act that resulted in the Sixties Scoop,[3] the Front de liberation du Québec (FLQ)/October Crisis in Quebec, which led to the implementation of the War Measures Act, as well as a growing awareness about environmental crisis.[4] Central, too, to the 1960s is the broad (if amorphous) movement for social justice. In America, the civil rights movement was underway. In Canada, Indigenous people did not have the right to vote until 1960 without losing their status. Additionally, feminist movements were developing what has come to be called Feminism's second wave, and organizing for what we now call LGBTQ2S+ rights was also reaching new levels of public awareness.[5] And while at times these movements intersected in mutually supportive ways, this was not always the case.

The 1970s saw a continuation of these issues, as well as the Vietnam War, which galvanized anti-American sentiment. More than 20,000 American draft dodgers were given refuge, thus reversing (for a time) the direction of immigration across the US/Canada border. The 1980s brought with them the patriation of the constitution with the *Constitution Act, 1982*, with its embedded Charter of Rights and Freedoms and the solidification of multicultural policy in the *Multiculturalism Act (1988)*. Despite the unifying intent of these legislative acts, tensions continue to emerge between the presentation of an inclusive and diverse country and the realities of deep and systemic inequities. Out of and amongst this large-scale reshaping of post-war Canada, new opportunities in cultural production emerged as the government responded to the findings of the *Massey Report*. At every point in this post-war period, the poets were writing. But significantly, there were emergent infrastructures in place to support and circulate this work.

Developing Poetic Infrastructures

George Woodcock has said of poetic production in the 1960s that the decade brought with it "an enormous quantitative expansion of Canadian writing" (*The World of Canadian Writing*, 13). This is true. Increased infrastructure meant increased production and, in turn, the increased circulation and consumption of Canadian literature and culture. Many small publishing houses were formed in this period—some of which, like Coach House and Anansi, remain benchmarks of literary and poetic publishing well into the twenty-first century. Indeed, the Council's establishment of subsidies and supports for small presses—along with individual grants awarded to poets—helped to grow poetic culture and production both in and beyond urban centres. While the Canada Council's support caused a sea change in the production and distribution of poetry in Canada, it is important to note that not all emergent literary culture was supported by the Canada Council. While the Canada Council aided in the establishment of small presses, many poets began to produce and circulate their work using then-new mimeograph technology. bpNichol's grOnk press and bill bissett's blewointment press are examples of these kinds of do-it-yourself publications which were influential but, due to their publication quality, were deemed inadmissible for Council funding.[6] Similarly, the formative publication from TISH, which we will consider more fully below, was produced from borrowed paper and access to a mimeograph machine in the English Department at the University of British Columbia.[7] Furthermore, the amplification of sound poetry and spoken word begins to happen in this decade. Once again, the poets were engaged in prolific production, as well as fostering more debate and conversation, but this growing field was now supported by a robust, if sometimes flawed, funding infrastructure.

In addition to new sites for publication, there was a growth of discourse that moved discussion about poets and poetry into a broader public. Again, while it should not be a stretch or a surprise, the evidence is clear: when publication venues are required to support Canadian content, focus on writers in Canada grows. For example, editor, scholar, and former TISH affiliate Frank Davey outlines that:

> [a]rticles about Al Purdy appeared in *Time* (Canadian edition) in May 1965, in *The Montreal Star* in July 1965, in *Saturday Night* in August 1971 and July 1972, and in the *Financial Post* in March 1972. Articles on [Leonard] Cohen appeared in *Maclean's* in October 1966, in *Saturday Night* in February 1968 and June 1969, and in *The Montreal Star* in June 1969. Articles on Atwood appeared in *Saturday Night* in June 1967, March 1971, and November 1972 (the issue's cover story), in the *Montreal Star* in November 1968, in *Maclean's* in August 1969 and September 1972, in *Chatelaine* in October 1972, in *Mademoiselle* in July 1972 and May 1974, in *The Financial Post* in April 1973, in *Toronto Life* in June 1972, in the *Toronto Star* in October 1972, and in *The Globe and Mail* in April 1973. An article about [Michael] Ondaatje appeared in *Saturday Night* in February 1971. Purdy published poems in *Saturday Night* eight times between February 1967 and September 1973, as well as in *Maclean's* (August 1969) and *Arts/Canada* (December 1971/January 1972). [Margaret] Atwood published poems in *Saturday Night* in June 1967 and October 1968, and in *Maclean's* in August 1969. ("Al Purdy, Sam Solecki, and the Poetry of the 1960s," 39).

Davey's intensive catalogue of now-infamous poets reaching magazine-cover heights of fame is effective in demonstrating that poets—often a handful of the same poets—were increasingly mainstream public figures. In addition to attention in periodical publications, which circulated poetry, new teaching-oriented anthologies of Canadian poetry were published in this period. These academic- or teaching-oriented anthologies did more than simply circulate poetic work; anthologies do a good deal of the work of canon formation.[8] Central among the academic anthologies of poetry in Canada in this period were those by Gary Geddes and Eli Mandel. While neither anthologies made substantive swerves away from more mainstream poetry—no visual poetry was included in either, for example—both anthologies were embraced by academics teaching Canadian poetry to students in post-secondary institutions.

Another benchmark change facilitated in great part by the formation of the Canada Council and its funding mandates was the development of the public poetry reading series across the country. One such—the Contact Reading Series—is a useful example in that it demonstrates the interconnectedness of the creation of the Council, the circulation of poetry, and the development of urban, regional, transnational, and international poetic discourses and communities. As Cameron Anstee writes, while not the first of its kind, the Contact Reading Series ushered in a cultural engagement with and platform for poetry that has lasting effects in the twenty-first century literary landscapes (76).[9]

The Contact Reading Series was funded by a Canada Council Grant and, as such, "stands apart as a result of the *reading series* model that it established," which is a "basic structure that continues to operate in Canada in the twenty-first century" (Anstee, 76). In his work on the series, Anstee identifies the series as stemming in part from the Canadian Writers' Conference which was held in July 1955 at Queen's University. Organized by George Whalley, the conference was attended by poets including Irving Layton, Louis Dudek, Miriam Waddington, Phyllis Webb, and Jay Macpherson, among others. Significantly, Anstee has tracked the effusive response of attendees to the poetry readings that were a part of the conference and highlights specifically from Macpherson's report that many poets found the readings the most useful part of the whole conference because many of them had not had "much opportunity of trying new poems out on a sympathetic ear" (137). When the Contact Reading Series applied to the Canada Council, the organizers made a clear connection between the need for poetry and poets to be in communication with one another and with listening publics.[10] The request for funding was successful: the series received $845 in funds under the category of "Opera, Theatre, Ballet, etc." thus underscoring how new the notion of poetry needing live publics was at this point. While much has been written about the ways in which arts and literature need public engagement, the fact that Contact's application for support for a reading series was categorized under performing arts is significant.[11] By 1972, requests to the Council for public reading supports were so ubiquitous that there was a new category developed for the adjudication of applications which was called "Public Readings by Canadian Writers" (Anstee, 79).

The Contact Reading Series managed to develop both a national platform for poets as well as a reciprocal international one. Over the five years that it ran, the Contact Reading Series brought poets from across Canada—including, significantly, from Quebec— to an audience in Toronto, and it also brought in American poets such as Amiri Baraka (then Leroi Jones), Denise Levertov, and Charles Olson. In turn, F.R. Scott, Irving Layton, and Leonard Cohen all read at the Poetry Center in New York in 1959. Thus, what the Contact Reading Series accomplished is clear: it brought together poets and audiences and fostered engaged literary publics. As Anstee writes:

> In 1957 there were no such regular events; by 1962 there were several. The performance of poetry also took on additional forms in the 1960s. Coincident with the establishment of the Contact Poetry Reading Series, Folkways Records issued two LPs: *Six Montreal Poets* (A.J.M. Smith et al. 1957) and *Six Toronto Poets* (W.W.E. Ross et al. 1958). Poets were regularly hosted on CBC radio, and the National Film Board of Canada produced numerous poetry-related projects (among them *Ladies and Gentlemen, Mr. Leonard Cohen* in 1965 and the Poets on Film series of the 1970s). Individual reading tours also grew more common.
>
> (Anstee, 79)

The literary reading series became a stable in Canadian literary and especially poetry communities in the late 1950s. A decade later, Raymond Souster observed that "Contact appears to have formed a bridge over into the Fifties in which the modern Canadian poetical movement could begin its slow determined march" (Gnarowski, 2).

While the conditions for the writing, publication, and circulation of poetry were expanding in exciting and innovative ways, there were attendant conversations growing about what Tanis MacDonald names as "poetry's position in cultural politics." MacDonald uses the term "culture wars" to describe the poetic landscape of these decades, and she does so deliberately, observing that since about 1960 there have been "significant changes and an equal, if not opposite, reaction to each of these changes in the cultural positions of Canadian literature in general and Canadian poetry in particular" (for more see MacDonald). One place to track these tensions is in the growing body of literary criticism that, often, was written in part by poet-critics. Take, for example, thematic criticism. Developed predominantly by Northrop Frye in his conclusion to Klinck's *Literary History of Canada* (1965) through his concept of the "garrison mentality," thematic criticism took on a life of its own and in Canada dominated academic and public conceptions of Canadian literature. Frye, who, as D.M.R. Bentley notes, was asked to provide a conclusion precisely because he had *not* read and researched the material in the book and thus could provide an arm's-length overview, observed that "a tone of deep terror in regard to nature" pervades "Canadian poetry" and creates in Canadian "communities" and "the Canadian imagination" what he termed "a garrison mentality" (see Bentley, "Rummagings"). This "garrison mentality" is deeply imbricated in settler colonialism and narratives of frontierism. For Frye, texts which exhibit a garrison mentality emphasize binary oppositions, as well as "coldness, wildness, loneliness, and other survivorist/frontier aspects."[12]

While a garrison mentality is not in and of itself negative, the concept was taken up to describe everything from Canadian population organization along the 49th parallel, to fear of American influence, to fear of a malevolent North.[13] Following his arm's-length diagnostic, Frye went on to shore up and develop his concept in *The Bush Garden: Essays on the Canadian Imagination* (1971), which directly influenced a generation or more of his students, including Margaret Atwood. Atwood's *Survival: A Thematic Guide to Canadian Literature* was published in 1972 and takes Frye's thematic criticism to a further pole. In *Survival*, which was read and embraced by a general public, as opposed to Frye's more scholarly work, Atwood figures people in Canada as "victims" and outlines a series of "victim positions" which can serve as thematic templates for literary criticism and analysis.[14] And, while Atwood's text was in part aimed at high school teachers interested in integrating Canadian material into their classrooms, and partly at a money-making effort for the House of Anansi Press, it nonetheless became a zeitgeist text, and a polarizing one at that. One particularly problematic aspect of *Survival* is its central focus on settler identity and total erasure of Indigenous presence. Indeed, the text is predicated on settler fear without naming what Terry Goldie identifies as settler fear and temptation which is predicated on the compartmentalized guilt of settler colonialism and its attendant rhetoric of white supremacy (*Fear and Temptation*, iv).

Atwood's was not the only volume of literary criticism to engage with thematic criticism. D.G. Jones's *Butterfly on Rock* (1970), John Moss's *Patterns of Isolation* (1974), and Robin Matthew's *Canadian Literature: Surrender or Revolution* (1978) are a few examples of thematic criticism that circulated widely and helped solidify this mode of literary and poetic discourse.[15] While other trends in literary criticism emerge, as MacDonald points out, the effects of thematic criticism have had a lasting and significant effect. Narratives that hinge around unpopulated "wilderness" ossify and legitimize land as unpopulated. In short, such narratives recapitulate the myths of *terra nullius* and erase Indigenous lives to make space for non-Indigenous ones. This is a founding problem of Canada, and in the 1960s and 1970s thematic criticism functioned as a kind of "literary version of cultural nationalism" that celebrated frontier spirit and continued to uphold images of Indigenous Peoples as Romantic figures outside of contemporary time. As we saw in the Preface and will address more fully in Chapter 5, to frame entire peoples as homogenized and nostalgic is one of the central tricks of white supremacy. Thematic criticism did many things, and this is one of its abiding legacies.

In her excellent introduction to poetry after 1960, MacDonald argues that poetry itself was a catalyst not just for literary but also for cultural debates happening in Canada. Poetry was central to debates about how artists were supported in Canada, how books were published, and what kinds of literatures were taught in high school as well as post-secondary classrooms. Because key figures in these debates were located *in* these classrooms, and because, like Frye for example, they were often engaged in poetic discourses, poetry became a central place in which these conversations—and contentions—happened. As literary canons were developed and "regional snobbery, racism, sexism, and classism" became more vital to address, poetry continued to be written by poets (MacDonald, 475). And while this might seem a simple statement—and is, to a certain extent—it is worth differentiating between the two. For, as MacDonald usefully reminds us, to reproduce, or even try to frame poetic production as only a linear process is to reify and ossify narratives of progress, linearity, and inheritance over innovation, political engagement, and aesthetics (MacDonald, 475). Smaro Kamboureli makes a similar observation in her introduction to the important collection of essays *Trans.Can.Lit.* While still centring the national, Kamboureli suggests that:

> CanLit is both firmly entangled with [the] national imaginary and capable of resisting it. The body literary does not always have a symmetrical relationship to the body politic; the literary is inflected and infected by the political in oblique ways, at the same time that it asserts its unassimilability.
>
> (viii)

In other words, the signifier of "CanLit" for literature written in Canada, or "CanPo" for poetry written in Canada, gets yoked with political and social culture, and yet it resists this unification. For, to suggest that literatures or poetries are ever singular is folly—and all the more so when homogenized and read as a synecdoche for the nation. Yet, this happens, and perhaps the roots of this work can be best located in the period under consideration in this chapter.

Significantly, MacDonald suggests that we readers consider that poetry written in Canada, and especially poetry when harnessed under the complicated singular signifier "CanPo," has been and remains "intentionally, declaratively, open-endedly engaged with public debate" and that this has been possible because poetry is the "lesser-read genre than the novel, a (usually) less-profitable publishing venture, and a genre whose various forms and anti-forms emphasize an ongoing interest in language, aporia, and power" (MacDonald, 479). Indeed, work from the period shores up this assertion. Dudek and Gnarowski's hugely influential *The Making of Modern Poetry in Canada* (1967) posits a break in poetics towards "open rage and revolt" (231). And, while to suggest that the break is new would discount the work of anti-fascist and transnational poets of the 1930s, it bears consideration on its own terms.

What can it mean to "give vent to open rage and revolt"? For George Woodcock, the changing poetics of the period revolted, as is so often the case, against the conventions of the previous generation. In this case, one form that "revolution" took was in the grassroots and working-class poetics of poets such as Milton Acorn, Alden Nowlan, and Al Purdy.[16] It also meant the introduction, via University of British Columbia professor Warren Tallman, of the Black Mountain College School of Poetics.[17] Similarly, it meant the creation of some key small presses including but not limited to Coach House Press, House of Anansi Press, Brick Books, Coteau Books, Turnstone Press, and the journals *Contemporary Verse II*, *Dandelion*, and *Room of One's Own* all in 1975. It also meant that in addition to a shifting poetics on the page, there was an increased gathering of poets and writers to discuss aesthetics as well as pressing issues for writers. Not only was The Writers' Union of Canada created in 1972, and several years before it in 1966, the League of Canadian Poets, but also conferences were held with more regularity. "Women and Words/Les femmes et les mots" was a landmark event in Vancouver in 1983 that aimed to claim space for women's writing in both English and French, and for which there had been neither space nor even consideration granted in the cultural nationalist project of the 1960s and 1970s. Of similar significance was "Writing Thru Race," a conference held in Vancouver over Canada Day weekend in 1994, 11 years after "Women and Words/Les femmes et les mots." This conference aimed to make space for diasporic writers and writing in Canada. This conference, attended by writers including Roy Miki, Dionne Brand, Larissa Lai, Lillian Allen, Lee Maracle, and Lenore Keeshig-Tobias, was a watershed event that held space for BIPOC writers and refused or restricted entry to white writers.[18] Given the systemic and ongoing barriers and gatekeeping that BIPOC writers experience in Canada, this was both a vital and a bold move. It created a media sensation and, unfortunately if not unsurprisingly, backlash against the work these writers were doing to leverage space and time together. As MacDonald observes, this choice to restrict attendance by white writers "neatly pointed out the central point of writing through race: that it is different from writing about race, and different from writing through the dominant culture" (486).

The 1960s–1980s saw many social and cultural changes; and with them, poetic developments. In order to give some context for these changes, we will turn our attention to several case studies of poets whose work and whose identities engage in some of the key concerns of the period. The case studies of this chapter do not necessarily focus on the most canonical poets of the period. Readers familiar with the material might be surprised that there is not a case study on Leonard Cohen or Margaret Atwood, for example. Instead, I begin with the poet Phyllis Webb, whose attention to both space and silence offers a different perspective of what MacDonald calls the "fracture mechanics" of the era. Webb's work moves from the centre to the margin deliberately. It also offers space in which to consider queer poetics and the possibilities of attention that arise in gaps, fissures, and gestures. From Webb, I move to consider the formation of the TISH group in Vancouver. This constellation of poets working to interrupt what they saw to be the status quo draws lines of connection across the 49th parallel and into the radical poetics happening in parts of the United States. It also offers a site from which to return to the notion of coteries from a different historical moment and to attend to the ensuing poetic attentions of some of the poets affiliated with the group. From TISH, I move to a case study on the Quebec writer Nicole Brossard whose feminist poetics mark a significant moment in English-French poetic translation. Brossard is a foundational figure not only in the collaborative feminist poetics coming out of Montreal, but also as a poet of international circulation and renown. The chapter closes with a consideration of the Kootenay School of Writing (KSW). Like TISH, KSW emerged from a particular moment of social and cultural activism, where poetry was a site for engaging with the material conditions of living and aesthetics were always already rich with political possibility. In focusing on these poets and groups, I aim to widen the scope of readerly attention to the work that poetry was engaged with in this period.

Case Study: Phyllis Webb, Poet of Space and Silences

To read Phyllis Webb's biography in any literary encyclopaedia is to encounter a life immersed in social and cultural action. Born in British Columbia in 1927, Webb went to the University of British Columbia, and later McGill University. In 1949, at the age of 22, she ran as a candidate for the Co-operative Commonwealth Federation (CCF), an action which foretold her lifelong commitment to socially engaged politics.[19] While she did not win her riding in the election, she did meet F.R. Scott who was serving as Chairman for the CCF at the time. Scott encouraged Webb to relocate to Montreal, and when she did, she met the poets involved with both *Preview* and *First Statement*. While she worked as an administrative assistant at McGill University, where she also took a qualifying year for graduate studies, Webb met Irving Layton, Louis Dudek, Eli Mandel, Gael Turnbull, Leonard Cohen, Al Purdy, and many others.[20]

Her first published poems appeared alongside work by Eli Mandel and Gael Turnbull in *Trio*, an anthology put out by Souster's Contact Press. Her following collection, *Even Your Right Eye*, was published in 1956 and the following year she was awarded the Canadian Government Overseas Award grant, which allowed her to go to Paris to study theatre. There, she encountered the existentialism of Jean-Paul Sartre, Albert Camus, and others; the influence of which is discernible in some of her poetry. Webb returned to the West Coast in 1960, initially to pursue graduate work. While she did not ultimately undertake studies, she did join a writing group that included Earle Birney, George Woodcock, and Jane Rule. These writers introduced Webb to the work coming out of the Black Mountain College—work by Charles Olsen, Denise Levertov, Robert Creeley, Robert Duncan, and Allen Ginsberg. Her third book, *The Sea Is Also a Garden*, came out in 1962 and marked another perceptible shift in Webb's poetics and themes. A few of the

Black Mountain writers attended the writing workshops in Vancouver in 1963, and their interest in radicality and experimentalism had an influence on Webb's own poetics. This radicality is most clearly evident in *Naked Poems*, which takes up themes of feminism, sexuality, and desire while defining a decidedly new relationship to the page.

Along with her earlier publications, *Naked Poems* (1965), *Selected Poems 1954–65* (1971), *Wilson's Bowl* (1980), *The Vision Tree* (1982), *Water and Light: Ghazals and Anti Ghazals* (1984), *Hanging Fire* (1990), *Nothing but Brush Strokes* (1995), and *Peacock Blue: The Collected Poems of Phyllis Webb* (2014) sketch a blueprint for a life and career in poetry and poetics, but of course a list is only the smallest sliver of a story. In addition to her decades-long writerly work, Webb was a central figure in the CBC's cultural interview series, *Ideas*. And, when she left that position at the height of her success in it, she shape-shifted into another long career as a teacher of creative writing at the University of Victoria in British Columbia. Webb's life and work is vital, and it has also been controversial. To understand her importance requires us to consider her poetic work on its own terms, and then to attend carefully and critically to the ways in which she was received and critiqued by some of the most vocal literary and poetic critics of the day.

Webb's early poetry, such as the poems published in *Trio*, demonstrates a preoccupation with confined movement. Her speaker identifies with nuns in their cloisters. As her poetics develop, Webb becomes increasingly engaged with embodied politics and philosophical complexities; and this gets borne out on the page itself. For our purposes, we will look at her watershed *Naked Poems* as an example of a kaleidoscopic poetics. Published in 1965, *Naked Poems* has been described as one of the most influential Canadian long poems, as it reimagined what was possible for a book-length poem.[21] While not a new form by any means, the long poem certainly developed new contours in the decades following E.J. Pratt's epics. By 1979, it was a form significant enough for Michael Ondaatje to publish *The Long Poem Anthology* with Coach House Press.[22] In his introduction, Ondaatje reflected that the long poem was "the most interesting writing being done by poets today" (ii). The long poem, which typically moves towards narrative trajectories typically expected of prose, remains dedicated to poetics. Line breaks matter. Poetic devices matter. Simply calling it a "long poem" requires that readers attend to the text's poetics, which, despite an engagement with narrative, are rooted in poetry. In her introduction to *The New Long Poem Anthology* in 1991, Sharon Thesen observes:

> Long poems belong by practice and definition to what Ezra Pound called "the prose tradition" in poetry; that is, their tendency to a narrative sense of the passage of time drives them by and into history beyond the capacities and preoccupations of the lyric.
>
> (9)

In Canada, Thesen goes on, the long poem becomes a form from which to manage and attend to the dis-ease of the "poetic associated with the lyric voice" which is often encountered and experienced as "a falseness, a colonizing wish overlaid upon the real" (14). As first Ondaatje's and then Thesen's anthologies suggest, there are many poets who have taken up the long poem in Canada: Robin Blaser, George Bowering, Dionne Brand, Robert Kroetsch, Daphne Marlatt, bpNichol, Fred Wah, and Michael Ondaatje are but a few of the poets Thesen includes in *The New Long Poem*. It is Webb's *Naked Poems* that offers both a wide-angle view as well as a specific example of how experimentation with form and content worked in conjunction with temporal context.

As noted briefly above, Webb started writing and publishing poetry amongst coteries examined in the previous chapter. Her work was well received and fostered by Scott, Woodcock, and others, and this in turn had an influence on her. Take, for example, Sharon Thesen's reading of "Poet," from her first publication *Trio*. Thesen suggests that "Poet" is an *ars poetica*, which is a meditation within poetry in what poetry can do.[23] To read "Poet" as a "self-referential *ars poetica*," as Thesen does, moves the meditation beyond simply what poetry can do into the realm of what the poet, specifically *this* poet, can do. Here is the excerpt that Thesen focuses on:

> I am promised
> I have taken the veil
> I have made my obeisances
> I have walked on words of nails
> to knock on silences. (1–5)

Notice the anaphoric repetition of "I, I, I, I" and how it situated the speaker—the titular poet—at the front of each line. The "I" becomes a door the reader must pass through, and in so doing enter the perspective of this poet's own experience and authority. The effect is subtle and significant when, in the fifth line, the "I" is abandoned for an enjambed line. After being promised, after taking the veil, after being deferential, and after walking on "words of nails," the speaker lands on silence and knocks against it. What are readers to make of this pilgrimage? For Thesen, there are traces of the "binding patriarchal traditions" that the feminized speaker has had to employ to navigate the masculinized company of poets and, perhaps, poetry itself.[24] In her early work, such as this poem in *Trio*, Webb's focus is on cloistered nuns and powerful yet tortured men such as King Lear and Vincent Van Gogh. But these polarized relationships to gender start to shift.

In an interview with Pauline Butling, Webb reflects that she was deeply influenced by the male figures in her life.[25] As she encountered both radical poetics and feminism in the 1960s and 1970s, she started to think through and engage with feminism in her work. "Finally," she related to scholar Janice Williamson, "I had this overbearing sense that there had been too many fathers, literary or otherwise … . I wrote a little piece in which I dispatched the fathers to the river Lethe, and I saw them sail away" (see Williamson). By the time she publishes *Naked Poems*, the fathers, literary or otherwise, have been cleared and what remains is space into which Webb's poetics grow.

Naked Poems unfurl in short lines that move their orientation on the page. Tracking a relationship—between two women, but also between the poet and the poem, between what is possible and what is beyond, between beauty and wanting—the collection is lofty with airy lines. Here, again, *ars poetica* is perhaps evident, but there is no mortification, no knocking or chafing against an inhospitable or exclusionary silence. Instead, even the page becomes a place on which to take up and inhabit space differently. Take, for example, the opening stanzas form "Suite I":

> MOVING
> to establish distance
> between our houses.
>
> It seems
> I welcome you in.
>
> Your mouth blesses me
> All over.
>
> There is room.
>
> (npag)

The movement on the page between lines and stanzas draws a dynamic line between the speaker and the lover. This movement is markedly different than the staccato "I, I, I, I" of "Poet." Instead, nearly each line is enjambed, and thus moves the reader in perception and thought unit from one place to the next and a languid but steady pace. That line is held taught, too, in the distance between the welcome and its appearance, between the room that the lover is welcomed into and the room that is established in the blessing of the lover's body. And yet, amidst all this movement, the lines are porous on the page. There is space, there is possibility, there is quiet, and for this moment there is no rushing. Reminiscent of Charles Olson's breath unit, Webb's spacious lyric spreads out, moving from page to page, from room to stanzaic room.[26] Indeed, as Rob Winger has keenly observed, Webb's poetic process in this collection is deeply referential to Olson's imperative in "Projective Verse" that "ONE PERCEPTION MUST IMMEDIATELY AND DIRECTLY LEAD TO A FURTHER PERCEPTION."[27] What is less possible to see in the format of this particular book you are holding is that in the original, Webb's poems in "Suite 1" exist primarily in the bottom quarter of the page. The reader must travers an expansive blankness, wonder and wrestle with it—what to do? Is this disorienting? Light streaming through an open window? Is it the quiet sometimes held between two lovers lying close, but not yet touching or speaking?

The poems reorient themselves, in "Suite 2" to the middle of the page:

While you were away

I held you like this
in my mind.

It is a good mind
that can embody
perfection   with exactitude.

Here, enjambment is maintained but stretched with spaces between some of the thought units. The effect, perhaps, is to slow the reader down to the reflective and self-referential pace of the speaker. Again, *ars poetica*, with reference to both what poetry can do and what this poet can do here, with silence, over time. Observe with me the extra space in the final line above—between "perfection" and "with exactitude," that is not a typo, but time. A two-beat pause, a breath pause in Olson's terms, that keeps us as readers in not just the lineation of the poem, but the speaker's own lungs and voice. Her thoughts, even, become embodied in our reading, if momentarily. When, towards the end of "Suite 2," the speaker still reflects on the absent lover, it is not literary fathers that crowd the line, nor the silent words. Instead, it is poetry itself that fills the lines:

You brought be clarity.

Gift after gift
I wear.

Poems naked
in the sunlight

on the floor.

Poems naked in the sunlight on the floor, made possible in part by the lover who brought not veils or nails but clarity. The trajectory of *ars poetica* which is also *ars erotica* reaches an astonishing set of reflections. In a section titled "Some final questions" the speaker moves discursively between an italicized set of questions and responses. When asked "*But why don't you do something?*" the response is declarative: "I am trying to write a poem." The question then becomes, "*Why?*" to which, after a few beats, response and question seem to come together in either one voice, or two that have joined:

Listen, If I have known beauty
let's say I came to it
asking

Oh?

Back to the left-hand margin, these questions and answers move away from singularity into something else. To land on "Oh?" moves the reader into both a question and an answer. Is it what the speaker asks of beauty while writing a poem? Is it the response of the querying interlocutor? Is it necessary for us to know, or to note the shift away from absolutism to possibility? Webb's poetic attention teaches the reader in turn ways of attending. Her spaces and silences are fulsome and invite the reader to pause without ever becoming complacent.

Case Study: TISH and Experimentations with Perception

Pauline Butling suggests that term "avant-garde" has referred to "both a social position—ahead of the mainstream—and a subject position" ("(Re) Defining Radical Poetics," 17). For Butling, herself a keystone writer and record keeper of this period of radical poetries in Canada, some of the vital moments that define radical or avant-garde poetics in English Canada stem from the reception of transnational modernist movements by Scott, Smith, and the McGill Group, and into the development of little magazines and small presses discussed in earlier chapters. If, in Canada, poetics—and especially "radical" poetics can trace transnational roots and routes—then this is perhaps especially true when we consider the interconnected work of poetry in Western Canada in this period. It is rare that we can look back across history and point to specific times and sites where things changed enormously, though it does certainly happen. September of 1961 in Vancouver is one such time and place. That September, the social and poetic discussions that had been happening amongst a group of students, professors, and other literary producers in and around the University of British Columbia coalesced in the form of a new little magazine. This one was called *TISH: A Poetry Newsletter, Vancouver* and it was produced on paper liberated from the Department of English at the University. The founding editors of *TISH* included George Bowering, Frank Davey, and Fred Wah, as well as other key figures involved in the production of the magazine and its contexts.[28] These key figures included but were not limited to Daphne Marlatt (then Buckle), Gladys Hindmarch (now Maria Hindmarch), Robert Hogg, and Lionel Kearns. Like the McGill Group, or the coteries that formed around *Preview* or *New Frontier*, the TISH writers were drawn together through a combination of shared aesthetic values and the beautiful coincidence of being in or being drawn to the same place at relatively the same time.

Most of the writers who came to be associated with TISH were from Western Canada and British Columbia more specifically. Remember, Canada is a vast geographic space, and yet Eastern and Central Canada—namely Toronto and Montreal—have held sway as urban, cultural, and ideological centres. Other parts of the country—Atlantic Canada, the Prairies, the West Coast, the northern most parts, the territories—are often left out of the cultural imaginary, not to mention the material and infrastructural realities. Many of these writers arrived in Vancouver, and specifically at UBC, in a flow of post-war economic booms that allowed people from working-class and lower-middle-class situations to attend universities in Canada. Many of these writers shared the experience of being the first in their families to attend university. And while they were able to attend university due to the post-war economic changes, the university and its prevailing class hierarchies had not changed in equal measure to its constituents. The result? While the writers associated with TISH were, on the one hand, exploring the "problem of [poetic] margins," they were also bumping up against the ongoing reality of social hierarchies in the university space.[29] Experiences of margin/centre in social and educational settings influenced their work in and on poetics.[30] The arrival of Black Mountain poetics in Vancouver was of paramount importance. Like McGill, decades earlier, we see an instance in which campuses and classrooms can be places of possibility and change. And while all this change is rife with excitement and energy, it was not experienced evenly by all who were engaged with it. As Butling observes, the TISH group began by publishing radical work rooted in the local, with the focus to amplify the work of marginalized writers. However, a decade after the first publication, many of the group had published a few books each, "acquired significant cultural capital as exemplars of cutting-edge, radical poetries in English Canada, and most had jobs teaching at universities or colleges" (55). And, while academic jobs were vastly more attainable in the 1970s than they have been since, it would be an enormous critical failure not to note, as Butling does, that their success "relates to their relatively high level of social capital as young, white, able-bodied men" (ibid.). Women, racialized writers, and queer writers associated with the TISH group would explore their own experiences of marginalization outside the centripetal force of TISH.[31]

In addition to bringing poets in Canada, and especially in the Western part of Canada into conversation with poets in the United States via Black Mountain College, perhaps one of the most significant evolutions in this moment was around the function of and focus on language and its materiality. Here again we see struggles with and against the traditional lyric I that has, historically, purported to represent a singular speaking subject. Yet, as with some experiments we saw in the previous chapters, poets of this era were also pushing against totality in representation. In the United States, experiments were afoot among those in the Language poetry movement.[32] Less geographically specific than Black Mountain, Language poets are interested in the ways in which language itself is a material to work with, rather than a de facto medium for clarity and communication. Some of these similar concerns were developing in the Canadian context, especially in relation to historical settler representations of place. As Pauline Butling observes,

> The importance of this shift to language-centred poetics has often been noted as part of the radical shift to open-form and locally based poetics in English Canadian poetry in the 1960s. Some forty years later, the notion of language as locus seems equally important as a shift away from

> the colonizing tropes of landscape poetry or what Mary Louise Pratt aptly names an "imperial stylistics."
>
> ("Poetry and Landscape, More than Meets the Eye: Roy Kiyooka, Frank Davey, Daphne Marlatt and George Bowering," 89)[33]

The suggestion made by Butling is that poets of this era—and specifically ones operating on the West Coast of Canada, most of whom were in proximity both with one another and with TISH and what is now the Emily Carr University of Art and Design—were refusing the colonial impulses of mastery implied in the deployment of the "I" as a consolidated poetic subject. Instead, they turned to both situatedness as a means of acknowledging agency (or lack thereof) and to language as a material of self-reflexive critique (Butling, 89).

To unpack the experimentations in perspective Butling turns to Mary Louise Pratt's concept of "imperial stylistics." For Pratt, the way colonial agents convey the act of seeing produces a colonial discourse of mastery and ownership. Pratt calls this the "monarch-of-all-I-survey genre" (201) and uses Richard Burton's narrative of his so-called discovery of Lake Tanganyika (1860) as an example. Here is Pratt analysing Burton:

> First, and most obvious, the landscape is *estheticized*. The sight is seen as a painting and the description is ordered in terms of background, foreground, symmetries between foam-flecked water and mist-flecked hills and so forth.
>
> (204)

As Pratt explains, these descriptions of Burton's *do* something beyond present a visual image of a place. The work Burton's words do is both subtle and insidious: the use of adjectives that tie this particular landscape to Burton's home country/the imperial centre coupled with the ways in which Burton centres his speaker/the viewing I as the sole human observer works together to thread through some "little bits of England" into the landscape Burton claims to have discovered. However subtle these imperial stylistics may seem, the effect is anything but: imperial stylistics work to naturalize and give primacy to a point of view, and in the case of Canada the view that has historically been naturalized is that of white upper middle class English-speaking cis-gendered men.

Butling makes the compelling observation that some poets working in the 1960s in this mainly West Coast context began working "*against* this 'monarch-of-all-I-survey'" aesthetics, and from this work an "anti-lyric poetics of the 'local' began to emerge" (91). Butling points to works such as Roy Kiyooka's *Kyoto Airs* (1964), Frank Davey's *City of the Gulls and Sea* (1964), Fred Wah's *Lardeau* (1965), George Bowering's *Rocky Mountain Foot* (1968), and Daphne Marlatt's *Vancouver Poems* (1972). To these examples we can add later works such as Lisa Robertson's *Occasional Work and Seven Walks from the Office of Soft Architecture* (2004), Rita Wong's *forage* (2008), and Jeff Derksen's *Transnational Muscle Cars* (2003).[34]

TISH was not the only site of radical poetics at play in this period. Another key nexus, to borrow Butling and Rudy's description, was the intersecting projects of grOnk/Ganglia and blewointment. blewointment began in Vancouver and was primarily associated with bill bissett, who is a multifaceted artist who works in textual, musical, and fine arts mediums. The author of more than sixty books thus far, bissett is renowned for his rejection of standardized English, and refuses the confines of punctuation and spelling in favour of a relationship with language that focuses on its elements. bissett founded blewointment press in 1964 with the focus on publishing chapbooks of poetry by new and emerging writers such as Margaret Atwood, Michael Ondaatje, and Gwendolyn MacEwan. bissett sold the press in 1983 and it continues as Nightwood Editions. In 2005, Nightwood launched a blewointment imprint.

Ganglia was a collaboration between bpNichol and Dave Aylward. Born of their time working at the University of Toronto library, *Ganglia* was a little magazine whose aim was to be both publication venue and tool for communication. For Nichol, the project was geared specifically at amplifying and circulating the experimental work of writers in British Columbia to poetic communities in Ontario.[35] *Ganglia* shifted between publishing the work of a single poet, such as bill bissett and Judith Copithorne, and publishing anthology issues. For Nichol, publishing was a means to communicate poetic developments as well as to enact friendship. In an interview with Geoff Hancock, Nichol observed, "The results [of publishing] were fantastic. We were able to send news from Canada to other writers we admired" (Hancock, 33). Nichol's focus on publishing as a means of connection can be seen in more recent small presses such as those run by rob maclennan of above/ground press, derek beaulieu of house press/No Press, Kate Siklosi and Dani Spinosa of Gap Riot, and Alessandro Porco of Happy Monks Press.[36] Though relatively short-lived, Nichol's project of radical poetics and radical generosity has had lasting effect on some poetic production and small-press publication in Canada.

The *Ganglia* project lasted a short two years and then gave way to a new iteration of irregularly published series of pamphlets called *grOnk*. This project was inspired directly by the work of TISH's newsletters in that it worked on a subscriber basis, which allowed the editors to have a sense of who was interested and how many pamphlets were needed in a given run.[37] Unlike *Ganglia*, which was Canadian in its scope and aim, *grOnk* engaged in an international poetic discourse. For example, the first issue which was published in 1967 included work by bill bissett, Victor Coleman, and David W. Harris, as well as j.f. bory and Pierre Garnier who were a part of the French spatialiste movement. The series was initially edited and published by Nichol, then by David W. Harris, bill bissett, and Steve McCaffery. The pamphlets, which were painstakingly constructed and packaged, are marked examples of the work small presses were doing. In addition, these pamphlets, like *Ganglia*, were attentive to radical forms of poetics including but not limited to concrete poetry, visual poetry, and experiments towards sound poetry. Both *grOnk* and *Ganglia* came to an end when, in 1988, bpNichol died unexpectedly.

Micro-presses like those created by Nichol and bissett have had an almost incalculable effect on literary culture in Canada. And, indeed, while the financial support and nationalist initiatives of the post-*Massey Report* Canada Council funding have had significant effect on the development and sustenance of small presses such as the venerable Coach House Press and House of Anansi, it might be equally interesting to note the community connections that made and, in many cases, keep these small presses alive. Coach House Press began in 1965 when printer and typesetter Stan Bevington arrived in Toronto from Edmonton, Alberta. Bevington rented a coach house and purchased a Challenge Gordon platen press, and with Dennis Reid, who now is a curator at the Art Gallery of Ontario, began to print and publish poetry. bpNichol's *journeying* and *The Returns* as well as Michael Ondaatje's *The Dainty Monsters* were early publications, and the press has maintained a two-pronged focus on book printing as well as book publishing. Innovation and craft was undoubtedly a part of what gathered many "now-luminary figures" in Canadian literature to the press in its early days (Coach House, "About"). Members of the editorial board in the 1970s and 1980s included Victor Coleman, Frank Davey, Linda Davey, Barbara Godard, bpNichol, Michael Ondaatje, Sarah Sheard, and David Young. The press changed ownership in the late-1980s and, under the management of Margaret McClintock, published books by writers including André Alexis, Ann-Marie MacDonald, and Anne Michaels. The press went dormant in 1996 due to government funding cuts but was revived in 1997 by Bevington. Editors included Hilary Clark and Victor Coleman, Darren Wershler, and is now under the editorial leadership of Alana Wilcox. Situated on bpNichol lane, where one of Nichols' poems—a/lake/a/lane/a/line/a/lone—is etched into the pavement, the press has evolved and yet manages to maintain its dual focus on innovative publishing and excellent and innovative book printing. Coach House also remains a community nexus.[38]

In the same era, The House of Anansi Press was formed. Anansi began two years after Coach House, in 1967, by Dennis Lee and David Godfrey, and was focused specifically on the amplification and circulation of "Canadian literature." Formed the same year as the centenary of the Canadian state, the concomitant Expo 67, the press was deeply influenced by the cultural nationalism of the period.

It is difficult to underestimate the effect of these groups, small presses, and micro-presses on poetic culture. Like the period explored in the preface, prior to the implementation of some of the *Massey Report* recommendations, writers struggled to find publishers without looking abroad. Karl H. Siegler of Talonbooks, for example, describes the realities of publishing in Canada this way: "Their dismissal was based on a colonial perception of our shared reality—most Canadian books in all genres were to be found on a single shelf near the back of the bookstore under the rubric 'Canadiana'."[39] Rosemary Sullivan writes that until the formation of presses such as Anansi and Coach House "foreign owned or branch-plant houses had a very bad track record in publishing original Canadian books" (199). The hard work of creating infrastructure for poetry fundamentally changed the way literature circulates in Canada.

Case Study: Nicole Brossard

Community building, while not central to all presses at all times, is certainly a recurrent theme in Canada. That we can read the work of Nicole Brossard in English is due to this work of connection that was happening in the 1960s and 1970s in some key literary locations. In 1974, under the editorial direction of Barbara Godard and Frank Davey, Coach House Press published *Daydream Mechanics* by Nicole Brossard. Brossard, a Quebecoise poet and writer, was already well known in francophone literary communities, but virtually unknown in English Canada. Writer, academic, translator, and editor Barbara Godard first translated Brossard's poetry for a reading with Adrienne Rich for the *Writers in Dialogue* conference (1978). Godard then translated Brossard's work for the journal *Room of One's Own* that same year, and, unsatisfied with the lack of discourse between feminist writers in English and French Canada, Godard then held the *Dialogue* conference (1981), which was aimed at bridging literary conversation across the two linguistic "solitudes" in Canada. It was from a similar desire—to foster creative conversation between English and French speakers—that led Godard and Frank Davey to create Coach House Press's Translation Series, which ran from 1974 to 1986 (see Davey, *A History*). In addition to being one of the first writers represented in this series, Brossard's work engaged with Continental French theory such as the work of Gilles Deleuze, and translating her work into English also introduced these Continental French thinkers to an anglophone readership. Now, Brossard is one of the most celebrated writers in Canada, recognized for her generative and generous poetics of sensibilities and sensualities.

Brossard's work extends into editing projects, such as *La Barre du Jour* (1965), *Les Têtes de Pioches* (1976), and *La Nouvelle Barre du Jour* (1977). She has also been involved in several noteworthy anthologies including *Anthologie de la poésie des femmes au Québec* (1991), *Poèmes à dire la francophonie* (2002), *Baisers vertige* (2006), and *Le Long Poème* (2011). She has also been involved in collaborative stage productions and monologues such as *La Nef des Sorcières* presented at the Théâtre du Nouveau-Monde in Montreal in 1976 (translated by Linda Gaboriau and published as part of Coach House Press's Quebec Translation Series in 1980 under the title *A Clash of Symbols*), and *Célébrations*, which was also presented at the TNM in 1979 as well as *Je ne suis jamais en retard* at the Théâtre d'aujourd'hui in 2015. Unquestionably, Brossard's poetics extend across genres, spaces, and generations.[40]

To enter Brossard's poetic space is to engage with language as a medium of queer possibility. What is more, Brossard's poetics insist on both pleasure and sensuality as vital for survival and for future-oriented thinking, especially for women and queer people. As the editors of *Avant Desire* note, "if it is laudable for us to recognize the importance of pleasure in 2020, imagine the subversiveness and danger of insisting on queer pleasure" half a century ago (Queyras, Robichaud, and Wunker, xiv). In order to move pleasure and desire into a textual space, Brossard's poetics engage the sensuality of language by developing her own lexicon of words. Across the decades of her poetic career Brossard's work is engaged in the active present and future-oriented project of desire. Her poetry works across languages and restrictions to face beloveds and forge community, connection, and, if needed, alternative geographies for belonging.

Take, for example, "Mauve," a poetic engagement of creation and collaboration—what the editors of *Avant Desire: A Nicole Brossard Reader* call "transcollaboration"—to build a poem that is also a conversation about futurity. The poem functions as both a conversation across languages and a braiding together of sense and perception between the two writers. Here is the first set of stanzas, in which Brossard's French leads and Daphne Marlatt's English picks up the thread and continues:

> La réalité est un sursis au-delá
> et du reel lorsqu'on observe
> en l'apparence virtuelle, courbes
> de ceci qui ressemble combine de fois
> les images: la bouche au féminin
> does de sens émotion dorsale
>
> Real that of the under-bent
> curves of the virtual we take for real
> a gap delayed that-over-there re
> semblance the images repeat
> mouth in the feminine, dos(e)
> of sense making a dorsal
> *commotion*
>
> (*Avant Desire,* 158)

Perhaps the first observation to make is that there is not an attempt at direct translation between the two stanzas. Instead, "La réalité" is rendered statement of fact: "Real that" into which "l'appearance virtuelle" is made no longer appearance but "virtual we take for real." The English stanza makes plain the gaps between speaking and understanding that can be exacerbated by a gap in fluency. The gap—"la bouche au féminin"—is both back bone (*dos*) and measure (*dos(e)*) of "sense making dorsal." Rather than call and response, Brossard's collaboration with Marlatt becomes a making grounded in the feminine and acknowledging the imperfect negotiations that we must undertake to reach one another across various kinds of abysses.

In addition to her constant attention to futurity for women and for queer futurities, Brossard's work maintains a connection to the deep violence of history. In some of her poetry, the speaker becomes a watchful, weary, and anguished record keeper who marks the violence of the present against the violence of the past and demands better. Brossard, who is deeply invested in Quebec history and culture, and invests through a loving criticism strident critique of its structural inequities, is most bracing in her work that addresses the murder of 14 women at L'École Polytechnique in Montréal on December 6, 1989. For readers unfamiliar with Brossard's oeuvre, this poetic essay keeps company with them as they encounter and experience the collective shock the women must have experienced when a gunman entered a post-secondary space of learning, separated the women from the men, called the women feminists, and then shot 14 of them dead. But, as Brossard demonstrates in "6 December 1989, Among the Centuries," this act of misogynistic violence is neither isolated nor unique, and to suggest it is anomalous would be to erase the deep history of violence against women. Brossard uses poetic lineation to establish the ways in which violence against women fractures and traumatizes:

> On December 7, 1989. I learn that a man has just killed fourteen women. The man, they say, separated the men and the women into two groups. The man called the women feminists; he voiced his hatred toward them. The man fired. The women dropped. The other men ran away. Suddenly,
> I/they are dead
> felled by a
> break in meaning. (*Avant Desire,* 95)

Here, Brossard begins with a long prose line in which the thought units get shorter and shorter as the speaker processes horror. Then, as the prose can no longer carry meaning meaningfully, the line breaks into a poetic one. Each line staggers, enjambed upon the next, and they do not end with any solace. Rather, Brossard leaves the reader in the broken "meaning" of misogynistic violence. This, the line suggests, is a reality that cannot exist and yet does.

Brossard is both record keeper, and future-maker. In "Smooth Horizon of the Verb Love" translated by poets Robert Majzels and Erín Moure, Brossard uses stanzas to build rooms of possibility.[41] The poem moves across time in the constant and constantly shifting landscape of Montreal:

> an urban image from the eighties
> when we hung out at Chez Madame Arthur
> and at the back of the room
> women wrapped their arms around
> nights of ink and dawn (*Avant Desire,* 152)

This reflection to an earlier decade places women in the urban space of Montreal in the 1980s, the same decade in which 14 of them were murdered as they studied engineering. Yet here, these women are safe, embraced; held and holding the tools of transcription, imagination, and a new day. The poem ends with women, and with a specific woman. It ends with the speaker focusing on the horizon, with an awareness of the peripheral dangers, but with a refusal to be contained:

> focus on yes, on the woman's
> eyelids
> caress not silence not word
> focus beyond. Hold me back (ibid.)

The negation—"not silence not word"—redoubles the focus on "yes" and on "beyond." The final utterance to "hold me back" is offered without punctuation and thus can be read multiple ways. A dare, a command, a taunt, a refusal; there is no way of being certain and thus readers are returned to what is: women in urban spaces, women writing, women wrapping their arms around night and around each other. There is consent and there is care and there is a horizon.

Notions of both care and future horizons are to be found in the wider feminist poetic hubs of this era. Evident in examples such as Godard's translation of Brossard in the Coach House Translation Series, as well as Brossard's and Marlatt's transcollaboration, it is possible to find numerous instances of feminist poetics at work. In addition to meetings and conferences such as *Dialogue* (1981) and *Women and Words/Les Femmes et les mots* (1984), two vital nodes of feminist poetic collaboration emerged in the early 1980s. The first of these nodes was a group that came to be known as *Theory, A Sunday*. In 1983, Nicole Brossard invited some feminist writers to discuss theory on a Sunday. These writers shared a feminist consciousness and the urban space of Montreal. As Lisa Robertson writes, women writing and talking about theory in the city is a radical act with historical precedence:

> Why do certain cities at certain times become the stages for intense social and cultural transformation? I think of early 20th century Paris, the city that was home for so many of the women expatriate writers .... From my admiring distance, and across the duration of many friendships, Montréal feels to me to be a place of comparable intellectual generosity and intensity. ("Theory, A City")

Feminism, Robertson concludes, is a galvanizing facet of urban culture. It binds together women-identified writers from different places through the shared experience of being in urban spaces. The collaborative, experimental poetics coming out of Montréal in the early-1980s was getting translated and published, and thus made accessible to feminist writers across the country in Vancouver. The Women's Press, Coach House and its Translation Series, journals like *Fireweed*, *Writing*, *Raddle Moon*, and *Room of One's Own* became hubs for intellectual, aesthetic, and political exchange (Robertson, "Theory,

A City"). From Quebec, from the perspective of feminist poetics, others began to more clearly understand the effects of The Quiet Revolution. Between 1960 and 1966 the political sphere in Québec changed dramatically, and this had significant effect on the lives of women.[42] Shortly after The Quiet Revolution, the Front de Libération du Québec was formed to protect and foster cultural and linguistic separatism through any means necessary. The FLQ was armed and used force to make its collective points, which culminated in Prime Minister Pierre Trudeau enacting the War Measures Act in 1970.[43] In the midst of these tumultuous and massive changes, feminists got together to theorize and write. The resulting text, translated as *Theory, A Sunday*, marks a watershed period in feminist poetics in Canada.

The second node of feminist poetic development in this period was *Tessera*. Began a year later, in 1984, as a forum for feminist literary theory and feminist writing, the editors of *Tessera* were invested in presenting the English and French contexts of feminist discourse alongside one another. The editorial collective, initially made up of Barbara Godard, Daphne Marlatt, Kathy Mezei, and Gail Scott who met at a feminist conference at York in 1981, used the term "fiction/theory" and "*fiction théorie*" to refer to the kinds of experimental feminist writing happening across languages. The journal, which ran until 2005, published cutting edge feminist writers and critics including Brossard, Louky Bersianik, Louise Cotnoir, Linda Hutcheon, Marlatt, Erín Moure, M. NourbeSe Philip, France Théoret, Audrey Thomas, Gail Scott, Donne Smyth, Lola Lemire Tostevin, and Aritha van Herk.[44] As both *Theory, A Sunday*, and *Tessera* demonstrate, one of the vital through lines of feminist poetics is interconnectedness and generative exchange.

Case Study: The Kootenay School of Writing, Expo '86, and The Giantesses

In 1984, the same year *Tessera* was founded, another hub of connection, collaboration, and exchange was founded. That year saw the Social Credit Government in British Columbia close the David Thompson University Centre (DTUC) in Nelson, British Columbia. This closure of a vital hub of both craft and conversation was political. As such, what came next was self-aware of politics and the role that poetry can and does play in political and social arenas. The KSW was formed after the closure of the DTUC and was comprised of some of the writers affiliated with the work that had been happening in the KSW largely located itself in Vancouver. KSW was focused on both writing practice and social organization located in urban space, as is evident in this excerpted mission statement published in the initial brochure:

> The Kootenay School of Writing is response to the failure of most public institutions to serve their artistic communities. It stands in opposition to the concept of "culture industry" in its recognition that theory, practice, and teaching of writing is best left to working writers. To this end, the School represents a new hybrid: a form of parallel gallery and centre of

scholarship, open to the needs of its own constituency and alert to the possibilities of all disciplines that involve language. (Kootenay School of Writing kswnet.org)

The School, which continues to function, brought together writers such as Jeff Derksen, Lisa Robertson, Fred Wah, Tom Wayman, Dorothy Trujillo Lusk, Meredith Quartermain, Nancy Shaw, and Catriona Strang, whose poetics share intersecting concerns around labour, gentrification, urban space, and racialized and gendered experiences. The poetics associated with KSW were rooted in the social and political turmoil that was happening in British Columbia, and especially Vancouver in the 1980s. As Clint Burnham notes in his critical study of the KSW, this was a moment in which

> poetry was political (not) only in terms of its content, but formally. A time when the politics of Vancouver, of British Columbia, meant large-scale demonstrations in the streets, and the threat of a general strike. A time when a shut-down, rural university writing program was reborn as an urban hotbed of experiment and cosmopolitan theory, with as much in common with Gramsci as with the anarchistic Direct Action group. ... a poetry movement—the KSW—that was as much about the street as the library, about art as literature, about politics as aesthetics, about community as the academy.
>
> (Burnham, 11–2)

Poetry written by KSW associates was deeply invested in both formal innovation and theoretical engagement. Like *TISH* before it, poets of KSW were in border-crossing conversations with American writers.[45] In this case, the Language poets, especially of the San Francisco Bay Area. It was also a poetic community deeply invested in and engaged with feminism.[46] Several women poets formerly associated with KSW—Lisa Robertson, Catriona Strang, and Christine Stewart and, before her death, Nancy Shaw—demonstrate across their poetic work this investment with feminism. We will turn to them now.

In 1986, Vancouver hosted Expo '86 the second world's fair held in Canada and the only one since the centenary Expo '67 in Quebec. Prior to the global event, mass evictions took place to make space for the expected arrival of tourists. In addition to enacting outrageous disregard for the people living in these spaces—specifically in and around False Creek and the Downtown Eastside—the evictions and other "clean up" initiatives made precarious the survival of cultural organizations such as the KSW. Organizing in response to the violent changes became a further part of the social and collective work of the KSW, and in so doing a connection among collaboration, cultural production, and social engagement was forged. As Lisa Robertson writes,

> [KSW Collective members] were resisting the totalizing movement of capital and its usurpation of both individual and collective time, but they were resisting by widely varying means: Marxist class critique,

> avant-garde experiment, conceptual rigor, feminist rejections of gendered hierarchy, woman-centred editing practices, queer identity explosions, post-colonial and anti-racist actions. Some used images, or alcohol, or archives, or housing, or sex as the resistant material, experiencing these inseparably from language. Myriad groupings of identifications and practices ripped through and animated the collective fabric. [...] Resistance became a form of life, a form of lived coexistence. This form of life included the structure of group conversations, the improvised ways decisions were made and tasks were allotted, [and] the chaotic fidelity with which records were kept and events and meetings were documented. (Robertson, "The Collective")

Scholar Julia Polyck-O'Neill suggests that here Robertson offers resistance as a conceptual organizing principle for the KSW's "shapeshifting, multiplicitous, and multifarious approaches to creative and critical cultural production" ("Lisa Robertson's Archive," npag). The work thus became rooted in poetics as a means of creative socially and politically engaged discourse. As KSW-member Nancy Shaw observed, "the formation of the Kootenay School of Writing ... and the collaborative practice that ensued, was a response to the collapse of support for interdisciplinary collaborative work," which "had become institutionalized in the 1970s" (Shaw, 103). Like the feminist poetic work happening in Montréal, the work of some KSW members such as Robertson and Shaw centred feminism and collectivity as central to poetic production.

Robertson, Strang, and Stewart, with Nancy Shaw, formed a group they called the Barscheit Nation. Within that group, they named themselves "Giantesses," wrote a manifesto, and started *Barscheit* magazine. As Robertson points out in an interview in *The Capilano Review*, they recognized that operating in a "more evolved Marxist discourse" did not mean that feminism was central. In claiming public space for their feminist poetics, The Giantesses of Barscheit Nation demonstrated how poetry and poetics can be a space of radical potential.

This Giantess Manifesto draws from modernist and avant-garde aesthetics and poetics. The visual effect of the block of all-caps text hails concrete and visual poetics, while the collective "we" signals collective action. "GIANTESSES ARE WAITING FOR THE WORLD TO CATCH UP. WE EXPECT TOTAL ACQUIESCENCE," the manifesto announces. This total refusal of the status quo gestures back to work of the Quebec *Refus Global*,[47] as well as to the kinds of feminist manifestos issued in the United States by Valerie Solanis, the Redstocking Collective, and the Combahee River Collective.[48] As Jenny Penberthy notes, KSW women poets in the 1980s–1990s were "inserting feminism into the discussion," because the "historical silencing of women writers was increasingly visible and irksome to the KSW women." The work, in part, became recuperative: KSW tended to "subordinate gender considerations to those of class" (45). In addition to the recuperative work of celebrating and amplifying historically marginalized or erased women writers, what we see in the Giantess Manifesto is once again evidence of the need to both make and take up poetic space.[49]

Conclusion

In this chapter, we have seen some of the ways that poets continue to build both infrastructure and communities in which poetry could circulate. As the study of Canadian literature became increasingly institutionalized, readerships extended. And yet, despite an increase in institutionalization and infrastructure, poetry and poets continued to recognize the need for pushing boundaries, asking questions, and making interventions with their craft. The creation of the Canada Council for the Arts fundamentally affected how writers could access material support for their work. In addition to the creation of grants that supported individual artists, the Council also facilitates support for small presses. And while there is always more room to make granting accessible, it is hard to deny the effect of material and infrastructural support on the creation and circulation of literature. The changing cultural landscape likewise plays a role in the production and circulation of poetry: feminisms, calls for and critiques of multiculturalism policy, and large celebrations of the nation all affected poets in a variety of intersecting ways. The study of Canadian literature became a more institutionalized part of post-secondary curriculums during this period, and many of the most influential small presses in the country were established. Experimentations in form and lyricism proliferated and, as we will see in the next chapter, a surge of writing by Indigenous poets began to build momentum. In her essay "Post *Halfbreed*," Janice Acoose relates how Louis Riel predicted that a century after his death Indigenous Peoples in North America would rise up led by "artists, musicians, poets, and visionaries" (40). The following chapter aims to consider the proliferation of Indigenous poetries Riel foretold.

Key Terms

Canada Council for the Arts: The federal government's main infrastructure for supporting the arts. The Council's mandate from the Parliament of Canada is to "foster and promote the study and enjoyment of, and the production of works in, the arts." The Council was created in 1957 as a partial fulfilment of the recommendations of the *Massey Report*.

Expos '67 and '86: Expo '67, "the Universal and International Exhibition," was a pinnacle of the Centennial celebrations of 1967. Initially planned for Paris, and then Moscow, the Exhibition happened in Montréal after the USSR cancelled. The exhibition was the first of its kind in North America and was planned as a tripartite partnership between the federal government, the Québec government, and the city of Montréal. Deemed a success, Expo '67 increased tourism to Montréal significantly. Expo '86, held in Vancouver, was a single-themed exhibition focused on transportation and communication. The exhibition has a complicated legacy. Some narratives highlight the ways in which the exhibition transformed Vancouver into a world-class city, while others underscore the devastation of the Downtown Eastside through displacement of poor and unhomed Vancouverites and flag the city's dubious reputation for unaffordability as connected to the exhibition.

Multiculturalism: A federal policy of multiculturalism was adopted in 1971 by the Liberal government under Pierre Trudeau. The policy arose out of the Royal Commission on Bilingualism and Biculturalism (1963–69) and was intended as a means of addressing rising francophone nationalism in Quebec as well as growing cultural diversity in Canada. It was the first policy of its kind in the world.

October Crisis: A portmanteau for a series of connected events that occurred in Quebec during the fall of 1970. Preceding the crisis the FLQ, a militant independence movement, undertook a series of attacks between 1963 and 1970. On October 5, 1970, the FLQ kidnapped British trade commissioner James Cross. Soon after, the FLQ kidnapped and killed Quebec Minister of Immigration and Minister of Labour Pierre Laporte. After the Quebec Premier and the Montreal mayor issued a plea for federal help, Prime Minister Pierre Trudeau deployed the Armed Forces. He also invoked the War Measures Act for the first and only time during peacetime in the country.

Quiet Revolution: Known in French as the Révolution tranquille, this was a time of enormous and swift change in Québec during the 1960s. The Union Nationale party had been in power since 1944 and was trending increasingly to the conservative right. In 1960, the Liberals under Jean Lesage defeated the Union Nationale and undertook a series of reforms including the 1964 Parent Report (so named for the Chair of the Commission of Inquiry on Education) which effectively separated the Catholic Church from the public education system, the economic nationalism promoted by Réné Lévesque, and the Royal Commission on Bilingualism and Biculturalism. Late in the decade, the passage of the Official Languages Act (1969) and the Constitution Act (1982) rounded out a period of enormous social and cultural change for the province.

Notes

1 See Ahmed, 90, 92.

2 See Sugars and Moss, "Introduction: Nationalists, Intellectuals, and Iconoclasts" (213).

3 The Sixties Scoop was an extension of the Indian Act that ran from 1951 through the 1980s. It entailed the forced removal—most often without parental or band consent—of Indigenous children from their families and placement of them in the homes of white settler families. As Niigaanwewidam James Sinclair and Sharon Dainard write, this was not due to inferior Indigenous parenting, but rather as a deliberate extension of the violent and paternalistic polices of cultural assimilation

and cultural genocide on the part of the Canadian government. Additionally, in 1969 the federal government produced its "White Paper" which proposed to replace the Indian Act and end treaties. The federal government claimed this would mean equity for Indigenous Peoples in Canada, but Indigenous critics such as Harold Cardinal refuted these claims and pointed instead to the ways in which this was a proposal for forced assimilation.

4 Sugars and Moss cite growing awareness of colonialism in this period as well as a growing awareness of environmental crisis spurred on in great part by the publication of Rachel Carson's *The Silent Spring* (1962) which helped raise awareness about the environmental and health effects of widely used pesticides such as DDT. They also note that environmentalist David Suzuki begins working to raise public awareness about environmental issues in this period. See Sugars and Moss, 215–16.

5 The acronym means lesbian, gay, bisexual, transgender, queer/questioning and the "+" acknowledges the multiple modes of identification not contained in the acronym.

6 See Frank Davey, "Al Purdy, Sam Solecki, and the Poetics of the 1960s."

7 See Wunker and Mason.

8 For a place to begin considering canon formation in Canadian literature, see Robert Lecker's edited volume *Canadian Canons: Essays in Literary Value.*

9 Anstee cites Heather Murray's *Come, Bright Improvement! The Literary Societies of Nineteenth-Century Ontario*, as a key example of scholarship plotting the literary societies' work as "cultural and educational" and geared at fostering "independent thought, public speech, and cultural democratization" (Murray, 155).

10 In the application to the Council, Raymond Souster wrote that:

> The organizers now wish to bring poets from further afield. It is proposed to pay a reading fee and travel expenses. For some this will be the first time that they have received money for their poetry … . This is not a complaint: it is a statement of a condition that can be changed.
>
> (in Anstee, 79)

11 For work on arts and publics see Michael Warner. See also Ann Cvetkovich. For a more recent consideration of literary readings in the Canadian context, see Moure and Shearer.

12 This is MacDonald's wonderful description, 471.

13 See Sherrill Grace, *Canada and the Idea of the North.*

14 It is interesting to note that Atwood's text totally ignores Canadian literature of the inter-war period, perhaps because the period would provide too many strong counterexamples.

15 A decade later, Davey's *Surviving the Paraphrase* (1983) would be hailed as a significant and formative break with thematic criticism.

16 See Woodcock, *Introduction*, 113.

17 See Hobby, Porco, and Bathanti.

18 The acronym BIPOC means Black, Indigenous, and Peoples of Colour.

19 Recall from chapter two that the CCF, founded by F.R. Scott and others, was the predecessor to the present day New Democratic Party. This was the same election that A.M. Klein unsuccessfully ran for the CCF.

20 See Robert Lecker, "Phyllis Webb."

21 Douglas Barbour, "Naked Poems."

22 It is useful to note, here, the revivification of the long poem in Canada in the immediate aftermath of the Canada Council's formation: with funds that

contribute to subsistence over time, the very forms and modes prevalent in a field can change.

23 The term *ars poetica* comes from the text of the same name written by Horace in 19 BCE. In this text, which translates from the Latin to "the art of poetry," Horace offers advice about the writing of both poetry and drama to other writers.

24 See Thesen, "Phyllis Webb."

25 See Pauline Butling, *Seeing in the Dark: The Poetry of Phyllis Webb.*

26 Worth noting, perhaps, that the word "stanza" which marks discrete sections of a poem is also the Italian word for "room."

27 See Winger, "How to Know Now: 'Zen' Poetics in Phyllis Webb's *Naked Poems* and *Water and Light.*"

28 When referring specifically to the publication, I will italicize *TISH*. When referring to the group I will not italicize.

29 See Butling for a detailed analysis.

30 Butling's citation of a conversation between Davey and Irene Niechoda and Tim Hunter is especially illuminating. Davey observes,

> I think we felt marginalized in a number of ways, having come from a small town. Marginalized by being Canadian in North America; marginalized by being from the West Coast and British Columbian, in the Canadian context; marginalized by becoming more and more interested in language rather than in content … .
>
> (Irene Niechoda and Tim Hunter)

"A Tishstory, edited by Irene Niechoda and Tim Hunter from an afternoon discussion at Simon Fraser University in 1985." In Douglas Barbour, Ed. "Beyond TISH. New Writing, Interviews, Critical Essay."

31 Both Daphne Marlatt and Fred Wah are examples of this marginalization within the culture of TISH. Marlatt has gone on to write genre-shifting works such as *Ana Historic* and, with Betsy Warland, *Two Women in a Birth* in which poetic form gets reworked to make space for women, queerness, and the materiality of feminized bodies in both history and the present. Wah's poetic biotext *Diamond Grill* addresses and explores his family history and undertakes a trenchant critique of systemic racism. Indeed, while TISH undoubtedly ushered conversations about poetry and poetics into a new phase in Canada, it was by no means a poetics or a coterie free from the social and cultural constraints of previous generations. See Butling and Rudy. See also Wah.

32 Or sometimes "L=A=N=G=U=A=G=E" after the little magazine of the same name edited by Charles Bernstein and Bruce Andrews between 1972 and 1981.

33 Butling is quoting from Mary Louise Pratt's text *Imperial Eyes: Travel Writing and Transculturation.*

34 We could also add works by Stephen Collis, Sina Queyras, Jordan Abel, and Canisia Lubrin that can perhaps be seen as working with this anti-lyric poetics, but, as we will consider in the coming chapters, situating it increasingly in discourses that work across anti-Indigenous, anti-Black, homophobic, and misogynist histories to unsettle the tyranny of a singular speaking subject.

35 "bpNichol." *Archives and Special Collections*. Ottawa, ON: Carleton University. https://asc.library.carleton.ca/exhibits/bpnichol-we-are-words-and-our-meanings-change/ganglia-gronk

36 rob maclennan of above/ground press has been publishing small runs since 1993 and cites Nichol, bissett, and Maggie Helwig as direct influences. Similarly, beaulieu, of house press and No Press has been publishing small, handsewn chapbooks for over two decades. Porco of Happy Monks Press refers to the project as "borderline invisible"—the print run is 25 copies, 10 of which go to the author. The more recent Gap Riot Press, run by Siklosi and Spinosa, is "anarchist at its heart and communal by nature." Siklosi is also the curator of the Small Presses of Canada interactive map: https://festivalofauthors.ca/small-press-interactive-map/

37 An early example of this method was *The Song Fishermen's Song Sheets*, which was run out of Halifax and circulated in the late-1920s.

38 As with nearly all cultural organizations, some individuals associated with Coach House have dealt with allegations in the #MeToo era. Several lawsuits are ongoing at the time of writing of this volume.

39 Siegler elaborates that writers were "strangers in our own land." See Sugars and Moss, 234.

40 See Sina Queyras, Geneviève Robichaud, and Erin Wunker.

41 From *Cahier de roses et de civilasation* (2003), trans. Robert Majzels and Erín Moure (2007) as *Notebook of Roses and Civilization*.

42 For example, in 1964 the Liberal government passed Bill 16 the aim of which was to "abolish a married woman's judicial handicap by which her legal status was that of a minor." See René Durocher, "Quiet Revolution."

43 The FLQ bombed the Montréal Stock Exchange and later kidnapped both British Consulate Member James Cross and Labour Minister Pierre Laporte. Laporte was murdered. The invocation of the War Measures Act effectively turned Montréal into a militarized space in which all civil rights were suspended.

44 See tessera.journals.yorku.ca and *Collaboration in the Feminine: Writings on Women and Culture from Tessera*, Ed. Barbara Godard for more.

45 Indeed, readers may not have noticed that some original TISH members such as Fred Wah became associated with KSW.

46 Burnham notes that the title of his study is a play on the many resonances of "matter" including Marxist materialism and *mater* as in the Latin for mother, signalling the school's abiding investment in feminist theory and poetics.

47 *Refuse Global* or "total refusal" was a manifesto published in Quebec by 16 young artists including Jean-Paul Riopelle and Françoise Sullivan in 1948. The manifesto emerged from the Automatistes who were deeply influenced by the work of French Surrealism. In it, the signatories decried the repressive culture of Quebec under the conservative and religiously right-leaning leadership of Quebec Premier Maurice Duplessis. *Refuse Global* is hailed for helping to usher in the Quiet Revolution in Quebec.

48 For a more thorough overview of radical feminism see Barbara Crow.

49 See Jenny Penberthy.

For Further Reading

Burnham, Clint. *The Only Poetry that Matters: Reading the Kootenay School of Writing*. Vancouver: Arsenal Pulp Press, 2011.

Butling, Pauline, and Susan Rudy. *Writing in Our Time: Canada's Radical Poetries in English (1957–2003)*. Waterloo: WLUP, 2005.

Collis, Stephen. *Almost Islands: Phyllis Webb and the Pursuit of the Unwritten.* Vancouver: Talonbooks, 2018.

Works Cited

Acoose, Janice. "Post *Halfbreed:* Indigenous Writers as Authors of Their Own Realities." *Looking at the Words of Our People: First Nations Analysis of Literature.* Ed. Jeannette Armstrong. Penticton: Theytus, 1993. 29–44.

Ahmed, Sara. *The Cultural Politics of Emotion.* 2nd ed. London: Routledge, 2014.

Anstee, Cameron. "'Poet and Audience Actually Exist': The Contact Poetry Reading Series and the Rise of Literary Readings in Canada." *Journal of Canadian Studies,* 49.1 (Winter 2015): 73–94. https://doi.org/10.3138/jcs.49.1.73

Atwood, Margaret. *Survival: A Thematic Guide to Canadian Literature.* Toronto: Anansi, 1972.

Barbour, Douglas. "Naked Poems." The Canadian Encyclopedia. 2018. www.thecanadianencyclopedia.ca/en/article/naked-poems

———, Ed. "Beyond TISH. New Writing, Interviews, Critical Essay." Special Issue *West Coast Line,* 25.1 (Spring 1991); and NeWest Press. Edmonton: NeWest, 1991.

Bentley, D.M.R. "Rummagings, 5: Northrop Frye's 'Garrison Mentality'." *Canadian Poetry.* N.d.

Brossard, Nicole. *Notebook of Roses and Civilization.* Trans. Robert Majzels and Erín Moure. Toronto: Coach House, 2007.

Burnham, Clint. *The Only Poetry That Matters: Reading the Kootenay School of Writing.* Vancouver: Arsenal Pulp Press, 2011.

Butling, Pauline. *Seeing in the Dark: The Poetry of Phyllis Webb.* Waterloo: WLUP, 1993.

———. "'(Re)Defining Radical Poetics'. Butling and Susan Rudy." *Writing in Our Time: Canada's Radical Poetries in English 1957–2003.* Waterloo: WLUP, 2004. 17.

———. "'Poetry and Landscape, More than Meets the Eye: Roy Kiyooka, Frank Davey, Daphne Marlatt and George Bowering'. Butling and Susan Rudy." *Writing in Our Time: Canada's Radical Poetries in English 1957–2003.* Waterloo: WLUP, 2004. 89–102.

Coach House Books. "About us." www.chbooks.com.

Cardinal, Harold. *The Unjust Society.* Vancouver: Douglas & McIntyre, 1969.

Crow, Barbara. *Radical Feminism: A Documentary Reader.* New York, NY: NYUP, 2000.

Cvetkovich, Ann. *An Archive of Feelings: Trauma, Sexuality, and Lesbian Public Cultures.* Durham: DUP, 2003.

Davey, Frank. *Surviving the Paraphrase.* Winnipeg: Turnstone, 1983.

———. *A History of Coach House Press's Quebec Translation Series.* Montreal: ACQL, 1995. http://publish.uwo.ca/~fdavey/c/chpque.htm

———. "Al Purdy, Sam Solecki, and the Poetics of the 1960s." *Canadian Poetry,* 57 (2002): 39–57.

Dudek, Louis, and Michael Gnarowki, Eds. *The Making of Modern Poetry in Canada: Essential Articles on Contemporary Canadian Poetry in English.* 1967. Toronto: Ryerson Press, 1970.

Durocher, René and Millette, Dominique. "Quiet Revolution". Encyclopedia Britannica, 13 Oct. 2016, www.britannica.com/topic/Quiet-Revolution. Accessed 4 August 2023.

Frye, Northrop. *The Bush Garden: Essays on the Canadian Imagination.* Toronto: Anansi, 1971.

———. "Conclusion." *A Literary History of Canada*. 1965. Ed. Carl F. Klinck. Toronto: UTP, 1973. 821–49.

Gnarowski, Michael. *Contact 1952–1954: Notes on the History and Background of the Periodical and an Index*. Montreal: Delta Canada, 1966.

———. *Contact Press 1952–67: A Note on Its Origins and a Check List of Titles*. Montreal: Delta Canada, 1971.

Godard, Barbara, Ed. *Collaboration in the Feminine: Writings on Women and Culture from Tessera*. Toronto: Sumach, 1994.

Goldie, Terry. *Fear and Temptation: The Image of the Indigene in Canadian, Australian, and New Zealand Literatures*. Montreal: McGill-Queen's UP, 1987.

Grace, Sherrill. *Canada and the Idea of the North*. Montreal: McGill-Queen's UP, 2007.

Hancock, Geoff. "The Form of the Thing: An Interview with bpNichol on *Ganglia* and *grOnk*." *Rampike*, 12.1 (Fall 2001): 33.

Harvey, Jocelyn. "Canada Council for the Arts." *The Canadian Encyclopedia* (March 7, 2022).

Hobby, Blake, Alessandro Porco, and Joseph Bathanti. *The Anthology of Black Mountain College Poetry*. Chapel Hill, NC: UNCP, 2022.

Kamboureli, Smaro. "Introduction." *Trans.Can.Lit.: Resituating the Study of Canadian Literature*. Eds. Smaro Kamboureli and Roy Miki. Waterloo: WLUP, 2007. vii–xv.

Lecker, Robert, Ed. *Canadian Canons: Essays in Literary Value*. Toronto: UTP, 1991.

——— "Phyllis Webb." *Open Country: Canadian Poetry in English*. Toronto: Thompson Nelson, 2008. 308.

Lee, Dennis. "Cadence, Country, Silence: Writing in Colonial Space." *Open Letter*, 2.6 (1973): 34–53.

MacDonald, Tanis. "Fracture Mechanics: Canadian Poetry since 1960." *Oxford Handbook of Canadian Literature*. Ed. Cynthia Sugars. Toronto: OUP, 2017. 471–94.

MacLennan, Hugh. "Where is My Potted Palm?" 1952. Rprt. in *The Other Side of Hugh MacLennan*. Ed. Elspeth Cameron. Toronto: Macmillan, 1978.

Macpherson, Jay. "Report on Poetry Readings." *Writing in Canada: Proceedings of the Canadian Writers' Conference, Queen's University, 28–31 July, 1955*. Ed. George Whalley. Toronto: Macmillan, 1956. 136–9.

Marlatt, Daphne. *Ana Historic*. Toronto: Anansi, 1988.

Marlatt, Daphne, and Betsey Warland. *Two Women in a Birth*. Toronto: Guernica, 1994.

Moure, Erín, and Karis Shearer. "The Public Reading: A Call for a New Paradigm." *Public Poetics: Critical Issues in Canadian Poetry and Poetics*. Eds. Bart Vautour, Erin Wunker, Travis V. Mason, and Christl Verduyn. Waterloo: WLUP, 2015. 310–29.

Murray, Heather. *Come, Bright Improvement! The Literary Societies of Nineteenth-Century*. Toronto: UTP, 2002.

National Film Board of Canada. National Film Act. Ottawa: Government of Canada, 1950.

Nichol, bp. "bpNichol." *Archives and Special Collections*. Ottawa, ON: Carleton University. https://asc.library.carleton.ca/exhibits/bpnichol-we-are-words-and-our-meanings-change/ganglia-gronk

Olson, Charles. *Human Universe and Other Essays*. Ed. Donald Allen. New York, NY: Grove, 1967.

Ondaatje, Michael, Ed. *The Long Poem Anthology*. Toronto: Coach House, 1979.

Penberthy, Jenny. "Listening's Trace: Reading Lorine Niedecker and Lisa Robertson." *Poetics and Praxis 'After' Objectivism*. Eds. W. Scott Howard and Broc Rossell. Iowa City, IA: UIP, 2018. 53–68.

Polyck-O'Neill, Julia. "Lisa Robertson's Archive, Singular and Collective." *ESC*, 44.2 (2018): 75–100.

Pratt, Mary Louise. *Imperial Eyes: Travel Writing and Transculturation*. New York, NY: Routledge, 1992.

Queyras, Sina, Geneviève Robichaud, and Erin Wunker, Eds. *Avant Desire: A Nicole Brossard Reader*. Toronto: Coach House, 2020.

Robertson, Lisa. "Theory, a City." *Theory, a Sunday*. New York, NY: Belladonna, 2014. 10–18.

———. "The Collective." *Avant Canada: Poets, Prophets, Revolutionaries*. Eds. Gregory Betts and Christian Bök. Waterloo: Wilfrid Laurier UP, 2019. 19–27.

Shaw, Nancy. "Expanded Consciousness and Company Types." *Vancouver Anthology*. 2nd ed. Ed. Stan Douglas. Vancouver: Talonbooks/Or Gallery. 91–110.

Sinclair, Niigaanwewidam, and Sharon Dainard. "The Sixties Scoop." The Canadian Encyclopedia. 2019. www.thecanadianencyclopedia.ca/en/article/sixties-scoop2019/

Sugars, Cynthia, and Laura Moss, Eds. "Introduction: Nationalists, Intellectuals, and Iconoclasts." *Canadian Literature: Texts and Contexts*. Vol 2. Toronto: Pearson, 2009. 213–41.

Sullivan, Rosemary. *The Red Shoes: Margaret Atwood Starting Out*. Toronto: HarperFlamingo, 1998.

Thesen, Sharon, Ed. *The New Long Poem Anthology*. Toronto: Coach House, 1991.

———. "Phyllis Webb." The Canadian Encyclopedia. 2018. www.thecanadianencyclopedia.ca/en/article/phyllis-webb

Wah, Fred. *Waiting for Saskatchewan*. Winnipeg: Turnstone Press, 1985.

———. *Diamond Grill*. Edmonton: NeWest Press, 1996.

———. *Faking It: Poetics & Hybridity, Critical Writing 1984–1999*. Edmonton: NeWest Press, 2000.

Warner, Michael. *Publics and Counter Publics*. New York, NY: Zone Books, 2005.

Webb, Phyllis. *Naked Poems*. Vancouver: Periwinkle Press, 1965.

———, Turnbull, Gael, and E.W. Mandel. *TRio*. Toronto: Contact Press, 1954.

Williamson, Janice. *Sounding Differences: Conversations with Seventeen Canadian Women Writers*. Toronto: UTP, 1993.

Winger, Rob. "How to Know Now: 'Zen' Poetics in Phyllis Webb's *Naked Poems* and *Water and Light*." *SCL/ÉLC*, 35.2 (2010), https//journals.lib.unb.ca/index.php/SCL/article/view/18331

Woodcock, George. *The World of Canadian Writing: Critiques and Recollections*. Toronto: Douglas & McIntyre, 1980.

———. *George Woodcock's Introduction to Canadian Poetry*. Toronto: ECWP, 1993.

Wunker, Erin, and Travis V. Mason. "Introduction." *Public Poetics: Critical Issues in Contemporary Canadian Poetry and Poetics*. Waterloo: WLUP, 2015. 1–25.

5 Indigenous Poetics

Post-Oka woman she's struttin' her stuff
not walkin' one step behind her man.
She don't take that shit
Don't need it! Don't want it!
You want her then treat her right.

Talk to her of post-modern deconstructivism
She'll say: "What took you so long?"

You wanna discuss Land Claims?
She'll tell ya she'd rather leave
Her kids with a struggle than a bad settlement.

(Beth Cuthand, from "Post-Oka Kinda Woman"
in Armstrong and Grauer 2001)

In Cree poet and teacher Beth Cuthand's "Post-Oka Kinda Woman," readers are taught to recognize the ways in which the watershed event has changed her and, in so doing, ushered in a renewed era of resistance, refusal, and reckoning. The poem requires readers to be able to locate themselves in relation to the central figure of the poem; you need to know what "Oka" signifies in order to begin to understand what it might mean to be a "Post-Oka woman."[1] This in turn expects that readers have a functional understanding of Indigenous histories in these lands called Canada. In centring an Indigenous woman's experience, Cuthand requires readers to encounter her on her own terms. Line breaks and breath pauses make readers wait for the woman to lead. The usage of institutionally associated terms such as "post-modern deconstructivism" are met with frustrated impatience on the part of the Post-Oka woman: "She'll say: 'What took you so long?'" And, in this excerpt, Cuthand deftly addresses the thorny history of settler land claims in short order: "She'll tell ya she'd rather leave/ Her kids with a struggle than a bad settlement." Cuthand's poem demands that any reader unfamiliar with the history and context leading up to Oka do the work to catch up. The work—reckoning with the history and presence of settler colonialism and white supremacy—will differ depending on a reader's lived experience.

DOI: 10.4324/9780429352966-5

Significantly, Cuthand focuses the mode of lyric address to readers who will recognize and understand her references. She foregrounds Indigenous experience and, in so doing, marks an important component of Indigenous poetry in the last three decades.

I begin with Cuthand's poem for two reasons. First, Cuthand's poetics engage with a lyric mode of address that acknowledges without reproducing European lyric circuitry. Who is the intended listener in this poem? It is decidedly *not* the Post-Oka woman. She is far ahead of the listener, waiting for them to catch up *if* they are lucky. In the same vein, who is the speaker? Certainly, it is someone deeply knowledgeable of the 78-day Mohawk resistance in the face of yet another act of violent colonial displacement. The speaker is someone who knows what a *pre*-Oka kind of woman is like, as well. And so, the first reason I begin with this poem is for its pedagogical poetics—its praxis. It teaches through both form and content. The second reason I have begun this chapter with Cuthand's poem is because of the poem's material history. Written in the aftermath of the resistance, it was first published in Jeanette Armstrong and Lally Grauer's *Native Poetry in Canada: A Contemporary Anthology* in 2001, the poem is not otherwise widely available in print. This dearth of publication and accessibility points to a larger systemic set of barriers Indigenous writers have endured in centuries of colonial presence and structural violence in Canada. In this chapter, which draws heavily on the work of Indigenous and allied scholars, the poetics of Indigenous writers point to the varied ways in which poetry is a powerful tool for both artistry and action.

Indigenous Poetics

In their entry for the *Cambridge History of Canadian Literature*, Lally Grauer and Armand Garnet Ruffo underscore the importance of poetry as a genre for Indigenous writers. "Poetry was the vehicle many early Indigenous writers used to approach literary writing, with its connection to the spoken voice and its flexibility of language and form," they explain. The space and shape of poetry is generative:

> It provided a popular form for protest and expression for many influenced by the songs of artists such as Buffy Sainte Marie. Writers whose lives were transient or who struggled to survive could write poetry without taking the extended blocks of time needed for a novel or a play.
>
> (499)

Poetry offers potential and possibility, even when a writer is working to fit the words in edgewise. When considering Indigenous poetry, and, indeed, poetics, it is important once again to pay attention to and ask questions about terminology. What does it mean to say "Indigenous poetics" in the context of a text about poetry in Canada, a country constituted in settler-colonial terms? Indeed, what does it mean when Marie Annharte Baker writes, "for me, a pictograph is a novel." The radicality of this statement is self-evident.[2] Yet, as we saw in the introduction to this volume in Lee Maracle's poem, the project of settler colonialism has been to disavow and actively suppress Indigenous culture of all kinds. Grauer and Ruffo explain that "Indigenous literature is intimately linked to knowing and rediscovering oral traditions, which include a vast body of poetry, narrative, and drama" (507). The traditions that are hailed by the portmanteau of "Indigenous literature" conveys "a sacred worldview in which humankind and the natural world are integrated into a holistic relationship based on kinship beginning in pre-settlement times and including many post-settlement narratives" (508). Moreover, they posit that all Indigenous literatures can be understood to be "counteracting erasure of identities and stories" (509). So, terminology matters. Thus, it is significant that Maracle suggested the framework of *poetics* to anchor the title for a key anthology on Indigenous literature and aesthetics. The book was named *Indigenous Poetics in Canada* at her suggestion and hinges around an attention to terminology. As the editor notes, Maracle suggested that he organize *Indigenous Poetics in Canada* around the concept of poetic rather than poetry because it requires that the reader shift their attention to Indigenous approaches to writing, and away from non-Indigenous terminologies.

Questions of terminology are thus vital, for language structures many modes of relationship. This is especially so when we consider the relationships between Indigenous Peoples and settlers in Canada. The same chasms between meaning and relationship that were opened by First Contact are present in the twenty-first century. The ways in which Indigenous literatures are understood, discussed, taught, and studied are one specific place where we can unpack the complexities of terminology. In a collaborative interlogue about critical approaches to Indigenous literatures in the Canadian context, Niigaanwewidam James Sinclair outlines the emergence of terminology debates. He writes:

> American Indian Literary Nationalism—what we will refer to … as Indigenous Literary Nationalism—is an intellectual movement that marks a range of committed critical responses to the calls throughout the 1980s and early 1990s for Indigenous-centered literary scholarship. (43)

As Sinclair documents, the call for Indigenous-centred literary scholarship required specific terminology and praxis that attended to the specificities of both aesthetics and contexts of Indigenous literary production. Keavy Martin underscores the necessity of mindfully integrating both discipline-specific terminology as well as Indigenous intellectual traditions into the university, where much literary criticism happens. For Martin, Indigenous-specific terminology is vital because the university cannot ignore intellectual traditions (45).[3]

I will follow the direction of the Indigenous Literary Studies Association in my use of the term "literatures" here, including poetry. In 2013, ILSA

(Indigenous Literary Studies Association) was formed to address the growing need for "a scholarly body based in lands claimed by Canada that focuses specifically on the study and teaching of Indigenous Peoples' literatures." In their governing codes, the Association explains the decision to employ the term "literature" this way:

> While the root of the word "literature" refers etymologically to letters—or to alphabetic written language—we use the term to refer much more broadly to "arts in the medium of language." Although Indigenous literary studies sometimes focuses on written texts, it remains inclusive of and connected to the study of a wide range of textual and rhetorical productions, including oral traditions, film music, graphic novels, and many other forms of creative expression.
>
> ("About")

Thus, the term "literatures" with its emphasis on plurality opens the limitations of English to pluralities. As Ruffo writes, while there was much literature written "since the colonial period *about* Indigenous people themselves" and an additional "body of translations from the oral tradition," until the 1980s and 1990s Indigenous literature "as a discursive field of study did not exist" ("Introduction," xxiii). Noting the importance of postcolonial studies and the ways in which questions and critical focus began to shift, Deanna Reder likewise underscores the relative recentness of Indigenous literatures as a discipline of post-secondary study (45).[4] And, as Reder further explains, the history of scholarship on Indigenous literatures is extraordinarily recent. "It was only in the late 1980s that scholarship on the image of the 'Indian' in CanLit emerged, and the early 1990s that articles on Indigenous writing were published," Reder details ("Introduction," 30).[5] Indeed, as Katherena Vermette succinctly puts it, the relatively recent surge of publications by Indigenous writers in all genres "is all about opportunity, not talent—there have always been exceptionally talented Indigenous writers" (xxi). In their timeline of Indigenous literatures in Canada, Vermette and Ruffo highlight 1884 and 1920 as vital moments in the attempted erasure of Indigenous cultural production. The first date, 1884, marks a key amendment to the Indian Act which made attendance at day school or residential school mandatory for all First Nations children. This government policy of aggressive assimilation focused on "getting rid of the Indian problem in Canada," as poet and Deputy Superintendent of Indian Affairs Duncan Campbell Scott wrote.[6] In addition to forcibly removing children from their communities and families, a key tactic of this aggressive assimilation project was to forbid the use of Indigenous languages and cultural practices. By 1920, school attendance for all Indigenous children between the ages of 7 to 15 years was mandatory. "Creativity [was] all but stifled for generations," write Vermette and Ruffo, and indeed, the record of publication by Indigenous writers of their own writing is extremely limited until 1967 when Chief Dan George performed his poem "A Lament for

Confederation" at the Vancouver celebration of the Canadian centennial.[7] Chief Dan George's poem works in the elegiac form to decry the incalculable violence experienced by Indigenous Peoples in Canada in the name of settler colonialism and the government's attendant policies.[8] The poem opens in a rhetorical mode that draws on language employed by Sir John A. MacDonald in his speech on Confederation in the Legislative Assembly (1865). In his speech, MacDonald hails listeners into his line of argument by signalling community and a shared sense of purpose. In a similar tactic, Chief Dan George foregrounds deep time and shared space, but with a difference: George differentiates between himself and settlers. Instead of focusing his lyric speech towards Canadians, George directs his rhetorical questions to the national signifier of "Canada":

> How long have I known you, Oh Canada? A hundred years? Yes, a hundred years. And many, many seelanum more. And today, when you celebrate your hundred years, Oh Canada, I am sad for all the Indian people throughout the land.
>
> (2)

The relationship between speaker and nation is quickly established beyond the parameters of colonial time. Bear in mind that George presented this at the Vancouver celebration of the centennial of Confederation, then note his deft rhetorical move. He has known Canada for a century, yes, and "many, many seelanum more." *Seelanum,* Findlay writes, is the Salish term for lunar months (44). By using an Indigenous word, George locates Indigenous presence on "Canadian" lands well beyond the short temporality of colonial presence. He then pans out further to include time immemorial as well as the present and future. As Canada celebrates—and the implication, given the performative location of this poem, is that people in Canada are celebrating as well—George's speaker expresses grief for all Indigenous Peoples. In so doing, George anticipates and refuses any tepid attempts to frame Canada as a "just society," as Pierre Trudeau would do shortly after. George's rhetorical focus then shifts to address the ruptures in Indigenous life and culture since the arrival of settlers:

> But in the long hundred years since the white man came, I have seen my freedom disappear like the salmon going mysteriously out to sea. The white man's strange customs, which I could not understand, pressed down upon me until I could no longer breathe.
>
> When I fought to protect my land and my home, I was called a savage. When I neither understood nor welcomed his way of life, I was called lazy. When I tried to rule my people, I was stripped of my authority.
>
> My nation was ignored in your history textbooks—they were little more important in the history of Canada than the buffalo that ranged

> the plains. I was ridiculed in your plays and motion pictures, and when I drank your fire-water, I got drunk—very, very drunk. And I forgot. (3)

Each stanza addresses a prevailing trope of Romantic primitivism, and then refutes that reductive frame. Instead, George offers insight, reflection, and self-awareness. The internal enjambment of each line piles degradation atop structural oppression until the speaker, ravaged by various colonial poisons, loses his grip on his story. This forgetting does not last, however. Whereas a literary lament traditionally expresses grief at a personal loss, George's lament is collective, communal, and refuses to rest in the present injustices. Looking into the past to draw knowledge and leadership from Indigenous histories, George projects Indigenous Peoples into a future that sees "young braves and our chiefs sitting in the houses of law and government, ruling and being ruled by the knowledge and freedoms of our great land" (3). George's vision for the future makes space for ongoing settler presence, and indeed at times acquiesces to an Indigenous need to "grab the instruments of the white man's success—his education, his skills," and with these new tools "build my race into the proudest segment of your society" (3). And, while this rhetorical choice may feel antithetical to the critique within the poem, it demonstrates George's fluency in the language of colonial Canada. The poem closes with a prophetic set of predictions that again bear resemblance to the rhetorical strategies employed by MacDonald and other politicians of Confederation. The difference, of course, is that George inhabits colonial rhetoric and inverts it, moving beyond the limitations of colonial imagination to hail a future for generations of Indigenous Peoples to thrive. "Lament for Confederation" directly addresses several of the ways in which Indigenous writers—and indeed Indigenous Peoples more broadly—are required time and again to contend, address, and navigate the repressive violence of colonial presence. With George's poem in mind, as well as the context of its initial performance, let us return to our consideration of the development of the study of Indigenous literatures in post-secondary contexts as well as the means and contexts of Indigenous literary production.

In his essay introducing the fifth edition of the *Oxford Anthology of Indigenous Literatures*, Ruffo plots a nexus of events that propelled a "literary resurgence or renaissance." These historical events and confluences include the return of soldiers from the Second World War and the Korean War who, upon returning to Canada, found that the socio-economic oppressions they had left behind remained. This, explains Ruffo, resulted in a mass migration to cities across the country, where "cultural and linguistic differences gave way to common socio-political concerns" (xxv). In addition, the civil rights movement in the United States encouraged people to create effective political organizations to work for social change (ibid.). As an example, Ruffo points to Harold Cardinal's *The Unjust Society* (1969) which addresses "the life of his people in the context of the [Trudeau] government's proposal to dismiss 500 years of historical record"(qtd. in Ruffo, "Introduction," xxv). The concurrent development of Indigenous literatures and an engaged literary criticism in Canada is markedly different than in the United States. Despite the tendency for Canada to be celebrated for its multiculturalism, there is only growing discussions in public spheres about structural and systemic racism in the country. Ruffo points out that while in the United States many Native writers were publishing texts that received awards and both national and international attention, in Canada this was not the case until much later. For example, he points to N. Scott Momaday's *House Made of Dawn,* which won the Pulitzer Prize in 1969 and observes that Momaday, like many of his American-based contemporaries, was a PhD holder trained at an American institution. "This was far from the case in Canada," Ruffo clarifies, "it would take another twenty-five years for Indigenous people to begin graduating from universities and colleges [in Canada] in substantial numbers" (xxvi).

In their timeline of Indigenous literatures in Canada, Vermette and Ruffo document a steady and significant increase in the presence and discourse around Indigenous literatures starting in the late-1970s and gaining momentum through the 1980s and 1990s. A few key events highlighted by Vermette and Ruffo include the formation of the En'owkin Centre[9] (1979), the incorporation of Pemmican Publications in Winnipeg by the Manitoba Métis Federation (1980), the incorporation of independent Indigenous publisher Theytus Books (1981), and the establishment of Native Earth Performing Arts in Toronto (1981). Significantly, these are all infrastructural developments, meaning they are spaces and places for creating and circulating Indigenous cultural production. Almost immediately after the establishment of these Indigenous teaching centres, publishers, and theatre company, landmark publications and creations by Indigenous creators impacted the arts and cultural scenes of the country. Vermette and Ruffo write that these included the publication of Beatrice Mosionier's (formally Culleton) *In Search of April Raintree* (1983) which is recognized as the first novel written by an Indigenous writer in Canada; the publication of Jeanette C. Armstrong's *Slash* (1985); the creation and production of Tomson Highway's play *The Rez Sisters* (1986); the publication of Lee Maracle's *I Am A Woman: A Native Perspective on Sociology and Feminism* (1988); the publication by Theytus Books of the first anthology of contemporary Indigenous poetry, *Seventh Generation: Contemporary Native Writing* (1989); and the publication in 1990 of Thomas King's *Medicine River* by Viking Canada, which was adapted into a nationally acclaimed made-for-television movie (xiii–xx). In the previous chapter, we considered at length the effects of the formation of the Canada Council on literary and artistic production in the country. While the benefits of the Council are undeniable, it is a stark reminder of the myriad ways in which Indigenous cultural producers were not immediately supported. Rather, Indigenous critics and literary historians point out, the development of Indigenous infrastructure by and for Indigenous cultural producers has always led the way, and settler Canada has yet to catch up.[10]

The late-1980s into the 1990s saw a growing momentum of Indigenous literatures being published as well as taken up by readers and winning national and international prizes. It was also a period in which vital interventions and solidarities emerged. Writers and playwrights such as Richard Van Camp, Eden Robinson, and Tomson Highway published first, and then second texts in the early- to mid-1990s. Highway, with Delaware poet and playwright Daniel David Moses and Ojibwe poet and storyteller Lenore Keeshig-Tobias formed The Committee to Re-Establish the Trickster. In 1988, they collectively published a manifesto to "reclaim the Indigenous voice in literature. To facilitate the creation and production of literature by Native people" ("Introduction," npag). Two years later, Keeshig-Tobias would publish a searing critique of non-Indigenous writers who appropriated both the voices and stories of Indigenous Peoples. "Stop Stealing Native Stories" appeared in the *Globe and Mail* on January 26, 1990. It opens this way:

> AAA-III-EEE-YAAh!
> Clear the way.
> In a sacred manner I come.
> The stories are mine.
> -Ojibway war song
>
> *Where the Spirit Lives* may be a bad film. *Bone Bird* by Calgary novelist Darlene Barry Quaife may oversimplify native spirituality. W.P. Kinsella's Hobbema stories may be insulting. But the real problem is that they amount to culture theft, the theft of voice.
>
> ("Stop Stealing Native Stories," npag)

Keeshig-Tobias goes on to underscore that "stories … are not just entertainment. Stories are power." Keeshig-Tobias's vital intervention opens a space to consider another set of solidarities and struggles. In Chapter 2, we encountered transnational solidarity, especially in the work of Dorothy Livesay. Keeshig-Tobias's intervention created a context in which Indigenous and racialized writers in Canada could come together to address systemic barriers to writing, publishing, and access to the support of grants and organizations such as The Writers' Union of Canada (TWUC). In the year following her article "Stop Stealing Native Stories," Keeshig-Tobias founded the Racial Minority Writers' Committee at the Writers' Union of Canada in collaboration with a group of writers. Erin Ramlo, whose doctoral work on the archives of TWUC contributes important findings, highlights that the aim was to address professional support and issues of gatekeeping and restricted access to publishing and other supports for Indigenous and racialized writers.[11] This work led first to The Appropriate Voice gathering of more than 70 Indigenous and racialized writers in Orillia, Ontario. One outcome of the meeting was a motion against cultural appropriation which was forwarded to TWUC and passed by the membership in 1992. A second outcome was the landmark Writing Thru Race conference in

1994. Conceived of as a meeting of Indigenous and racialized writers, the conference was hosted by TWUC, and met with controversy which, on the whole, can be summed up by a catch-all phrase: "white fragility." Organized to address appropriation of voice controversies and other issues, the conference organizers also made space for Indigenous and other racialized writers to meet together without the presence of white writers or journalists. Larissa Lai observes that the aim of the Writing Thru Race conference was to open discursive space for thinking through the complex struggles of Indigenous writers as well as other racialized writers in Canada. However, rather than being met with openness and generosity, the agenda was "hijacked by incendiary comments from the reactionary right, and the subsequent last-minute withdrawal of funding by the Department of Canadian Heritage" (214). The conference, which was organized both by members of the Writers Union of Canada Racial Minority Writers' Committee as well as writers who were outside these structures is significant. Lai, an organizer of the conference, reflects:

> The fact that the impulse for the conference structure came from outside … is important because it counts directly to the existence of a community in need of precisely the kind of space the policy demanded—one in which white guilt, anxiety, anger, and apology did not need to be attended to.
>
> (215)

Instead of listening to Indigenous and racialized writers and colleagues who were clearly articulating the need for more literary supports, founding members of the Writers' Union scolded the organizers publicly. As Lai outlines, both Pierre Burton and Margaret Atwood admonished the organizers for asking for financial support from taxpayers to hold a conference that created safe and closed spaces for Indigenous and other racialized writers to talk to one another. As Makeda Silvera pointed out, Indigenous Peoples and people of colour *also* pay taxes (see Lai; see also Ramlo). The hypocrisy of both Burton and Atwood is, in the twenty-first century, even more glaring. And yet, controversies around appropriation of voice, as well as structural racism and misogyny continue to rage on.[12]

The remainder of this chapter is made up of case studies. I begin with E. Pauline Johnson, whose complex poetics both on the page and on the stage offer a rich site from which to consider Indigenous poetic work. From a case study on Johnson, I move to focusing on the work of Rita Joe and Annharte. Though working in vastly different idioms, the poetry of both Joe and Annharte demonstrates modes of resistance and subversive rebellion against the stultifying languages of colonization. The next focus of a case study is Jeanette Armstrong, whose work as a poet, writer, literary historian, editor, and teacher is palpable in her poetry. The work of Armand Garnet Ruffo likewise offers readers a site from which to consider how poetry aids in the work of historical engagement and re/vision. From Ruffo's work,

I turn to Kateri Akiwenzie-Damm, whose poetry crosses lines of genre, operating both on the page and, like Johnson, on the stage. Here, though, the work is spoken word. Of equal import is Akiwenzie-Damm's work of building Indigenous poetic and literary infrastructures. The penultimate case study is Jordan Abel, whose conceptual poetics engage deeply with the ways settler languages of extraction and accumulation accrete in stories of place and belonging. The chapter closes with a consideration of some of the next generations of Indigenous poets.

Case Study: E. Pauline Johnson

Mohawk/settler writer E. Pauline Johnson was a prolific performer and poet who is also credited with being the first Indigenous literary critic.[13] In her lifetime, she was a complex and controversial public figure. Her legacy can be found in a huge range of places—from personal anecdote to scholarly and cultural catalysts. One such example comes from Armand Garnet Ruffo. In 1978, Ruffo notes that he was asked to start a "literary corner" in *The Native Perspective Magazine* that began with a short biographical piece on E. Pauline Johnson. That Ruffo was asked to focus on Johnson is significant. Mohawk writer Beth Brant refers to Johnson as "the revolutionary … the spiritual grandmother … to those of us who are women writers for the First Nations." To this Ruffo adds that Johnson is "the spiritual grandmother to *all* Indigenous writers" (xxxiii). To trace a form of linage Brant and Ruffo acknowledge, I will consider both Johnson's poetics and her complex navigation of her mixed-race Indigenous heritage through her public persona and her literary production.

The tensions between poetic production and reception develop in the late-nineteenth century and lay the foundation for policy, publics, and poetic production in the twentieth and twenty-first centuries. Emily Pauline Johnson, also known as Tekahionwake, was born in 1861 on the Six Nations Reserve in what was then Canada West. Johnson went on to become a poet, writer, artist, and performer whose fame rivalled that of Bliss Carman. Yet, her relationship to the literary canon, especially of her own time, is complicated and instructive. While she is sometimes categorized by scholars as loosely associated with the Confederation Poets, and while some of her poems are included in W.D. Lighthall's *Songs of the Great Dominion* (1889), she is notably absent from Smith's *Oxford Book of Canadian Verse.* Moreover, Smith went so far as to say that her poems were "minor Victorian escape poems" and suggested that her poetry was "theatrical and crude" ("Our Poets," 89–90). It is important to take note of the schism here, between popular reception of Johnson's writing, recitation, and performances and the mixed critical reception by her writing peers. The schism points to extant and ongoing trends in the settler colonial reception of Indigenous poetics. Whereas the other Confederation Poets are celebrated for their poetry, which elevated writing in Canada towards the "national literature" sought by critics, Johnson's work was either too derivative and too experimental, or too personal and too popular (ibid.). Smith's criticism points to his own interest in bifurcating poetic production in Canada into two categories: the native and the cosmopolitan. As we will see in the final chapter, it also lays the foundation for thinking through the deep critical divisions between lyric and conceptual poetry, and issues raised by BIPOC, LGBTQS+, and women poets that become increasingly evident throughout the twentieth and twenty-first centuries.

Johnson was born to an English mother and a Mohawk father. Her grandfather, John Smoke Johnson, was a celebrated hero of the War of 1812.[14] She and her siblings were raised at Chiefswood, her family's home on the Six Nations Reserve near what is currently called Brantford, Ontario. There, Johnson and her siblings were taught to love what her parents loved, which included "nature … the Anglican Church … the British flag … Queen Victoria … books and animals." But what her parents loved most of all were "the Indian people" (McRaye, 19). The tension between her two cultural heritages is taut and gets replicated in fascinating and complex ways in her page and performance poetry. Johnson's work exemplifies parental lineage and values, insofar as it oscillates between a lyric nationalism that echoes much of the sentiment Smith observes in anthologists of the period and a performance poetics that inhabits and uplifts her Indigenous heritage.

As a poet, Johnson deliberately performed a complex grammar of signification in her public performances. Whether on stage at The Young Men's Liberal Club in Toronto or performing in private parlours, Johnson would first recite a series of her poems dressed in an "Indian" costume of her own design. The buckskin costume, which was ordered from the Hudson's Bay Company and altered by Johnson, was comprised of rabbit pelts, moose hair, porcupine quills, a bear claw necklace, wampum belt, hunting knife, and a Huron scalp that had belonged to her grandfather, Jacob Tekahionwake (see Ferris and Jones). What do we make of this bricolaged performance costume? At the very least it suggests a deep awareness on Johnson's part of who her audience would be, and who her publishers were. As Tekahionwake, she performed what she referred to as her "Native" poetry. These poems are distinct in her substantial oeuvre, and they were unusual for the period as well: more performance art than page poetry, these poems often take the form of dramatic monologue and are, for the most part, now the poems that editors anthologize. Upon the first performance of "A Cry from an Indian Wife," a poem that, while written in heroic couplets, is spoken by the wife of a Native man involved in the Northwest Rebellion, a reviewer in the *Globe* stated that it was "like the voice of the nations who once possessed this country … speaking through this cultured, gifted, soft-voiced descendant" (Sugars and Moss, 392). The second part of Johnson's performance came after a brief intermission and was meant to represent the other facet of her identity: seated on a formal chair and dressed in formal Victorian eveningwear, with her hair up and her eyes downcast on the page, Johnson read her so-called white poems as a self-styled embodiment of dominant settler-colonial culture. Audiences loved this dichotomous representation of two disparate cultures. Indeed, she performed in front of thousands.

A woman performing in public, Johnson embodied the contradictions mapped onto her racialized, gendered body. In the same decade that Duncan Campbell Scott vowed to rid the nation of "the Indian problem," Johnson refuted all narratives of Romantic Primitivism by performing two sides of her identity on stage for all to see. Carole Gerson and Veronica Strong-Boag describe Johnson's bifurcated persona as a dialogic imagination. For Gerson and Strong-Boag, Johnson attempts to "embrace an enlarged view of the British Empire and the Canadian Nation" that required embodying often contradictory viewpoints in her writing (178).

Johnson's work—her transformative and disunified aesthetic practice—becomes even more astonishing. For, while literary history remembers Johnson as a writer, her contemporaries came to know her best as both a writer and a performer. It is notable that Johnson worked in mediums of both text and embodiment to, as she puts it, "upset the Indian Extermination and Non-education theories" of the day. In the same year, she debuted her performances as Tekahionwake, she also published an editorial in *The Toronto Globe*, entitled "A Strong Race Opinion: On the Indian Girl in Modern Fiction."[15] In it, Johnson critiques the stereotypical depiction of Indigenous women as "squaws." Preceding Terry Goldie's important writing on the use of semiotic control in representing Indigenous subjects in Canada by a century, Johnson outlines the ways in which representational strategies render Indigenous women both hyper-public and simultaneously absent. The Indigenous woman's body is stripped of its specificity and mapped over with colonial desires. She is both public property and a marginalized—if not effaced—subject.

Employing satiric tactics that were making contemporaries such as Sara Jeanette Duncan popular, Johnson underscores the ways in which Governmental policies of extermination were working at the level of literary production. Rather than depict a "real live Indian girl," Johnson provides another argument:

> the general author gives the reader the impression that he has concocted the plot, created his characters, arranged his action, and at the last moment has been seized with the idea that the regulation Indian maiden will make a very harmonious background whereon to paint his pen picture, that, he, never having met this interesting individual, stretches forth his hand to his library shelves, grasps the first Canadian novelist he sees, reads up his subject, and duplicates it in his own work.
>
> (401–2)

Johnson's editorial makes plain that in Canadian literature and culture the Indigenous woman is hyper-present and indelibly absent as she gets deployed and redeployed in the service of colonial, white fantasy.

Taken alongside her deft criticism within this article, how do we read Johnson's complex public performances of gender and race on both the page and the stage? Critics have made much of Johnson's doubled, even contradictory tactics at the same time they celebrate her performative strategies. Contemporary critics from Beth Brant to Janice Fiamengo, Gerson, and Strong-Boag flag her importance and her complicated strategies. They note she could be ambivalent and self-contradicting (Gerson and Strong-Boag, 180).

By tracing the material conditions of Johnson's publishing history, Sabine Milz characterizes Johnson as deliberately public in both her performance choices and her publication strategies. Milz underscores not only that Johnson's self-fashioning was synthetic, but also, and most importantly, that it was *self-consciously* synthetic. Milz suggests, Johnson's Indigenous costume was deliberately and consciously inauthentic (see Milz, 130-32). Like the Victorian gown, itself a costume signifying gendered, racial, and class identity, Johnson's Indigenous costume was a deliberate and public performance that was woven into the fabric of her texts. I want to suggest that her doubled and contradictory navigation of racial and gendered politics on both the page and the stage represent an early and important intervention. As a mixed-race Indigenous woman writer and performer, Johnson debuted new tactics in Canadian literary culture as a public figure. However, that ground is never solid. Gregory Younging observes that, after her death in 1913, "nearly six decades were to pass before another Aboriginal author was published in Canada" (182). It is important to ask what role anthologists, editors, and critics played in this literary gatekeeping. For example, while Margaret Atwood writes a full chapter on Indigenous characters in literature, in her popular guide to Canadian literature, *Survival*, she does not include an Indigenous writer in her volume.[16] Upon reflection, nearly two decades later, Atwood muses at her omission of Johnson that, "perhaps because, being half-white, she didn't rate as the real thing, even among Natives" ("A Double-Bladed Knife," 243). Atwood's comments, made in 1990, were written in an essay on Thomas King in which she reflects on her omission of Indigenous writers from *Survival*. The derision and purity narratives are clear and may with good reason strike readers as resonant with the assimilationist rhetoric of figures such as Duncan Campbell Scott.[17]

Despite her critics' derision and her omission from many literary anthologies and other literary-critical accounts, Johnson's influence is undeniable. Her work was popular and significant in her own day. She was able to engage wide audiences in Canada and abroad on topics including racism, gender inequity, class, and Indigenous issues. Her work has been inspiring and meaningful for Indigenous writers who came after her including but not limited to Rita Joe, Lee Maracle, Jeanette Armstrong, and Joan Crate. And while there are recovery projects underway to reread Indigenous authors into Canadian literary history—whether they were published under pseudonyms, anonymously, or simply unnoticed by literary history—the fact remains that Johnson's radically public presence on the page and on the stage did not alter the relationship between Indigenous Peoples and the Canadian imaginary. Instead, I offer this reading of Johnson as an example of the ways in which instances of public poetics intervene in the status quo, and yet remain risky. They remain risky for the individual herself, and they underscore pernicious systems of oppression. Johnson's reading tells us as much about how literary and popular representations of Indigenous women remain, as I have suggested, both hyper absent and indelibly present.

Think of Johnson performing "A Cry from an Indian Wife" in front of an audience that included Duncan Campbell Scott, a man whose working life was built on carrying out genocidal projects. He witnessed Johnson's performances, yet his work for Indian Affairs continued. In short, he was not transformed. Rather than being a cause for celebration, the historical presence of women in Canada's literary culture has created a false sense of equality and valuation where there *structurally* is not one. Or, as Louise Bernikow puts it, "What is commonly called literary history is actually a record of choices" (58), and those choices need to be both articulated and questioned regularly and publicly.

Case Study: Rita Joe and Annharte

Mi'kmaq poet Rita Joe was born in Whycocomagh, Cape Breton in 1932. When she was 12 years old, by her own account she put herself into the Indian Residential School in Shubenacadie and observes, "that school plays an important part in my life, along with Native upbringing by many mothers" (Vermette and Ruffo, 112). Deeply invested in intergenerational education, Joe was engaged with diverse groups of people. "My education is my people," she wrote, "I have a front seat to see and feel their needs, the major one being that we, too, live with ideal productiveness" (ibid.). Joe won a writing competition held by the Writers Federation of Nova Scotia in 1974, and this recognition served to further underscore her platform to address Indigenous and a specifically Mi'kmaq cultural past, present, and future. Her poetry is celebrated both for its accessibility—it is lyric and often employs deceptively direct syntax—as well as for its sustained elevation of generosity and generativity. Take, for example, what may be one of Joe's best known poems: "I Lost My Talk." The poem opens with a complex couplet that moves swiftly to a second couplet that relies on enjambment to solidify its sobering point:

> I lost my talk.
> The talk you took away.
> When I was a little girl
> At Shubenacadie school. (1–4)

The opening line situates the speaking subject in a position of agency: subject, verb, and object line up with an end-stopped period. The suggestion of this opening line is that the speaker is in control of the loss. This assumption is swiftly negated with the second line: "The talk you took away." Here, again there is an end-stopped line, but this time the sentence is fragmented. The introduction of "you" establishes a traditional lyric circuitry of speaker, addressee, and lamented loved one—but does so with a difference. The lost love is *talk*, and it has been both lost and taken. This double absence links the lines together as a couplet. They are bound not by rhyme but by loss and by structure. The loss hinges the lines together, and the periods that stop the reader at the end of each line punctuate the double loss. The stanza closes with an enjambed line. The poem opens with loss: the talk was taken from the speaker when they were a child at the Shubenacadie Indian Residential School. Immediately the power dynamic is flipped: the speaker has agency, and that agency is rooted in the speaker's ability to identify the loss and the theft of language. "You" has agency, but that agency was abusive and abused:

> You snatched it away:
> I speak like you
> I think like you
> I create like you
> The scrambled ballad, about my word. (5–9)

These lines punctuate loss with specificity and effect. The speaker's talk was taken from her, and the results are that she is made in the violator's image. Even her poem—the "scrambled ballad"—is created in the image of the thief. But rather than rest in the violation alone, Joe's speaker makes a turn. After acknowledging that two ways of speaking and seeing live in the speaker, but that "your way is more powerful," she makes a generous entreaty. The speaker reaches out her hand towards the "you" and asks to be granted the capacity to find her talk "so I can teach you about me." In a generous inversion of student and teacher, and especially in the context of the violence of the Residential School System, Joe's speaker offers reciprocity in the face of the thief of her language and culture.

Joe's poetry is recognized not only for its directness of speech, but also for its poetics of generosity. Billy Johnson posits that this generosity is evident not only in Joe's poetry, but also in her deliberate choices for publication. Noting that she published first in *The Micmac News* (1978), and that this trend can be seen through *Song of Eskasoni: More Poems of Rita Joe* (1988) Johnson suggests:

> Joe's poetics form a strategy that stresses the continuity between historical and contemporary forms of Mi'kmaw representation and communication, oral and material, over the notions of discontinuity and rupture that so often form the focus of colonial narratives of European-Indigenous contact.
>
> (144)

Lee Maracle, who edited Joe's second collection of poetry, observed of Joe that her "poems pen for the reader that most important love of all—the love of people in their quest for a just society" (qtd. in Vermette and Ruffo, 113).

The continuity that is visible in Joe's poetics is likewise identifiable in the work of Salteaux Anishinaabe poet Annharte, though the tone and use of humour differs almost totally. Born on the prairies a decade after Rita Joe, Marie Baker aka Annharte is a writer whose work is grounded is wordplay and humour. Rather than reach out a hand to invite the non-Indigenous reader to be taught, Annharte's poetry demands the reader keep up with her. Indeed, Amy De'Ath suggests that Annharte's lyric mode of address bifurcates readers, separating them into Indigenous and non-Indigenous readerships. Annharte's discursive tone uses humour to hail Indigenous readers into a circle of shared experiences, while the lyric address is often directly to non-Indigenous readers and figures. When asked to describe her own work, Annharte explained herself as a cultural worker whose aim is to produce "films, plays, and books that celebrate cultural survival after five hundred years of resistance to settler lit(ter) (not literature)" (Vermette and Ruffo, 182). Let's turn to a few of Annharte's poems.

In a mode similar to that of Rita Joe's work, some of Annharte's poetic oeuvre draws on free verse stanzas that are periodically punctuated with internal or end-stopped rhymes. In a poem entitled "How to Write About White People" Annharte suggests:

> From a distance & keep them outside
> even if it seems cruel to do that.
> They will sit on the prairie horizon
> left to silhouette as grain elevator
> once you rode up on a spotted stallion. (1–4)

The opening lines utilize enjambment in order to land the reader in medias res, already outlining how to deal with white people. Deftly, swiftly Annharte directs her lyric address in this poem to an Indigenous readership. The division between an Indigenous "you" who "once rode up on a spotted stallion" and the non-Indigenous "They" is stark.

> The white chief told me he ran from the city.
> He was made lumpy and grumpy.
> Innoculations were frequent.
> They tried every day to kill him.
> Psychology was what they called the war. (8–12)

In this penultimate stanza, each line is punctuated with an end-stopped period that pulls the reader up short. The effect is a staccato rhythm that is interrupted with the deliberate internal rhymes and introduction of a second, even more sinister "They." The poem ends with a deeply apocalyptic two-lined stanza: "Laboratory used to be his first name./ He changed his address after the millennium" (16–18). Here, the ways in which European sciences of "discovery" have been weaponized are laid bare in the use of personification. The double entendre—to change address could mean both place of habitation and means of speaking—and hinged to the twenty-first century and left both abstract and unsettled. In a review of Annharte's *Indigena Awry*, Lorraine Weir observes that while some critics have sought to connect the technical and poetic experimentation in her work to that of the Kootenay School, this would be a limitation and mistake. Rather, "in her commitment to technical experimentation, Annharte's work ranges from dub to lyric, from spoken word to elegy … in which the 'experimental is never separate from a passionate rejection of white bourgeois aesthetics'" (134). As such, Weir suggests, Annharte's work is far more aligned with the visual and multimedia aesthetics of Skeena Reece and Rebecca Belmore in "crafting of an 'enemy language' to do the work of resurgence" (135).

Case Study: Jeannette Armstrong

The work of writer, poet, visual artist, language advocate, and teacher Jeanette C. Armstrong demonstrates another branch of interconnected poetics. Recall Maracle's use of the term as a means of indicating in English the need for the settler-reader to shift their perspective from poetry to a more expansive term. Armstrong (Okanagan) embodies expansiveness. She is a writer of many genres, an award-winning visual artist, a fluent Nsyilxcen speaker, and a cultural worker. Her work is grounded in her belief that Indigenous cultures are unique and specific, and as such are integral to Indigenous-led resurgence. In their introduction to her selection of works, Vermette and Ruffo quote Armstrong on why she writes: "it is a way to contribute to the vast dialogue of the human spirit and its course through time" (213).

> It is a way to reach others I may never meet in person now and in the future. I appreciate voices from the past like Pauline Johnson and my own great aunt, Mourning Dove. They are windows to a time and place I can never experience. I write because oral literature is now extremely vulnerable.
>
> (qtd. in Vermette and Ruffo, 213)

Armstrong's first collection of poetry, *Breath Tracks*, was published in 1991. It is a stunning collection of poems that moves between left-aligned stanzas and poems with spatial chasms that hail embodiment and the breath that moves the title of the book. Like Joe and Annharte, Armstrong's poetry works in and alongside the lyric, with keen shifts that refuse settler-poetic categorization. Take, for example, this opening stanza from "History Lesson":

> Out of the belly of Christopher's ship
> a mob bursts
> Running in all directions
> Pulling furs off animals
> Shooting buffalo
> Shooting each other
> left and right (1–7)

At first reading it might be tempting to attend to these lines as visually engaging free verse, and it wouldn't be incorrect to do that. However, if we left our observations there then we would be missing the nuanced decisions Armstrong has made. Eschewing the punctuation of English, Armstrong uses instead capitalization to both guide and, perhaps, cause readers to pause. The potential enjambment of the first two lines requires the reader to rush, like the mob, only to pull up short, staccato, in the following three lines which feel, when read aloud, as though they are lineated observations. A few lines later, the speaker again flags key references to settler-colonial violence and does so in such a way that the reader needs to do the work of association:

> Pioneers and traders
> bring gifts
> Smallpox, Seagrams
> and rice krispies (15–18)

These "gifts" are deadly. Smallpox ravaged Indigenous populations across Turtle Island because it was a previously unencountered disease for which the people had no immunity. Later, under the leadership of Jeffery Amherst, Hudson's Bay blankets deliberately infected with smallpox were distributed amongst Indigenous communities.[18] Rice Krispies, of course, is a cereal made by the Kellogg's corporation, the founder of which, among other things, was a proponent of eugenics and forced sterilization. Meanwhile, "Seagrams" metonymically references the Seagram Liquor corporation, which at one point was the largest in the world.[19] In four short lines, Armstrong underscores the so-called gifts of colonialism. The poem ends with a damning diagnosis of the effects of European history:

> Somewhere among the remains
> of skinless animals
> is the termination
> to a long journey
> and unholy search
> for the power
> glimpsed in a garden
> forever closed
> forever lost (39–47)

Hardly Eden, the final vision of Armstrong's lesson is one of apocalyptic degradation and loss. This unflinching explanation of the effects of colonial presence, oppression, and violence on Indigenous Peoples is consistent throughout Armstrong's poetry. In a later long poem entitled "Indian Woman," the speaker opens by listing the epithets and negative stereotypes that are cast upon Indigenous women. The short free verse lines catalogue a litany of abuses and false assumptions. Midway through the poem, the speaker intervenes and refuses the slurs hurled at her. "Someone is lying," she says. "I am an Indian Woman." The second half of the poem reorients the reader to beauty inherent in Indigenous women. The speaker both inverts and refutes all the negative descriptions of her, outlining the worlds within Indigenous women as well as their world-making capacities. The poem ends with a strong statement of self and place: "I am a sacred trust/I am Indian woman" (52, 93–94). While this poem does not let go of or deny the violent damage of settler colonialism, racism, and misogyny, it moves from a place forever lost to a people indomitable. Across her decades of poetic production, Armstrong's work keeps watch, teaches lessons, and uplifts Indigenous Peoples. Her work as a writer, poet, and educator keeps time with what Grauer and Ruffo identify as a moment in which Indigenous writers were seeking out other modes for publishing as well as collaborating. Grauer and Ruffo remind readers that the late-1980s and early-1990s were an important span of time in which misrepresentation and appropriation by non-Indigenous authors and publishers was called out in meaningful ways. It was also a moment in which more Indigenous writers such as Ruffo, Thomas King, Louise Halfe, Marilyn Dumont, and Annharte became affiliated with university spaces in a variety of ways. While these affiliations are never neutral, they do open up possibilities for connection and community building in important ways.[20]

Case Study: Armand Garnet Ruffo

Indigenous poets are dynamic and ingenious. In Robert Warrior's terms, Indigenous poets work for "intellectual sovereignty" which is an "intellectual and critical praxis" (iii). This can mean working within, as well as against the linguistic violence of English and French, to create possibility as well as resistance.[21] The challenges of writing poetry within the context of colonialism cannot be underestimated. And yet, Indigenous poets create poetry that attends to Indigenous pasts, presents, and futures in multifaceted and innovative ways. Some, such as Armand Garnet Ruffo, Joan Crate, and Armstrong, weave the past together with the present in their poetic work.[22] For example, in some of his key earlier works, Ruffo (Ojibwe) uses poetry as a means of interrogating the past from his location in the present. The effect is not simply dialogic, but something more temporally and philosophically complex. Like the work of Métis playwright Marie Clements, whose stage directions open layers of space and time in a single moment, Ruffo's engagements with historical events and figures transcend the moment of the poem itself. A prolific writer, artist, filmmaker, and scholar, Ruffo has earned numerous prestigious awards for his cultural production. He is the recipient of a "Life Membership Award" from the League of Canadian Poets, and at the time of this writing, he is a professor of Indigenous Literature and Creative Writing at Queen's University in Kingston, Ontario.

The author of five books of poetry, Ruffo works across and on the edge of genres. Drawing on the work of Marvin Francis, Warren Cariou has suggested that Indigenous poetry and poetics is "edgework." In other words, if poetry and poetics in a non-Indigenous epistemology denote a series of categorical boundaries, then Indigenous poetics, which has been cordoned off through colonial practices, make the boundaries—the edges—visible by moving along and through them to constantly create (Cariou, 31).[23] Ruffo's poetic engagements with historical figures and events can be understood as a kind of edgework. *Grey Owl: The Mystery of Archie Belaney* (1996) is a long poem in which Ruffo constructs a poetic biography of the Englishman Archie Belaney.[24] *At Geronimo's Grave* (2001), which won the Archibald Lampman Poetry Award, uses the life of Geronimo to reflect on the erasure of countless Indigenous Peoples' lives in Turtle Island. In *The Thunderbird Poems* (2015), Ruffo constructs a series of poetic engagements with the visual art of Norval Morrisseau. His most recent collection of poetry, *Treaty#* (2019), is a tripartite engagement with the language and legacies of treaties between the British Crown and Indigenous Peoples. By definition, a treaty is a contract based in good faith and undertaken for the future. In practice, the shared nation-to-nation obligations of the treaties have not been upheld by settler governments in Canada. Instead, they have been undermined at their core—the friendship and good faith have been extracted. And yet, they remain. Ruffo's most recent collection addresses the promises, the futurity, and the realities of broken treaties. The collection won the 2020 Latner Writers' Trust Poetry Prize and was shortlisted for the 2019 Governor General's Award for Poetry. Across his oeuvre, Ruffo moves between past and present with the future in mind, often employing the legal language of settler colonialism to draw attention to hypocrisies and refute negative representations of Indigenous Peoples.

Take, for example, an early poem entitled "Poem for Duncan Campbell Scott," published in *Opening in the Sky* (1994). One of Scott's poems that is often anthologized, entitled "Onondaga Madonna," is written from the perspective on a non-Indigenous person looking at an Indigenous woman holding an infant. The poem is a Petrarchan sonnet, and as such sets out a problem in the octave which is addressed and resolved in the sestet. The "problem" of Campbell's poem is the Indigenous woman who is personified as a member of a "weird and waning race." Drawing on the tenets of both salvage ethnography and Romantic primitivism, Scott's poem "solves" the problem of Indigenous presence by switching focus to the infant, whose skin is lighter than his mother's. The "solution" of Scott's sonnet is to place Indigenous Peoples in the past—especially women. The only way forward is to eradicate Indigeneity from the children, according the poet's logic. Ruffo's poem refuses the sonnet structure and shifts perspective from one to many. The opening query undermines both Scott and the lyric perspective of his poem. Whereas Scott's poem opens with authority—the speaker captures and pins down the Indigenous woman in his gaze—Ruffo *de*personifies the settler entirely asking, "Who is this black coat and tie?" Scott is pared down to his "Christian severity": and his belief in "work and mission." Scott's authority is undermined deftly. For example, when he says he comes from "Ottawa way," Ruffo's speaker corrects: "Odawa country." Moreover, the lyric perspective in Ruffo's poem is collective rather than singular—there is reference to a collective "our" as well as references to many voices in conversation "some whisper this man lives in a house of many rooms," "some don't care, they don't like the look of him," "others don't like the way he's always busy writing." This collective set of observations both accrues group knowledge and draws attention to the settler's ostentatious "authority." Ruffo ends his poem with lines that directly draw from Scott's own:

> Him,
> he calls it poetry
> and says it will make us who are doomed
> live forever. (32–35)

Lifting the language of "doom" from Scott's work, Ruffo both underscores Indigenous knowledge in the past, and places it in a future where readers encounter living knowledge and living people who survive despite all attempts to eradicate their lives and cultures. For Ruffo, a through line that connects Indigenous poets is the recognition that language is power. He goes on to observe that while there are inevitable differences and unique qualities in each poet's work, there are many points of intersection including language, tradition, land and environment, and systems of oppression and racism. Moreover, Ruffo points out, many Indigenous poets express and explore concerns with writing in the language of the colonizer and some, such as Maria Campbell, inject Indigenous language and diction into English which she describes as "the dialect and rhythm of my village and my father's generation" (2). Other examples of these kinds of poetic tactics flagged by Ruffo include work by Gregory Scofield, Louise Halfe, and Marilyn Dumont (Ruffo, "Introduction," xxxiii). To this list, I would add Joshua Whitehead, whose debut collection of poetry *Full-Metal Indigiqueer* integrates languages of gaming, LGBTQS+ communities, and social media into English and Cree.[25] In her first collection, *Disintegrate/Dissociate* (2019), Arielle Twist broadens poetic language to encompass trans vitality in all its multiplicities, drawing attention to the ways in which settler languages cannot encompass such multitudes.[26] And, in her multi-modal poetic work *Slow Scrape* (2020), Tanya Lukin Linklater works across documentary poetics, concrete-based installations, event scores, memory work, Cree, and Alutiiq to develop a transhistorical engagement with space, place, and Indigenous connections.

Case Study: Kateri Akiwenzie-Damm

Poetry is a means of connection. It has the power to connect through language, as well as through embodiment. We read the words the poet has placed on the page, and through those words we are reminded of the breath, blood, and body that carried the words to the page in the first place. Embodiment and the connection that embodiment can bring is perhaps even more apparent in oral poetry and spoken word. Leanne Betasamosake

Simpson offers the insight that in poetics embodiment is a means in which "our [Indigenous] bodies collectively echo the sounds of our ancestors, the sound of the land, and (o)depwewin, the sound of our hearts" (107). In a similar vein, Janet Rogers observes that "we, as poets, are here to witness, ruminate, and creatively express our stories, in verse to all that has gone, all that is now, and visions of the future."[27] The poetry and work of Kateri Akiwenzie-Damm exemplifies the ways in which poetics and embodiment in Indigenous poetics are modes of connection in the present for the future.

Akiwenzie-Damm is a member of the Saugeen Ojibway Nation, Chippewas of Nawash Unceded First Nation, on the Saugeen Peninsula in Ontario. A poet, educator, writer, spoken word artist, Indigenous arts advocate, and publisher, Akiwenzie-Damm is an Assistant Professor of creative writing, Indigenous literatures, and oral traditions in the Department of English at the University of Toronto Scarborough. In 1993, she founded Kegedonce Press, which is Ontario's longest-running Indigenous literary publisher. Of her spoken word Akiwenzie-Damm observes that it "arises from Anishinabek art, literary, and oratory traditions and practices that encompass songs, chants, oratory, storytelling, poetry, speeches, stories, and music as well as other art forms both old and new" ("Gitookl Say It," 9). Connection—to family, to community, and especially to Indigenous women and Indigenous writers—is at the core of Akiwenzie-Damm's work. As Dallas Hunt writes in his introduction to *(Re)Generation: The Poetry of Kateri Akiwenzie-Damm*, her influence on the field of Indigenous literature "has come in many forms and cannot be overstated" (xvii). In addition to founding Kegedonce Press in 1993, running it, and acting as editor and mentor for countless writers, Akiwenzie-Damm is also a preeminent spoken word artist and poet and writer of what Hunt names "sovereign erotic" literature. For Akiwenzie-Damm, centring much of her writerly focus on pleasure is a tangible means of articulating Indigenous futurity in the present. In the introduction to *Without Reservation: Indigenous Erotica*, she quotes Joy Harjo on the vitality and necessity of Indigenous modes of embodiment and erotics, "To be 'in the erotic' is to be alive … [and] [to] deny the erotic, to create absence of erotica, is another weapon in the oppressor's arsenal. When this part of us is dead, our future survival is in jeopardy" (*Without Reservation*, 99). In writing, in publishing, and in performing, Akiwenzie-Damm foregrounds connection.

Consider, for example, the opening of her poem "fish head soup":

mmmmmmm
this delicious longing

for you
is

a lick
of seaweed
stretched in the sun (1–7)

The poem opens with a sonic utterance that must come from the back of the sternum, up through the throat, and into the mouth. As sound moved from poet to page to reader, the line drops to three cascading enjambed lines that leap from longing to a lick of seaweed. The connection between desire for "you" and the "coastal craving" is described as "an ocean/of oolichan/oiling the earth." Oolichan, a fish that bears similarities to a smelt, is native to the Pacific Northwest and is so oily that it can be burnt like a candle (see World Wildlife Foundation, "Oolichan"). The elision of desire with geographic and species specificity centres the speakers longing in an Indigenous context. Here, pleasure and culture are mutually constitutive.

Idle No More

As I hope is clear, plotting a linear trajectory of poetry is the work of scholars, not the work of poets. Poetry is dynamic, engaged in both its own contexts and in conversations across time and space with other poets and poetic works. There are few contexts in which this is truer than with Indigenous poetics. It should be stated again, I am a settler scholar: my observations are rooted in some of the central structures and systems of oppression that continue to effect Indigenous writers. My aim in this chapter is to draw on the work of Indigenous scholars, critics, and writers in order to plot some lines of flight, rather than to assume a position of interpretive authority over Indigenous texts, as many settler critics and anthologists have done in the past. With this methodology and positioning again in mind, I turn to the more recent trajectories in Indigenous poetry and poetics knowing, as we do so, that the poetry that comes out of the last decade is not emerging from a vacuum. Rather, as Katherena Vermette points out, there has never been a dearth of Indigenous writers, there has been a centuries-long process of repression, oppression, and erasure, but there has never been a shortage of Indigenous cultural producers.

Land is intimately connected to Indigenous cultures, communities, histories, and futures. Land is at the heart of settler arrival to Turtle Island. Divergent and opposed understandings of how to be in relationship with land structure a great part of settler-Indigenous relations, both past and present. Or, as Mi'kmaw poet, ecologist, and storyteller shalan joudry writes, "in this landscape there have been many ends of the world / as one knows it" (23). And indeed land—and the care and respect for it—is deeply connected to recent events in activism, allyship, and, indeed, poetry. One place to begin is in the fall of 2012 as conversations started circulating on the Internet about the Jobs and Growth Act, more commonly referred to as omnibus Bill C-45. The Bill, which was over 450 pages long, was the second such omnibus bill passed by the Conservative government in order to implement its 2012 budget. Bill C-45 did many things, including transforming the Navigable Waters Protection Act into the Navigation Protection Act. Indeed, both omnibus bills came under criticism and scrutiny for their breadth as well as the number of motions proposed that had little or nothing whatsoever to do with the federal budget. The change to the Navigable Waters Protection Act fell under this category of non-budgetary change. The transformation from the Navigable Waters Protection Act into the Navigation Protection Act removed *water* from the title as well as the intent and practice of the bill. Whereas previously the Act protected the right to navigate water from interference of logging operations, bridges, pipelines, and other forms of industrial development and infrastructure, the new act only protects specific bodies of water named in the act itself. This means the Navigation Protection Act excluded 99.7% of Canada's lakes and more than 99.9% of Canada's rivers from federal oversight. Moreover, the new act specifically exempted pipelines, and so when Navigation Protection Act approvals are required—less frequently in this new iteration—they no longer trigger environmental assessments (Clogg, npag). The reconfiguration of this act also radically affected how Indigenous Peoples are able to care for and be consulted about reserve lands. In short, as lawyer Jessica Clogg writes, the act "now provides for surrender of reserve lands for leasing without the majority support from eligible voters" (Clogg, npag). In short, Bill C-45 proposed to fundamentally undermine the treaties that are foundational to settler-Indigenous relations.

In November of 2012, a teach-in was held in Saskatoon, Saskatchewan to educate and mobilize resistance to Bill C-45. Organized by Nina Wilson, Sheelah Mclean, Sylvia McAdam, and Jessica Gordon, the grassroots organization describes its history as a collaboration among Treaty people from Alberta, Manitoba, and Saskatchewan coming together to protest:

> ... the Canadian government's dismantling of environmental protection laws, endangering First Nations who live on the land. Born of face-to-face organizing and popular education, but fluent in social media and new technologies, Idle No More has connected the most remote reserves to each other, to urbanized Indigenous people, and to the non-Indigenous population.
>
> (INM, "About the Movement")

This teach-in, and a tweet using the hashtag #IdleNoMore, set off a wave of protests, teach-ins, and acts of solidarity across Turtle Island. And while, as McAdam reminds, "Idle No More began long before in different names, different locations through generations since the arrival of Europeans," this iteration brought with it new contours (65). Some of these new contours included what Ken Coates catalogues as affective: "it was joyous—more celebratory than angry. It was cultural more than it was political. Drumming and singing, long marches and Round Dances are its legacy, not speeches and slogans" (iv). Yet, as Gillian Roberts outlines, drawing on work by Glen Coulthard, in addition to Round Dances and teach-ins, by early 2013 the movement had expanded to include blockades (64). The grassroots nature of the movement, coupled with access to social media and other forms of open access information sharing, meant that popular awareness of the movement's increasing foci spread widely.[28] That late-fall and early-winter Round Dances popped up across the country, especially in shopping malls. The mall provided a warm space to gather, hold hands, dance, and raise awareness. The Round Dance, in turn, joyfully interrupted the consumer-driven flow of late-capitalism; inviting unsuspecting shoppers to join the circle and dance together. At teach-ins across the country, speakers shared space with testimonies and spoken word artists and poets. Language, shared, became a way to share information, history, and hope.

To this catalogue, we might also add a host of poets—both page poets and spoken word poets—whose work engaged with, was amplified by, or published soon after the emergence of Idle No More in 2012–13. In the four years following the emergence of Idle No More Indigenous poets such as Jordan Abel (Nisga'a), shalan joudry (Mi'kmaq), Liz Howard (European/Anishinaabe), Joshua Whitehead (Oji-nêhiyaw), Billy-Ray Belcourt (Cree), Dallas Hunt (Cree), Brandi Bird (Salteaux Cree), Leanne Betasamosake Simpson (Anishinaabe), Arielle Twist (Cree), and Tanya Tagaq (Inuk) to name but a few published first collections of poetry. Indeed, in the lead up to the sesquicentenary of Canada, there was a marked increase in media focus on Indigenous Peoples and cultural production by Indigenous Peoples.[29] And while the amplification of Indigenous voices has been beyond overdue, as Alicia Elliott (Tuscarora) has written, the continued tendency in mainstream media has been to infantilize and silo Indigenous Peoples.[30] Indeed, structural barriers to Indigenous publishing persist well into the twenty-first century.

Yet—and it is a significant yet—the proliferation of Indigenous brilliance in poetics is reaching new heights. The proliferation is the work of generations of Indigenous writers, and it is also the work of mentorship and community amongst Indigenous writers for one another. For, as Dallas Hunt observes, citing a CBC headline declaring "Indigenous authors celebrated as readership skyrockets across Canada," it is vital to attend to the ways in which Indigenous writers are engaged by the publishing industry.[31]

There are, in the work of Indigenous poets who have published first collections in the handful of years since Idle No More, lines of connection. Though formally unique from one another, many of these publications note friendship and community in the acknowledgements, as well as in the collaborative moves around editorial work and the work of providing "blurbs" for one another's books.

Case Study: Jordan Abel

To encounter the work of Nisga'a poet Jordan Abel is to enter a dizzying visual and aural soundscape where settler violence is placed squarely in the present. Abel's work is both conceptual and procedural. His first collection,

The Place of Scraps (2013, winner Dorothy Livesay Prize for Poetry), used erasure poetics to engage with the salvage ethnography of Marius Barbeau. Barbeau's work was aligned with the tenets of Romantic primitivism that framed Indigenous Peoples as a dying race; his practice was to purchase and remove items such as totem poles from the Nisga'a Nation. In his attempts to "salvage" Indigenous culture, Barbeau was in fact participating in dismantling and dispersing it. Abel's poems engage Barbeau's text *Totem Poles* and, in erasing Barbeau's text, Abel renders porous and present the repercussions and effects of salvage ethnography's tactics. As Mercedes Eng explains in a review of the book, totem poles tell histories of the people who made them (npag). Using Barbeau's text as source material, Abel excavates his memory, the source text, and language itself to reveal the losses wrecked by settler colonial intervention. Consider the following:

> 25.12.2010
>
> The poet exchanges gifts with his family; he gives his mother a book, a graphic novel, which is read immediately. The poet's mother identifies a section of the text and indicates that the page [in] question is a shared component of their past. The page depicts a totem pole in the Royal Ontario Museum. The poet's mother inquires if he remembers being there. But the poet does not hold that memory. The poet simply recalls the train car and the heat. Momentarily, the poet is surprised and ashamed that the pole that was removed from his ancestral village has also been excavated from his own memories. (npag)

Abel inhabits the form of Barbeau's observational writing. The dated entries are written in long blocks of prose poetry that ask readers to encounter them as poetry and in so doing consider the effect of genre. What does it mean to move prose into a poetic line and encounter it on those terms? What does it mean to excavate memory and history and encounter it on these terms? A poem-entry dated about a year later offers insight:

> 05.08.2011
>
> Of his own volition, the poet returns to Toronto, confident that he will be reunited with the totem pole removed from the Nass River by Marius Barbeau. The poet confronts the admission staff member at the ROM, explains that he refuses to pay to see a totem pole that was taken from his ancestral village. The staff member initiates a lethargic request to allow admission under special circumstances but is unable to contact any of his superiors. The staff member shrugs, verbalizes his apathy, and allows the poet into the museum. The pole towers through the staircase; the poet circles up to the top. The pole is here; the poet is here. (npag)

Totem poles can claim territory, can declare, "we are here." Abel's work is an important reclamation of territory, removing Sakau'wan's totem pole from the colonial museum, establishing a space for it within *The Place of Scraps*.

Part of the power of Abel's poetic excavation is in his capacity to invert the colonial tactics and, in so doing, declare enduring Indigenous presence. The western temporality of the lyric is likewise inverted, or even made obsolete. In centring both pole and poet, Abel reorients the lyric circuitry away from a longed-for person or thing. Instead, pole and poet encounter one another as speaker and longed-for thing. Together they exist beyond lyric time and extend into both a shared past and present.

Abel's subsequent collections of poetry each employ and explore conceptual and procedural methodologies as means to engage with the poet's personal history and the histories and present tenses of settler colonialism. In *Un/inhabited* Abel combined novels in the Western genre available for public access on Project Gutenberg and, using the CNTRL + F function—the search and find function—he sought out words having to do with the political and social aspect of land, land ownership, and territory. Upon locating a relevant work, Abel conducted a contextual study to determine how the word was deployed in the context of the sentence and the larger narrative. These contextual studies were then rendered poetic representations of trace, or absence, and ultimately of a visual representation of both the image of "a public domain" and what is left when it is erased or removed. His third collection, *Injun*, again employs compilation as a means of creating a large source text from which the long poem is produced. Here, the source text is collated from Western novels published at the height of pulp fiction (1840–1950). Using the racist epithet "Injun" as the target term, Abel again refines his contextual study. The result works in the documentary long poem tradition, but with a marked difference. Instead of penning the poem himself, Abel lets the racist representations of Indigenous Peoples presented in the novels speak for themselves. Stripped of their narrative dressing and amplified through his procedural poetics, the text demands that non-Indigenous readers confront layers of linguistic and narrative violence on his terms. The collection, which won the Griffin Prize for Poetry, is a presencing of Indigenous experience.

Conclusion

The present of Indigenous poetry is dynamic, extraordinary, and exciting. A brief catalogue of a few winners of major poetry prizes in the country testifies to these claims. When *Injun* was awarded the Griffin Prize for Poetry in 2017, it followed *Infinite Citizen of the Shaking Tent* by Liz Howard (Anishinaabe), which won the prize the previous year. In 2018, Billy-Ray Belcourt (Driftpile Cree) was awarded the Griffin for *This Wound Is a World*. Together with Abel, Howard and Belcourt mark a significant shift in poetics as well as Indigenous poetics. In each case the poets address theoretical, historical, and perspectival issues from within innovative poetic form. Howard's poetics draws on her work in neuroscience to "dream a science that would name me."[32] Belcourt's poetics make use of queer and affective theoretical methods and philosophies to make history "lay itself bare." In his hands, the elegiac is transmuted into both lamentation and prayer, where grief is both emplaced and a window to futurity. World making that is rooted in Indigeneity and theoretical and aesthetic experimentation is a hallmark of the most recent (at the time of this writing) company of Indigenous poets. The work of Joshua Whitehead (Oji-nêhiyaw, Peguis First Nation) similarly takes up experimental poetics. In his debut collection *Full-Metal Indigiqueer*, Whitehead conjures an Indigiqueer figure who fuses the organic and the technologic as a means of "re-beautifying and re-membering queer Indigeneity."[33] The collection manoeuvres around and through figures of the white western poetic canon such as Edmund Spencer, Shakespeare, and Milton and brings them into contact with figures of pop culture such as Lana Del Rey, Peter Pan, and the app Grindr. In so doing, Zoa the Trickster infects and pollinates each with queer indigeneity in order to centre Two-Spirit subjects at the heart of poetic matter. And while it is undeniable that Indigenous poets are at the vanguard of innovation, it is more likely that Leanne Betasamosake Simpson articulates the current moment of Indigenous poetics within the title of her book: *As We Have Always Done*.[34]

Key Terms

Cultural appropriation: The unacknowledged or inappropriate adoption of the customs, practices, ideas, beliefs of one group of people by members of another group often who are more dominant with relation to power.

Indian Act: Created in 1876, the Act aimed to force First Nations people to assimilate with settler culture through a series of violent interventions and regulations. The Act has been amended many times, including significant changes after the Second World War, and again in the 1980s. The Act has been responsible for the forced removal of children from their families, the creation and enforcement of Residential Schools, and complex and oppressive regulations around "status." In 1999, the government passed the First Nations Land Management Act giving First Nations governments somewhat more power, but this did not abolish the Act.

Oka/Kanesatake: A 78-day standoff (July 11–September 26, 1990) among Mohawk warriors, the Quebec police, and the Canadian Army. Catalysed by the proposed expansion of a golf course and suburb into the lands that included a Mohawk burial site, the crisis escalated. The army was called in, and while the expansion was cancelled, there has been no transfer of land to the Mohawks of Kanesatake. The resistance ignited solidarity actions across Canada and has been connected to calls for inquiries into missing and murdered Indigenous women and girls as well as to the Idle No More movement.

White Paper: In 1969, the government under Prime Minister Pierre Elliot Trudeau published a "White Paper" which advocated for the assimilation of First Nations people into settler society. In so doing, First Nations peoples would lose a great majority of their rights and benefits. Harold Cardinal, then-President of the Indian Association of Alberta, published a "Red Paper" in which he outlined First Nations' rejection of the White Paper. The government backed down.

Notes

1 Oka is a town in Quebec which borders on *Kanehsatà:ke* also known in English as Kanesatake, a Mohawk settlement. In 1990, the town of Oka approved plans to expand a golf course onto lands sacred to the Mohawk people, who in turn protested the development as a violation of their sacred land. The city escalated the development of the land while the Mohawk protected the land by building a barrier while trying to obtain a moratorium on the development. On July 11, the provincial police (*Sûretè du Québec*) raided the barricade. The result was a 78-day resistance on the part of the Mohawk Nation against the SQ and, eventually, the Canadian Army. The resistance is detailed in Alanis Obomsawin's essential NFB documentary *Kanesetake: 270 Years of Resistance* (1993).

2 For more, see Neal McLeod's introduction to *Indigenous Poetics in Canada*.

3 Martin writes, "Myths are easy for the university to sideline, but *intellectual traditions* it must contend with" (45).

4 In her portion of the collaborative interlogue, Reder writes, "with the advent of postcolonial studies, scholars began to ask about the function of the image of, and then of the work by, the *indigene*" (45). As she, like Ruffo, goes on to detail, it took more time still for Indigenous literary critics to survive the colonial university system and develop Indigenous literary criticism.

5 Reder highlights scholarship such as that by Thomas King, Calver and Hoy, and Terry Goldie, as well as W.H. New's *Native Writers and Canadian Writing;* Jeanette Armstrong's *Looking at the Words of Our People*, and Helen Hoy's "Nothing But the truth," as well as the key monograph by Janice Acoose, *Iskwewak—Kah'Ki Yaw Ni Wahkomakanak: Neither Indian Princess nor Easy Squaw* (1995) as path-building texts in the study of Indigenous literatures in all forms.

6 Scott, who is hailed as one of the more skilled poets of the Confederation period, worked in the Department of Indian Affairs.

7 There are a few exceptions, note Vermette and Ruffo, including the work of Mohawk writer Dawedine (Bernice Loft Winslow), Anahareo (Gertrude Bernard), a Mohawk woman who was married to the Indigenous imposter Archibald Belaney who passed himself off as an Indigenous man named Grey Owl. Additional examples cited by Vermette and Ruffo are, as they note, predominantly collected, edited, and published by non-Indigenous writers and ethnologists (see Vermette and Ruffo, xii–xx).

8 In his essay "Intent for a Nation," Len Findlay expands on this assertion and reads Chief Dan George's poetic tactics alongside and against George Grant's 1965 *Lament for a Nation*. Grant's work, which plots the political fate of the Progressive Conservative Diefenbaker government, has been hailed for provoking a surge in Canadian nationalism after its publication. Findlay argues that Chief Dan George both acknowledges and refutes this nationalism in his poetic work.
9 The En'owkin Centre is governed by the Okanagan Indian Educational Resources Society and is a registered private training post-secondary institution.
10 But one example of settler Canada's failure to "catch up" in the recognition and meaningful change in relationship to Indigenous Peoples is the 1991 Royal Commission on Aboriginal Peoples. Administered by both Indigenous and non-Indigenous commissioners, the report is more than 4000 pages long and details the ways in which Canada has an ongoing colonial relationship to Indigenous Peoples. The report was shelved, meaning it was not taken up in any meaningful or structural way.
11 In an unpublished dissertation, Erin Ramlo uses archival evidence to demonstrate the ways in which the Writers' Union of Canada systematically made equity a near-impossibility for Indigenous and racialized writers.
12 For example, in 2018 Book*hug press pulled and pulped Shannon Webb-Campbell's second collection of poetry, *Who Took My Sister?*, after allegations that she did not follow protocol in contacting the families of women whose stories were addressed in the poems (Millar, npag). After working with writer and elder Lee Maracle to address issues of protocol, Webb-Campbell published *I Am a Body of Land* (Book*hug 2019) which includes a preface from Maracle reflecting on the process of working with Webb-Campbell to address her mistakes. In her preface, Maracle addresses the work of mentorship she undertook and the work of learning that Webb-Campbell undertook with her. Another instance of complex engagement with Indigenous identity and allegations of appropriation occurred in 2020 when, several months after being awarded the Governor General's Award for Poetry for her collection *Holy Wild* (Book*hug), Gwen Benaway was named in an open letter calling for clarification of her claims to Indigeneity. Signed by five Indigenous cultural workers including Alicia Elliott, Terese Mailhot, and Joshua Whitehead, the letter, which circulated on Twitter, was prefaced with a statement on care and mindfulness:

> This is a collective call for Gwen Benaway to be accountable to the Indigenous communities she has claimed. It was written with deep consideration, caution, care and love for community. Please read the entire letter, and be mindful of how you respond.
>
> (GB2020, npag)

The signatories open the letter foregrounding the care and community amongst Indigenous artists, and cautioning non-Indigenous readers to "be mindful of their ignorance regarding our kinship systems, and therefore be sensitive to the nature of the contents of this letter" (GB2020, 1) The letter goes on to outline ten instances of Benaway discrepantly referencing claims to her Indigenous heritage and asks for "accountability without being cruel" (GB2020, 3). The letter closes by highlighting the beauty when "NDN people can bond and collaborate with each other" and that it is "even more beautiful when we feel safe to do so, and can freely collaborate and bond without our trust being violated."

Highlighting Indigenous collaboration, the letter is also pedagogical in teaching readers modes of requesting accountability that are not built on "being violent or cruel" (GB2020, 4). These ways in which Indigenous writers took on the labour of addressing these two recent examples—of breaching Indigenous protocol and of allegations of appropriation—demonstrate a model of care that has different contours than previous examples.

13 See Reder and Morra, *Learn, Teach, Challenge.*

14 In their editorial preface to Johnson's selections, Vermette and Ruffo also point out that Johnson's mother's family were well-known Loyalists (37).

15 Recall, again, that this is recognized as the first piece of Indigenous literary criticism. See Reder and Morra.

16 See the UBC-initiative *CanLit Guides* for not only a thorough introduction to Johnson's work and life in context, but a suite of guides aimed at student-learners. The guides cover all genres of literature in Canada.

17 It is notable, then, that when Atwood was commissioned to write a libretto for an opera on Johnson's life she "put her back into the *Oxford Book of Canadian Verse in English* in 1983." She explains that she included "Ojistoh," which she describes as "a hair-raiser about rape and murder," and notes that she'd "heard all this stuff about her being inferior to [Archibald] Lampman, but she is a creditable nineteenth-century poet in her own right—in her lyric work. Her dramatic work is often on par with, for example, Longfellow" (Clark, npag). See Clark, "Double Meaning: Margaret Atwood on Pauline." For another engagement with Johnson's life and work see the work of Mohawk poet and spoken word artist Janet Rogers who, in 2020, started Ojistoh Publishing on Six Nations Reserve.

18 See, for example, Jaimie Isaac's research.

19 Scholars such as Harold R. Johnson (Cree) have outlined in detail the ways in which the settler introduction of alcohol to Indigenous Peoples has had devastating effects. See, for example, Johnson's *Firewater: How Alcohol Is Killing My People (And Yours).*

20 Grauer and Ruffo draw connections between these writers. See especially pages 504, 507.

21 See, for example, Niigaanwewidam James Sinclair, "The Power of Dirty Water: Indigenous Poetics."

22 See for example Joan Crate's *Pale as Real Ladies: Poems for Pauline Johnson* (1991) in which the poet engages with the interior life of Johnson.

23 See also Marvin Francis, "Edgewalker." *City Treaty: A Long Poem.* Winnipeg: Turnstone Press, 2002.

24 Archibald Stansfeld Belaney, commonly referred to as Grey Owl, was a British born trapper and conservationist who appropriated Indigenous ancestry. Belaney reached international fame for his advocacy of conservation.

25 Whitehead's collection was shortlisted for the 2017 Lambda Literary Award for Transgender Poetry, the 2018 Stephan G. Stephansson Award for Poetry, and the 2018 Indigenous Voices Award for Most Significant Work of Poetry in English by an emerging Indigenous writer. In what the *TIA HOUSE* calls a moving act of radical kinship, Whitehead published an open letter explaining his withdrawal from the Lambda Award. After opening with sincere gratitude to the nominators and the jury, Whitehead goes on to explain that he is Two-Spirit and "to put it in the easiest terms for Western languages to understand, I live my life as a gay-femme and not a trans Indigenous person" ("Why I'm Withdrawing From My

Lambda Literary Award Nomination," npag). Whitehead's act of public pedagogy is significant.

26 Twist's collection is the winner of the Writers' Trust of Canada's Dayne Ogilvie Prize for LGBTQ Emerging Writers (2020) and the Indigenous Voices Award (2020).

27 Transcription of Indigenous Poetics Workshop, Trent University, Peterborough, November 4 and 5, 2010. See Neal McLeod, "Introduction."

28 See Coates who writes

> harness[ing] the power of the 'participatory web' and 'open source' ideology, [was] instrumental in giving Aboriginal people a platform and providing unprecedented access to audiences among Indigenous peoples and supporters in Canada and around the world.
>
> (173, 192)

29 A headline in CBC news from February 2020 reads "Indigenous authors celebrated as readership skyrockets across Canada." See Maryse Zeidler.

30 See "A Memo to Canadians" and *A Mind Spread Out on the Ground.*

31 See Hunt. See also Zeidler.

32 See Liz Howard. *Infinite Citizen of the Shaking Tent.* Toronto: M&S, 2015.

33 See CBC Best Poetry of 2017, www.cbc.ca/books/full-metal-indigiqueer-1.4148550

34 Simpson's book, *As We Have Always Done: Indigenous Freedom through Radical Resistance* (2021), identifies Indigenous political resurgence as "practice rooted in uniquely Indigenous theorizing, writing, organizing, and thinking" and calls for "unapologetic, place-based Indigenous alternatives to the destructive logics of the settler colonial state" (ii).

For Further Reading

Justice, Daniel Heath. *Why Indigenous Literatures Matter.* Waterloo: WLUP, 2018.

McLeod, Neal, Ed. *Indigenous Poetics in Canada.* Waterloo: WLUP, 2014.

Reder, Deanna and Morra Linda. *Learn, Teach, Challenge: Approaching Indigenous Literatures.* Waterloo: WLUP, 2016.

Simpson, Leanne Betasamosake. *As We Have Always Done: Indigenous Freedom through Radical Resistance.* Minneapolis, MN: UMP, 2021.

Younging, Gregory. *Elements of Indigenous Style: A Guide for Writing by and about Indigenous Peoples.* Edmonton: Brush Education, 2018.

Works Cited

Abel, Jordan. *The Place of Scraps.* Vancouver: Talonbooks, 2013.

———. *Injun.* Vancouver: Talonbooks, 2016.

———. *Nishga.* Toronto: Penguin, 2021.

Acoose, Janice. *Iskwewak—Kah'Ki Yaw Ni Wahkomakanak: Neither Indian Princess nor Easy Squaw.* 1995. 2nd ed. Toronto: Canadian Scholars, 2006.

Akiwenzie-Damm, Kateri, Ed. *Without Reservation: Indigenous Erotica.* Neyaashiinigmiing: Kegedonce Press, 2003.

———. "Gitookl Say It: An Anishnaabe Perspective on Spoken Word." *Canadian Theatre Research* 130 (Spring 2007): 9–14.

Armstrong, Jeanette. *Breath Tracks.* Vancouver: Theytus, 1991.

———, Ed. *Looking at the Words of Our People: First Nations Analysis of Literature.* Vancouver: Theytus, 1993.

Armstrong, Jeanette, and Lally Grauer, Eds. *Native Poetry in Canada: A Contemporary Anthology.* Peterborough: Broadview, 2001.

Atwood. "A Double-Bladed Knife: Subversive Laughter in Two Stories by Thomas King." Native Writers & Canadian Writing. Spec. Issue of *Canadian Literature* 124–125 (Spring/Summer 1990): 243–50.

Baker, Annharte. *Exercises in Lip Pointing.* Vancouver: New Star, 2003.

———. *Indigena Awry.* Vancouver: New Star, 2012.

Barrera, Jorge. "Author Joseph Boyden's Shape-Shifting Indigenous Identity." *APTN News* (December 23, 2016). www.aptnnews.ca/2016/12/23/author-joseph-boydens-shape-shifting-indigenous-identity/

Belcourt, Billy-Ray. *This Wound Is a World.* Edmonton: Frontenac, 2017.

Bernikow, Louise. *The World Split Open: Four Centuries of Women Poets in England and America, 1552-1950.* New York, NY: Vintage, 1974.

Campbell, Maria. *Stories of the Road Allowance People.* Penticton: Theytus Books, 1995.

Cardinal, Harold. *The Unjust Society: The Tragedy of Canada's Indians.* Toronto: Douglas & McIntyre, 1969.

Cariou, Warren. "Edgework: Indigenous Poetics as Re-placement." *Indigenous Poetics in Canada.* Ed. Neal McLeod. Waterloo: WLUP, 2014. 31–8.

Clark, Rebecca Anne. "Double Meaning: Margaret Atwood on Pauline." *My Scena* (September 1, 2015). https://myscena.org/rebecca-clark/double-meaning-margaret-atwood-on-pauline-2/

Clogg, Jessica. "Bill C-45, First Nations Rights, FIPA." *West Coast Environmental Law* (2013). www.wcel.org/blog/jessica-clogg-explains-bill-c-45-first-nations-rights-fipa

Coates, Ken. *IdleNoMore and the Remaking of Canada.* Regina: URP, 2015.

Coulthard, Glenn. *Red Skin, White Masks: Rejecting the Colonial Politics of Recognition.* Minneapolis, MN: UMP, 2014. https://doi.org/10.5749/minnesota/9780816679645.001.0001

Crate, Joan. *Pale as Real Ladies: Poems for Pauline Johnson.* Kingston: Brick, 1991.

De'Ath, Amy. "Decolonize or Destroy: New Feminist Poetry in the United States and Canada." *Women: A Cultural Review,* 26.3 (2015): 285–305.

Deerchild, Rosanna. "'It's Important to Challenge These Narratives': MMIWG Family Member Takes Issue with Book, *Who Took My Sister?*" *CBC Radio Unreserved* (April 13, 2018). www.cbc.ca/radio/unreserved/who-gets-to-tell-indigenous-stories-1.4616308/it-s-important-to-challenge-these-narratives-mmiwg-family-member-takes-issue-with-book-who-took-my-sister-1.4619203

Edwards, Stassa. "What Can We Learn from Canada's 'Appropriation Prize' Literary Fiasco?" *Jezebel* (May 16, 2017). www.Jezebel.com/what-can-we-learn-from-Canadas-appropriation-prize-lite-1795175192

Elliott, Alicia. "A Memo to Canadians." *The Globe & Mail* (2017). www.theglobeandmail.com/opinion/indigenous-memo-to-canada-were-not-your-incompetent-children/article37511319/

———. *A Mind Spread Out on the Ground.* Toronto: M&S, 2018.

Eng, Mercedes. "Jordan Abel's *The Place of Scraps.*" *Jacket 2* (2014). https://jacket2.org/commentary/jordan-abels-place-scraps

Erasmus, Georges, and René Dussault. *Report of the Royal Commission on Aboriginal Peoples*. Ottawa: The Commission, 1996.

Ferris, Neal and Manina Jones. "Flint, Feather, and other Material Selves: Negative Performance Poetics of E. Pauline Johnson." *American Indian Quarterly*. 41.2 (2017): 33-157.

Findlay, Len. "Intent for a Nation." *ESC*, 30.2 (2004): 39–48.

Francis, Marvin. "Edgewalker." *City Treaty: A Long Poem*. Winnipeg: Turnstone Press, 2002.

GB2020 [@GB20209]. "This Is a Collective Call for Gwen Benaway to be Accountable to the Indigenous Communities She Has Claimed." *Twitter* (June 15, 2020). https://twitter.com/gb20209/status/1272608805034000385?lang=en

George, Chief Dan. "A Lament for Confederation." *Native Poetry in Canada: A Contemporary Anthology*. Eds. Jeanette C. Armstrong and Lally Grauer. Peterborough: Broadview, 2001. 2–3.

Gerson, Carole and Veronica Strong-Boag. *Paddling Her Own Canoe: The Times and Texts of E. Pauline Johnson, Tekahionwake*. Toronto: UTP, 2000.

Grant, George. *Lament for a Nation: The Defeat of Canadian Nationalism*. 1965. Ottawa: Carleton UP, 1991.

Grauer, Lally, and Armand Garnet Ruffo. "Indigenous Writing: Poetry and Prose." *The Cambridge History of Canadian Literature*. Eds. Eva-Marie Kroller et al. Cambridge: Cambridge UP. 2009. 499–515.

Howard, Liz. *Infinite Citizen of the Shaking Tent*. Toronto: M&S, 2015.

Hoy, Helen. "Nothing but the Truth: Discursive Transparency in Beatrice Culleton." *ARIEL: A Review of International English Literature*, 25.1 (1994): 155–84.

Hunt, Dallas, Ed. *(Re)Generation: The Poetry of Kateri Akiwenzie-Damm*. Waterloo: LPS, 2021.

Idle No More. "About the Movement." (2012) https://idlenomore.ca/about-the-movement/

ILSA: Indigenous Literary Studies Association. "About." (2019) www.indigenousliterarystudies.org/home

Isaac, Jaimie. "Uncovering the Complicated History of Blankets in Indigenous Communities." *CBC Unreserved* (2019). www.cbc.ca/radio/unreserved/uncovering-the-complicated-history-of-blankets-in-indigenous-communities-1.5264926/the-complicated-history-of-the-hudson-s-bay-point-blanket-1.5272430

Johnson, Billy. "Impressions Sincerely Given: Publishing Rita Joe's Poetics of Continuity." *SCL/ÉLC*, 43.2 (2018). https://doi.org/10.7202/1062919ar 144

Johnson, E. Pauline. "A Strong Race Opinion: On the Indian Girl in Modern Fiction". *E. Pauline Johnson, Tekahionwake: Collected Poems and Selected Prose*, edited by Carole Gerson and Veronica Strong-Boag. Toronto: University of Toronto Press, 2002.

Johnson, Harold. *Firewater: How Alcohol Is Killing My People (and Yours)*. Regina: URP, 2016.

joudry, shalan. "Raising Forests." *Walking Ground*. Kemptville: Gaspereau, 2020.

Keeshig-Tobias, Lenore. "Introduction." *The Magazine to Re-Establish the Trickster*, 1.1 (1988).

———. "Stop Stealing Native Stories." *Globe & Mail* (January 26, 1990). www.theglobeandmail.com/news/national/cultural-appropriation-stop-stealing-native-stories/article35066040/

Kröller, Eva-Marie, and Coral Ann Howells, Eds. *The Cambridge History of Canadian Literature*. Cambridge: Cambridge UP, 2009.

Lai, Larissa. *Slanting I, Imagining We: Asian Canadian Literary Production in the 1980s and 1990s.* Waterloo: WLUP, 2014.

———. *Iron Goddess of Mercy.* Vancouver: Arsenal Pulp Press, 2021.

Lukin Linklater, Tanya. *Slow Scrape.* Montreal: Anteism, 2020.

McAdam, Sylvia. "Armed with Nothing More than a Song and a Drum: Idle No More." *The Winter We Danced: Voices from the Past, the Future, and the Idle No More Movement.* Ed. Kino-nda-niimi Collective. Winnipeg: Arbeiter Ring, 2014. 65–6

McGregor, Hannah, Julie Rak, and Erin Wunker, Eds. *Refuse: CanLit in Ruins.* Toronto: Book*hug, 2019.

McLeod, Neal, Ed. *Indigenous Poetics in Canada.* Waterloo: WLUP, 2014.

McRaye, Walter. *Pauline Johnson and her Friends.* Toronto: Ryerson UP, 1947.

Millar, Jay, and Hazel Millar. "A Statement from the Publishers Regarding *Who Took My Sister?* By Shannon Webb-Campbell." *Bookhugpress.ca* (March 30, 2018). https://bookhugpress.ca/a-statement-regarding-who-took-my-sister-by-shannon-webb-campbell/

Milz, Sabine. "Publica(c)tion: E. Pauline Johnson's Publishing Venues and their Contemporary Significance." *SCL/ÉLC* 29.1 (2004): 127–45.

Mosionier, Beatrice Culleton. *In Search of April Raintree.* Winnipeg: Portage & Main Press, 1983.

New, William H., Ed. *Native Writers and Canadian Writing.* Vancouver: UBCP, 1991.

Obomsawin, Alanis. *Kanesetake: 270 Years of Resistance.* Toronto: NFB, 1993.

Ramlo, Erin. "Towards a Critical History of the Writers' Union of Canada, 1972–1992." PhD dissertation. McMaster University, 2021. http://hdl.handle.net/11375/26928

Reder, Deanna. "Introduction." *Learn, Teach, Challenge: Approaching Indigenous Literatures.* Eds. Deanna Reder and Linda M. Morra. Waterloo: WLUP, 2016. 7–18.

Reder, Deanna and Linda M. Morra, Eds. *Learn, Teach, Challenge: Approaching Indigenous Literatures* Waterloo: WLUP, 2016. 7–18.

Roberts, Gillian. "Writing Settlement after Idle No More: Non-Indigenous Responses in Anglo-Canadian Poetry." *Journal of Canadian Studies/Revue d'Etudes Canadiennes*, 51.1 (Winter 2017): 64–89.

Ruffo, Armand Garnet. *Opening in the Sky.* Penticton: Theytus Books, 1994.

———. "Introduction." *Oxford Anthology of Indigenous Literatures: Voices From Canada.* 5th ed. Eds. Katherena Vermette and Armand Garnet Ruffo. OUP, 2020.

Simpson, Leanne Betasamosake. "'Bubbling Like a Beating Heart': Reflections on Nishnaabeg Poetic and Narrative Consciousness." *Indigenous Poetics in Canada.* Ed. Neal McLeod. Waterloo: WLUP, 2014. 107–20

———. *As We Have Always Done: Indigenous Freedom through Radical Resistance.* Minneapolis, MN: UMP, 2021.

Sinclair, Niigaanwewidam James, Keavy Martin, Kristina Faga, Daniel Heath Justice, Sam McKegney, and Deanna Reder. "Canadian Indian Literary Nationalism—A Criticism of Our Own?" *Cultural Grammars of Nation, Diaspora, and Indigeneity in Canada.* Eds. Christine Kim, Sophie McCall, and Melina Baum Singer. Waterloo: WLUP, 2012. 43–64.

———. "The Power of Dirty Water: Indigenous Poetics." *Indigenous Poetics in Canada.* Ed. Neal McLeod. Waterloo: WLUP, 2014. 203–16.

Smith, A.J.M. "Our Poets: A Sketch of Canadian Poetry in the Nineteenth Century." *UTQ*, XII (1942): 89–90.

Sugars, Cynthia, and Laura Moss. *Canadian Literature: Texts and Contexts*. Vol. 1 and 2. Toronto: Nelson, 2008.

Twist, Arielle. *Disintegrate/Dissociate*. Vancouver: Arsenal Pulp Press, 2017.

Vermette, Katherena. "Preface." *Oxford Anthology of Indigenous Literatures: Voices From Canada*. 5th ed. Eds. Katherena Vermette and Armand Garnet Ruffo. Oxford: OUP, 2020. 203–16.

Vermette, Katherena and Armand Garnet Ruffo, Eds. *Oxford Anthology of Indigenous Literatures: Voices From Canada*. 5th ed. Oxford: OUP, 2020.

Warrior, Robert. *Tribal Secrets: Recovering American Indian Intellectual Traditions*. Minneapolis, MN: UMP, 1995.

Weir, Lorraine. "Review of Annharte [Marie Baker]." *Indigena Awry*. Vancouver: New Star Books, 2013. In *Tracking CanLit*. Spec. Issue of *Canadian Literature* 220 (Spring 2014): 134–5.

Whitehead, Joshua. *Full Metal Indigiqueer*. Vancouver: Arsenal, 2017.

World Wildlife Foundation. "Oolichan... More than Just a Fish." https://wwf.ca/stories/oolichan-more-than-just-a-fish/.

Younging, Gregory. "Aboriginal Peoples' Estrangement: Marginalization in the Publishing Industry." *Looking at the Words of Our People: First Nation Analysis of Literature*. Ed. Jeanette Armstrong. Penticton: Theytus, 1993.

Zeidler, Maryse. "Indigenous Authors Celebrated as Readership Skyrockets across Canada." See Maryse Zeidler, *CBC News* (February 16, 2020). www.cbc.ca/news/canada/british-columbia/indigenous-authors-celebrated-as-readership-skyrockets-across-canada-1.5465622

6 Contemporary Poetics and Planetary Engagements

what people will take and give,
the passive lines, the passive guards,
if passivity can be inchoate self-loathing

all around, and creeping

self-righteous, let's say it, fascism,
how else to say, border,
and the militant consumption of everything,

(Dionne Brand, from *Inventory*)

And the women, with their pickaxes, unmaking.

(Sina Queyras, from *Expressway*)

it is better this way, or I would have no reason at all to write to you
what folds your ear sideways to my mouth, I slip into,
wondering what we might have become were we not so alive.

(Canisia Lubrin, from *The Dyzgraph*[x]*st*)

The previous chapter on Indigenous poetics aimed to trace some of the streams of poetic creation across generations of Indigenous writers. Unlike other chapters which are organized broadly around start and end dates, the chapter on Indigenous poetics did not work within those same parameters. In part, this is because Indigenous poetics exceed the parameters of this book. Additionally, the closer to the present this text gets, the more difficult it becomes to look at the context and pull out narrative and causal threads. It is this latter point—the complexity of addressing the present from within the relative present—that is our point of departure here. The three epigraphs that open this chapter attend to the complexities of addressing the current moment without losing touch with the past. It is here—the intersection of past and present—that this chapter begins.

In his study of Canadian poetry from 1960 to 1990, J.A. Weingarten proffers that poets have been "participating in the reinvention of history" (3). This reinvention is primarily a move away from metanarratives of so-called national unity and towards an increasing attentiveness to the local, the

DOI: 10.4324/9780429352966-6

particular, and the quotidian (ibid.). Weingarten's study focuses on writers such as Atwood, Al Purdy, and Barry MacKinnon. Weingarten highlights their work with the "lyric I" as central to the project of reinventing history:

> Their distrust of conventional history has spurred a new discourse that uses the particularities of region and family instead of the nation at large for the base of historical writing. In so doing, they have reimagined history as a lively and lyrical expression of the "I," rather than as an elite grand narrative told solely by academics.
>
> (4)

He goes on to detail the ways in which the poets of his study renovate the "lyric I" and bring it to a broader public in a historical context of concomitant reflection on the nation. And while there is evidence of lyric invention—as well as intervention—prior to 1960, the shifts that Weingarten observes, and which Chapter 4 addresses, evolve well into the twenty-first century. Texts such as Roy Kiyooka's *Transcanada Letters* (1975), a multimodal sustained engagement with self, other, and culture; George Elliott Clarke's *Whylah Falls* (1990), which engages with "Africadian" history; and Robin Blaser's *The Holy Forest* (2008), a serial poem which spans five decades of the poet's life, offer other examples that work in and build on this mode. The poets whose epigraphs open this chapter fall outside the parameters of Weingarten's study, yet there are significant similarities. In the work of Brand, Queyras, and Lubrin, the present is encountered, processed, and contemplated through lyric perspectives. The "I" is present, in other words. Their speakers orient the reader to the space and time of the poem. In each of these collections, the complexities of history collide with the complexities of subjectivity. Rather than look only backwards, the lyric speakers of these poems undo not just history, but also the possibility of a "lyric I" itself, and in so doing point to some of the changes the future deserves.

The Long Poem

Recall that, as we learned in earlier chapters of this book, the long poem is one that tells a story. It is a poem whose length and shape contribute to the story that is being told. And, while the parameters of a long poem are porous (Smaro Kamboureli once referred to the long poem as a "genre without a genre"), we tend to know them when we see them (Kamboureli, *On the Edge*, 101). bpNichol's durational project *The Martyrology* (1972) and Robert Kroetsch's *Field Notes* (1981) are both canonical long poems in Canada, and both, at the root, aim to engage with time and all its shifting chimerical qualities. Rachel Blau DuPlessis has suggested that for writers outside the patriarchal framework—women, for example—the expanded form of the long poem demonstrates "anti-authoritarian ethics at the level of structure," while Sharon Thesen observes that the long poem "can combine epic size with intimacy of voice" (Thesen, "After-Thoughts," npag). Thesen, the editor of two editions of *The New Long Poem Anthology*, highlights Lisa Robertson's *Debbie: An Epic* (1997) as an example of a long poem that intertwines epic size with intimacy of voice in an exemplary and innovative fashion. Similarly, works such as Michael Ondaatje's *The Complete Works of Billy the Kid* (1979) and much of Daphne Marlatt's work—*Steveston* (1974), for example—use the epic form to interrogate stories from multiple angles and approaches. That these works are poetry rather than prose is central to their functioning (Thesen, "After-Thoughts," npag). The long poem is a form in which thinking is given room to unfurl, and where the tactics of poetry—think, for example, of enjambment, erasure, elision—structure that thinking into lineation.

Also recall, while the long poem is hardly a form specific to Canada, it is one that has complex and vital histories, presents, and futures. A documentary long poem, so named by Dorothy Livesay, is a long poem with a particular social angle rooted in the impulse towards reportage in the 1930s (Livesay, *The Documentary Poem*). Donna Bennett and Russell Brown describe the documentary poem as one:

> in which historical or other "found" material is incorporated into a writer's own thoughts, in order to create a dialectic between the objective facts and the subjective feeling of the poet. The effect is often ironic; it is always intensely personal.
>
> (482)

As previously mentioned, J.A. Weingarten states that since around 1960 "Canadian poets have been participating in the reinvention of history" (4). His observations are relevant to discussions of the long poem and the documentary poem insofar as they remind us of some of the ways in which poets have been at times deeply engaged in complex projects of historiography that intersect with the trajectory of the settler-colonial project of Canada. As Weingarten outlines, the shifts in social and political narratives after the Second World War were significant, to say the least. We overviewed many of these shifts in the opening portions of Chapter 3, and Weingarten articulates the effect as a "convenient conflation of 'nation' (a cultural community) and 'state' (a politically governed community with clear geographic borders) by presuming that Canada's national character could be synonymous with its predominating systems of political power" (ibid.). In other words, in the period beginning around 1960, Weingarten sees a significant and sustained rise in the number of poets writing persistent engagements with the stories that make up histories of Canada. Many poets engaged with what Jean-Francois Lyotard referred to in his *The Post-Modern Condition: A Report on Knowledge* as "metanarratives," or dominant ideologies such as religion that structure modes of interacting with one another and one's own relation to a place. And, while there are significant nuances required to unpack the ways in which dominant ideologies intersect with individual or communal lived experience (one cannot ethically suggest that the effects of racism or misogyny are a metanarrative, for example), these poetic engagements with history are remarkable for the ways in which they participate in, subvert, and sometimes reify narratives of the nation.

From Reinventing to Reorienting History

The first epigraph that opens this chapter comes from Dionne Brand's long poem *Inventory* (2006) and it keeps company with work from Sina Queyras's *Expressway* (2009) and Canisia Lubrin's *The Dyzgraphxst* (2020). Published with a decade and change between them, these collections each address some of the prevailing poetic concerns of the most recent years. In the hands of each poet, poetry is both tool and tale; the poems are tools for navigation, investigation, and renovation of form and of the context of our shared existence on earth. The poems are also tales, weaving their own specific stories that draw on lyric tendencies, innovate on those traditions, and, when found wanting or lacking, make new poetics to fit the work each does. The three poets whose work opens this chapter are engaged with what Lyotard called "an incredulity towards meta narratives" (3). These three poets are also deeply engaged in interrogating the ways that history is never singular and always mediated by story. Using poetic tactics such as planetarity, lyric conceptualism, and an expanded lyric I, Brand, Queyras, and Lubrin exemplify some of the poetic engagements that exceed national narratives and attend to wider fields of experience.

The work of witnessing and the call to collective action is also evident in this small excerpt from Sina Queyras's *Expressway*. This line—"and then women, with their pickaxes, unmaking"—comes from the end of a collection that navigates the ways in which infrastructures made to connect people and places have in fact depersonalized and, in the case of the environment, devastated connections. Roads lead nowhere. A tollbooth operator on the Jersey Turnpike composes sonnets from each group of 14 cars passing her open window, while a solitary woman walks the median seeking cell service. Somewhere in the middle of this transit-centric critique, excerpts from Dorothy Wordsworth's journal are repurposed as source material for considering the effects of the Romantics on our understanding of both the lyric and human's relationship to Nature. Has something vital been lost in the masculinized reification of nature as both sublime and other? In Queyras's hands, the expressway and the things that manage to grow in ditches and back pockets of history are means of interrogating both late-capitalism and the tensions between lyric and conceptual poetics. Drawing on tactics of both, *Expressway* reorients the traditional lyric. And, like Brand's work in *Inventory*, the result is an imperative: reader, we must do better.

The final epigraph that opens this chapter is taken from Canisia Lubrin's book-length poem *The Dyzgraphxst*. Winner of the Griffin Poetry Prize, the Derek Walcott Prize, the OCM Bocas Prize for Caribbean Literature, and shortlisted for the Governor General's Award for Poetry in English, *The Dyzgraphxst* navigates how to represent the self. More specifically, the question of how to represent the self is explored within complex and intersecting experiences of the Black diaspora. Composed in seven acts, the poem prises open the pronoun "I" to make space for multiple modes of being in the world. The central speaker is Jejune. Described as "the voice addressed, every page," we are told that Jejune is "the chorus, the you, the we/unnavigable self. The character never leaves the stage" (ii). Jejune, who is marked "by and through diasporic life," questions methods of making, finding, and being at home in the world (ibid.).

Each of these collections push the limits of form and in the push make something that is both new and connected to what came before. Brand, Queyras, and Lubrin each address inequity at individual, communal, and global levels and simultaneously forge meaningful modes of being in contexts and places that are hostile to their speakers' thriving. In these collections, the rise of fascism, climate disaster, anti-Black racism, and transphobias and homophobias are centred; they become the terrain of poetry. And while poetry has long engaged with pressing social catastrophes—think of the transnational solidarities in the 1930s, for example—the work here exemplified a shift to what Heather Milne names a poetics of engagement. Milne traces a poetics of engagement in the early years of the twenty-first century to events such as the founding of Poets against the War in the United States. The group was created in 2003 by Sam Hamill in direct response to then-First Lady Laura Bush's decision to cancel a White House poetry night in fear that it might be "political." As Milne explains, a "flurry of antiwar poetry anthologies was published in the United States and Canada between 2003–2005," which both situated poetry as a fertile space for dissent and conjured legacies such as that of the 1960s anti-Vietnam War poetry (Milne "Introduction," 3). Rather than dissipate, as the earlier iterations did, Milne identifies a poetics of dissent that ranges from Poets Occupy Wall Street, to American poet Juliana Spahr's *That Winter the Wolf Came*, Amy King's Poets for Living Waters, the Enpipe Line Collective, and the collaborative poetics of Rita Wong's "#J28."[1] In short, for Milne, one of the defining characteristics of poetry of the twenty-first century is its capacity to address and engage with "matters." Milne suggests that the concept of poetry as, and engaged with, matter is fertile because of the connections not just to something mattering—as in being meaningful—but also to "the materiality of language, or bodies, and of the physical world of objects, ecosystems, and geographies" (3–4).

The poets in this final chapter may not all adhere directly to the definition Milne offers, but I harness her concepts here as a helpful organizing principle. In the twenty-first century, poetics in Canada matter. Brand, Queyras, and Lubrin, along with the other poets highlighted in this chapter each take up form as a means of engaging with history in service of the future. Working at the interstices of the long poem, the documentary poem, and innovations on the lyric form, these poets use poetry as a means of bearing witness and of interrupting the inadequate status quo. This chapter does not move in a strictly linear fashion. Instead, with case studies of some contemporary poets as anchors, I aim to trace lines of connection backwards with the hope of finding, if not direct lines of conversation and concern, then at the very least, lines of flight. The chapter uses case studies—of Dionne Brand, Erín Moure, Sina Queyras, Anne Carson, and Canisia Lubrin—as anchors to consider the flux and flow of poetics and contextual events in the more recent parts of the twenty-first century.

Case Study: Dionne Brand

Essayist, novelist, poet, teacher, editor, mentor, artist: Dionne Brand defies categorization. And yet, her work, which spans four decades and counting, has clear through lines of concern. Belonging, place, gender, race, movement, transit, and justice are recurrent themes that cross genres in her literary work. In this case study, her 2008 publication *Inventory* is central. *Inventory* is a long poem which catalogues atrocities both large and small. This catalogue is recorded and felt by the lyric speaker who is the anchor of the poem. Over the course of the collection the "I" of *Inventory* accounts for losses of all kinds. Unable to pull away from the television, her speaker documents and updates the "bristling list hourly" (99). The collection works in the tradition of both the long poem and the documentary long poem and does so with a difference.

Like Dorothy Livesay's work before her, Brand's long poem is itself an archive of its context. Penned in the months and years after 9/11, after the declaration by former American President George W. Bush of war on terror, *Inventory* witnesses at both the level of the street and the global. The speaker of the poem who catalogues her list in a fever is both omniscient and deeply rooted in place. Witness to both airstrikes in the Middle East and crying babies on a residential block of Toronto, the speaker of the poem sees and feels everything. She has the capacity and compulsion to enact what Diana Brydon describes as "affective citizenship" wherein the speaker of the poem mobilizes affect as a means of claiming citizenship not simply with places, but more properly with people engaged in global struggle (990). The speaker of Brand's *Inventory* is able to register both international atrocity and deeply intimate experiences of emotional intensity. The result is a long poem that bears witness and demands that the reader take up the work of witness, too. Brand's lyric witness bears similarities to Rachel Zolf's Janey in *Janey's Arcadia* (2014) in which a single figure bears witness to compounded human violence. In the case of Zolf's Janey, however, the figure is a cyborgian composite of Janey Canuck and Janey Smith, and Zolf's tactics of cataloguing are deeply invested in feminist mash-ups of conceptual poetics.[2] Not so with Brand's witness, who retains clear connections to a traditional lyric voice. One crucial innovation Brand makes on the lyric witness is rooted in her ethical relationship to her act of witnessing as well as her position regarding her own subjectivity.

"Nothing personal is recorded here," the lyric witness of Brand's poem reports (22). This statement—distant, clinical, bureaucratic—stands in contradistinction to what we tend to expect from the speaker in a long poem. As mentioned earlier, critics such as D.M.R. Bentley and Smaro Kamboureli have written in detail about the generic qualities of the long poem in Canada.[3] What matters for Brand's poem here is that the long poem has been framed as an in-between or ambivalent genre which tends to be addressed towards a public. This address towards a collective is, as Cheryl Lousley explains, a move that is epic in its tactics, but has quite different results:

> The long poem is addressed to a public, a collectivity, like the epic, but tends to deflate the epic's grand and totalizing vision through narrative discontinuity, autobiographical self-reflexivity, and attention to local particularities.
>
> (37)

Brand's long poem deviates from this formula in an important fashion: the poem, as Lousley highlights, "is tempered with ethical detachment" (38). In other words, Brand fuses the kind of objective distance associated with the epic with the expectations of facing a public that has become associated with the long poem's address. The effect is stunning. While it is almost too broad to say that contemporary poetry in Canada addresses its own moment of production, the fact remains. While, as we have seen throughout the course of this volume, Canadian literary critics have tended to frame literary production in relation to nation, region, language, and contexts of subjectivity such as race and gender, many critics—sometimes the same ones—also call for a "retooling" of critical approaches in order to address the changing contexts of poetic production on both a national and global scale.[4] Brand's *Inventory* accomplishes this complex labour. In attending to the local and the global, the broad and the particular, and the shifting allegiances of collective and individual perspectives, Brand models new modes of belonging in relation not just to nation, but to the planet.

In their foundational work *The Communist Manifesto*, Marx and Engles make the observation that capital and its flows have made the world a site of colonization.[5] The ways in which capital keeps growing and expanding markets globally as a way of trying to fix its own contradictions suggest that capitalism in this global contest—aka globalization—elides differences and projects universality. Within this context, there has been a significant "transnational turn" in literary studies.[6] It is into this temporal context I will introduce Gayatri Spivak's notion of "planetarity": Spivak explains that the concept of planetarity is a way to push against globalization. Rather than functioning as anti-globalization, which is perhaps best envisioned as the other side of the same coin, Spivak sees planetarity as a way to "overwrite the globe" as a way of articulating and envisioning how we inhabit the world (72). Spivak's notion of planetarity is an invitation to reconfigure our understandings of relationality—with the world on a grand scale, as well as with one another, with the environment, and with deeply specific experiences. The notion of planetarity is a useful one to help us think through the shifts in Canadian poetry in the twenty-first century because it offers a way of thinking across large concepts.[7] Let us consider the opening lines of *Inventory*:

> We believed in nothing
>
> the black-and-white American movies
> buried themselves in our chests,
> glacial, liquid, acidic as love
>
> the way to Wyoming, the sunset in Cheyenne,
> the surreptitious cook fires, the uneasy
> sleep of cowboys, the cactus, the tumbleweed,
> the blankets,
> the homicide of Indians,
> lit, dimmed, lit, dimmed
>
> (3)

A collective "we" opens the long poem with a pronouncement steeped in loss. Instead of rootedness, and a sense of both belonging to place and people, the "we" of the opening stanzas are instead saturated by the flattening effects of American black-and-white movies. Images of the West are undergirded with ideologies of Manifest Destiny, expansionist projects, and cultural genocide. The narcotic quality of light which dims and then reappears, dims and reappears draws past and present together in uneasy relation. The dimming light is both flickering television in the rooms of we, watching, and also the passage of days, weeks, months, years of oppression, and violence against Indigenous Peoples. From the outset, Brand's speaker announces relationality—between the collective "we" and the "they" of "uneasy cowboys" and "Indians," as well as between the then and now of expansionist projects.

The "we" of the opening lines are not bystanders, however, nor does the "we" function as a Grecian chorus whose function is to comment on the central action of the drama from a remove. Instead, readers quickly encounter the ways in which "we" are bound up in the ills of global capitalism and extraction:

> We waited, we waited sticklike and nervous,
> did what we could when allowed
> ....
> the steel we poured, the rivets we fastened
> to our bare bones like cars,
> we stripped, so fastidious,
> the seams of dirt excised from apples and gold
> all the railways
>
> everywhere, and the forests we destroyed,
> as far as

> the Amazonas' forehead, the Congo's gut,
> the trees we peeled of rough butter,
> full knowing there's something wrong
> with this
> ....
> we did all this and more
>
> (6–7)

Ecological exploitation from South America to Africa is aligned with colonial projects in North America to demonstrate the global scale of atrocities. The "we" of *Inventory* denotes responsibility that places individuals in relation with one another and, in so doing, activates the possibility to change. And yet, as Brand demonstrates, while "we did all this and more," there are additional agents in this calculus of living.

Brand activates three additional pronouns in *Inventory*, each of which thickens the complexity of relationality in her lyric witnessing. In the remainder of section one, "they" are set in opposition to the "we" of the opening pages:

> they waited, watched,
> evaluated all our good lyrics
> of the goodness, of the science, the delicious
> being of more than, well more,
> so hard now to separate what was them
> from what we were
>
> (8–9)

Who are "they" in relation to "we"? Perhaps "they" are larger forces animated by individuals—corporations, governments. Perhaps "they" are oppressive structures, again animated by individuals: racism, homophobia, misogyny, capitalism. Despite the difference between "we" and "they," the implication the poem offers is this: without recognition of culpability, without constant reciprocity, "how imprisoned we are in their ghosts" (7–8). The speaker's references to ghosts, and especially the ghosts of others, mark a distinct shift from poets who positioned Canada as a place without ghosts half a century earlier. In his 1962 poem "Can Lit," Earle Birney writes "We French, we English, never lost our civil war,/ endure it still, a bloodless civil bore; / no wounded lying about, no Whitman wanted./ It's only by our lack of ghosts we're haunted" (116). Many writers, teachers, and critics take this slim poem as evidence either of the *terra nullius* narrative, or, more recently, as evidence of settler imagination overwriting Indigenous presence. Evidence of these intersecting perspectives can be found earlier still, Catharine Parr Traill wrote "As to ghosts or spirits, they appear totally banished from Canada. This is too matter-of-fact country for such supernaturals to visit" (153). And while Atwood and others have written about the presence of ghosts and haunting in Canada, the other critics focus on how this absence of ghosts overwrites Indigenous presence, and by association the possibility of Indigenous spirits on these lands.[8] In her hybrid work of creative non-fiction, *Map to the Door of No Return: Notes on Belonging* (2002), Brand considers haunting on lands scarred by colonialism and situates her own status as an arrivant of colour in relation to the larger questions of haunting and colonial legacy.[9] In *Inventory*, she returns to the questions posed in *Map to the Door of No Return* and broadens them further. As sections of *Inventory* unfurl, a singular "she" enters the poem. "She" "felt ill" and wishes to address directly the "fascism" that she sees and feels everywhere (16–17). The urgency that "she" carries in her body shifts from disease to "weeping," but her vigilance never wavers. From this third-person position, "she" catalogues bombings and killings in the Middle East, fire bombings and mass shootings in the United States, racialized violence in England and France, deportations across Europe, mass migrations across Europe, South America, and the globe. With each catalogue, the potential for being overwhelmed with detail and devastation becomes more inevitable, yet she maintains her vigilance. Until, that is, she shifts her genre. Halfway through the second section of *Inventory* "she" relays that "she's written a letter, / an account of her silence" (34). From here, the third-person voice gives way to the first-person "I." The shift occurs at an enjambment: "don't pray it only makes things worse, I know." The remainder of the poem moves between this "I," the "she," a "you," and the "they." Listener, speaker, agent, and subject are split, joined, and recombined within the body of the speaker and the body of the poem itself. The poem ends with the final lines in the mouth of the first-person lyric I:

> I have nothing soothing to tell you,
> that's not my job,
> my job is to revise and revise this bristling list,
> hourly
>
> (100)

Revision of the individual in relation to others is taken alongside the need to revise collective relationality. Without constant vigilance and constant tending, the list never bristles and the "lyric-I" never rests. The possibility of planetary ethics is sketched across the archiving work of this long poem, but not promised. Instead, from within the long poem, Brand revises the form and in doing so enacts some of the methodologies we might need to address the bristling list of our shared planetary woundedness.

We can connect the transnational and planetary ethics enacted in *Inventory* with the work of poets such as M. NourbeSe Philip, Rachel Zolf, and, as the final case study in this chapter demonstrates, Canisia Lubrin.[10] Each of these poets attends to questions of belonging in their work and centre their poetics on queer and or racialized experiences, histories, and poetics. Networks of poetic communities extend globally and locally and the trajectories of movement—literary and literal—are living networks of writers who address intersecting histories of transit from the complexity of the present.

Case Study Erín Moure

The historical and cultural context of Canada from the end of the twentieth to the beginning of the twenty-first century was, once again, a period of significant change. If the late-1980s and early-1990s were a time of cultural changes—marked by the passing of the Multiculturalism Act, the North American Free Trade Agreement, the Gulf War, and environmental crises—the most recent decades in Canadian history have been marked by protest and controversy. Global events such as attacks on the World Trade Centre on September 11, 2001, and the global collapse of financial markets in 2008 reasserted the connection between the country and the rest of the world. Indeed, as Smaro Kamboureli and Robert Zacharias suggest, these global events strengthened the nation as both a state of mind and as a "structuring principle" just at a moment when critics and citizens alike were prepared to declare the so-called success of globalization (xii). Literary critics once again break into factions along categorical lines. These are, predominantly, questions about what makes a national literature, and tensions between lyric and conceptual practices in poetry. A careful look at both of these dominant concerns reveals questions about power and value that are both revelatory and concerning.

In the field of fiction, conversations—many of them incendiary—were concerned with who "counted" as a Canadian writer. Did a writer need to be born in Canada? Write about Canada? Live in Canada? Some particularly vociferous commentators critiqued the international success of Canadian novelists as evidence of the relentless progress of globalization.[11] Others, such as Kit Dobson and Libe García Zarranz, offer a more complex view of the development of both literary nationalism and literature in the nation. In *Transnational Canadas*, Dobson reframes the trajectory: he writes that "while it was formerly popular to celebrate the nation as a bastion against globalization on the left, today it seems that the national and the global are, instead, interlocking scales of capital" (x). Zarranz, meanwhile, posits that post-9/11, the material conditions and realities of borders have increased, while dreams of borderlessness have, paradoxically, also increased with significant effects on border-crossing subjects such as queers, refugees, and activists.

In poetic contexts, the questions seemed more specifically rooted in what the Russian formalist Roman Jacobsen termed *literariness*. Literariness is the quality of language organization that makes something literature rather than another kind of text. In critical conversations around poetics, discussions of power and value were tangled up in concurrent discussions of what counted as literary. In an essay entitled "Crossing," poet and translator Erín Moure articulated her own poetics and what Tanis MacDonald reads as Moure's "challenges to reading and writing practices" as well as Moure's "resistance to poetry as a consumable genre." Here is what Moure writes:

> Reading practices are not just embodied but are determined by ideology, culture, and history. They are codificaitons and decodifications I

> wanted a poetry that refused erasure. That clamoured … . I wanted, and want, a poetry that could not simply be consumed. Not a consumer poetry. I wanted a poetry that lets us think.
>
> (251–2)

This reflection on "poetry that lets us think" and "consumer poetry" demonstrates Moure's capacity to reflect on the context as well as practice of writing. Steeped in feminist thinking, Moure's poetics is, as MacDonald writes, "a statement that takes the temperature of Canadian poetry in the second decade of the twenty-first century" (471).

A poet, essayist, and translator whose work engages questions of philosophy, language, memory, and feminism, Erín Moure is the author of twenty books of poetry thus far. Moure consistently trusts that the reader is capable of thinking with her work. Steeped in feminist and philosophical discourses, Moure describes poetry as a "conversation that crosses borders and breaks institutional rules in creating new paradigms and possibilities as it pursues a course of freedom, listening, celebration, support" ("About," npag). Her view on poetry and poetics is radical, expansive, and demonstrative of her own intergenerational engagement. Shannon Maguire in her introduction to Moure's selected poems describes the effect of Moure's work as altering "the conditions of possibility for poets of several generations" (ii). Indeed, Moure's own conditions were likewise altered by her experience of the Women and Words conference in 1983. In a conversation with Pauline Butling and Susan Rudy about how and why her poetics changed so significantly in *Furious* Moure reflected that:

> … the real catalyst of turning point for me was the Women and Words conference in 1983. It opened up my thinking about women and language.
>
> ("Why Not Be Excessive?" 43)

Recall that the conference was attended by more than a thousand women and that speakers included a diverse set of writers such as Nicole Brossard, Claire Harris, Betsy Warland, Maria Campbell, Phyllis Webb, Makeda Silvera, and Louise Cotnoir. Moure recalls that in her presentation, Cotnoir relayed to the listeners that "Language is biased and (women) are the ones that suffer the bias … we are fighting against the social order that has defined us by its language" (qtd. in Wheelwright, 1). The relationship between situated, lived experience and the possibilities of language became tools for Moure.

Deliciously difficult to definitively categorize, Moure's is a poetics of attention. Rooted in her characteristic wordplay and capacity to construct alternative possibilities through poetic innovation, Moure is iconoclastic. Her experimental poetics draw deeply on multilingualism—she writes and translates in French, Catalan, Spanish, and Galician (so far)—as well as on radical feminist poetics, including the networks of bilingual and francophone feminist thinkers and writers in Montreal. Her collection *Furious* (1988) won the Governor General's Award for poetry. The collection takes on German philosopher Immanuel Kant's notion of "pure reason" and interrogates languages of power. It is also a collection which addresses political frustrations through the lens of female experience. Work, family dynamics, and gender and sexual identity are examined as part of a project to "inhabit freely the civic house of memory I am kept out of" (91). Indeed, across Moure's oeuvre is a sustained consideration of the ways in which belonging and citizenship are restricted or refused to many people.

In *Furious*, for example, Moure uses feminist poetics to survey the context of the "here" of Canada. The speaker finds the context to be lacking. Consider this excerpt from a section entitled *The Acts*:

> It's the way people use language makes me furious. The ones who reject the colloquial & common culture. The ones who laud on the other hand the common & denigrate the intellect, as if we are not thinking. The ones who play between the two, as if culture were a strong wind blowing in the path of *honour*. It takes us nowhere & makes me furious, that's all.
>
> (86)

The speaker's fury over a kind of ideological and cultural "stuckness" as well as a misguided understanding of "honour" connect with the concerns of poets who have likewise addressed social and cultural rifts in Canada. The speaker attempts, in an eponymous section, to speak with a "mouth, hurt" by both colonial and misogynistic language. Writer and scholar Sonnet L'Abbé considers this a "manifesto of sorts" in which Moure lays out a poetic praxis: "Behind their fury is a deep faith that language can be used more consciously, more ethically, to take us somewhere. That somewhere," observes L'Abbé, is "a kinder world, a place of respectful and joyous interrelation" (iii). Exemplified in this excerpt, the female speaker of *Furious* consistently balances deep philosophical reflection with quotidian experiences. rob maclennan writes that Moure is "one of those rare poets that seems to have created her own school out of disparate, desperate, and seemingly unrelated stands of other writing, other histories, and other lines of thinking, becoming something entirely her own" (maclennan, npag). Though, in the threads across her many publications where she addresses working-class life, she is rarely grouped with those poets harnessed under the signifier of "People's Poetry."[12] Instead, Moure may be more generatively read as an experimental poet whose capacity for connection—through the poetics in her work, as well as her work as a translator—situates her, and her work, as a keen-eyed thinker whose feminist poetics and linguistic experiments render her a beacon.

Case Study: Sina Queyras and Lyric Conceptualism

Interlopers, those figures whose poetics render them complex to categorize, pose an exciting challenge to the work of literary historians and literary critics. The work of defining coteries, schools, groups, and, sometimes, factions is often work that happens belatedly. Whether through the labour of literary historians, critics, or members themselves looking backward, definitional work, or the "naming" of a group rarely happens in the moment. Tanis MacDonald describes this process of defining trends and groups as a:

> series of gestures of making and unmaking: for example, the proposal of a certain aesthetic or poetic approach as Canadian in either tone or approach, and a near-simultaneous refusal of that same gesture on the basis of its limitations or its provenance.[13]

Examples of this gesture of qualification abound. Following Tanis MacDonald's flagging of A.J.M. Smith's rejected preface to the 1936 anthology *New Provinces* and Michael Gnarowski and Louis Dudek's *The Making of Modern Poetry in Canada*, I would add introductions of more recent anthologies including Gary Geddes's *15 Canadian Poets x 3* (2001); derek beaulieu, Jason Christie, and a.rawling's *Shift & Switch* (2005); Sina Queyras's *Open Field: 30 Contemporary Canadian Poets* (2005); and Jim Johnstone's *The Next Wave: An Anthology of 21st Century Canadian Poetry* (2018).[14] Events, such as "The Cage Match of Canadian Poetry," which was presented in terms that would be relevant in a wrestling match, actively worked to amplify what MacDonald identifies as "gestures of making and unmaking." The event pitted Carmine Starnino, a Montreal-based writer, editor, and literary critic against Christian Bök, a poet and scholar whose collection *Eunoia* won the Griffin Poetry Prize in 2002. Described by an organizer as the "future of Canadian poetry" where Bök and Starnino were positioned as "Canada's very own Pound and Eliot," the Cage Match was organized and advertised in pugilistic terms. Even the reference here to T.S. Eliot and Ezra Pound is significant in that it suggests an overdetermined polarization of aesthetics and projects the global influence of infamous modernists onto two Canadian men who were willing to play out such theatrics in public. Indeed, the event was hyped as a spurious debate between a traditionalist (Starnino) and an experimentalist (Bök).[15] However, attempts to broaden and amplify the importance of poetic differences through a single event were unsuccessful. Instead, as poet and novelist Gary Barwin writes in his reflection on the event,

> I don't know why we can't have both approaches as part of a vital and active poetry world. Sometimes poetry is research, exploration of the hadronic structure of a conceptual alphabet of supernovae. Sometimes it is renovation, rejuvenation, development, and refinement. I like my Blues atonal and with a seventeen and a half bar form. But I also like good ol' 12 bar blues with just the three chords, well executed, sometimes with old words, sometimes with new words that talk about sex, lost love, and microwaveability.
>
> (Barwin, npag)

Barwin's insight underscores the strangeness built into desires for strict schools, styles, and groups. In a few short lines infused with characteristic wit, he reminds readers what poetry can do when desires for purity or strict divisions are refused. In their introduction to *Prismatic Publics: Innovative Canadian Women's Poetry and Poetics* (2009), editors Kate Eichhorn and Heather Milne make a similar suggestion. They describe the through lines that bring the poets in the anthology together noting that while they do not share a common methodology or aesthetic, each poet they include engages with language as a mode of inquiry.[16] Thus, while there are many examples of resistance to hybrid or innovative poetic methods that move between the lyric and the experimental, there are also significant examples of the exuberant possibilities that come from working in this mode.

Fast forward to the spring of 2012 when a manifesto appeared on the America Poetry Foundation's *Harriet the Blog*. Entitled "Lyric Conceptualism, a Manifesto in Progress," it set out a series of aphoristic statements about a new hybrid poetics. Here are a few of the opening lines:

> The Lyric Conceptualist has moved beyond the indigestible and the unreadable, in fact, beyond all gestures that have made pleasure the enemy of reading.
> Still, the Lyric Conceptualist remains true to her politics of inclusion, appreciating the thinkership of conceptual poetry, the revelations in mass assemblages that concretize the ephemeral textuality of daily life. Yet she stubbornly continues to bask in the reverie of solitude.
> Lyric Conceptualism indulges in the excess of language while appreciating the clean lines of the minimal.
> Lyric Conceptualism does not confuse clarity with simplicity.
> Lyric Conceptualism rejects naïve notions of truth and beauty.
> Lyric Conceptualism is not simply expressionism.
>
> (Queyras, "Lyric Conceptualism" 62)

Written by Sina Queyras, the manifesto in progress both outlines a hybrid poetics and addresses current tensions and fissions in poetic camps. Recall that the "Cage Match of Canadian Poetry" which pitted traditionalist lyric poetry against avant-garde conceptualism had only happened three years prior. In "Lyric Conceptualism" Queyras rejects narratives of genre purity. Instead, Lyric Conceptualism—which, in the manifesto, is both personified and gendered—draws tactics and inspiration from lyric and conceptual poetry as well as the "ephemeral textuality of daily life." The quotidian and the complex are not mutually exclusive, nor does one hold some strange primacy over the other. Instead, Queyras works across these scales and sites.

Conceptual poetry's genealogy is often plotted through the development of Conceptual Art. As Caroline Bergvall writes, Conceptual Art from the mid-1960s onwards was "a mode of working that, true to avant-gardist modes, was critical of the commodified art object and of art institutions themselves. The art machine needed further untooling. The aesthetic credos of originality and progress needed stripping right down" (Bergvall, 18). Philosophy, linguistics, and other modes of social and critical theory became tools for "untooling," and groups of likeminded practitioners emerged. Writing groups engaged in conceptual tactics included Mass Observation, OuLiPo, and L=A=N=G=U=A=G=E poets, all of whom were interested in procedural, collective, and constraint-based modes of addressing the function of the author (19). While conceptual methodologies were ostensibly engaged with writing, Bergvall observes that in the art world, "Conceptual Art turned quickly into a small coterie of largely given, largely male, largely white art stars" (20). Is the same true of poetry? The answer is complicated. For, while there are unequivocable examples of gatekeeping, in the Canadian context reality is much more complex than a binary opposition can ever represent. Moreover, as Gregory Betts details in his comprehensive study of the earliest iterations of avant-gardism in Canada, there is a significant and long history of these kinds of aesthetic practices.[17] And, as Bergvall and others observe, exploring, disrupting, and navigating the power politics and possibilities of language is the material of writing itself.[18] However, not all writers whose work can be read as conceptual find richness and company in the categorization of "conceptual," and this is important. Part of the discomfort with such identifications comes from the actions of some vocal few, where (for example) some egregious acts of literary racism have been presented under the portmanteau of conceptual writing.[19]

In "Lyric Conceptualism," Queyras succinctly and evocatively addresses some of the dangers of strident gatekeeping and poetics devoid of an awareness of the human. Instead, they focus on the possibilities that exist in the interstices of lyric and conceptual work. Like the poetry of Rachel Zolf, Queyras addresses questions of subjective and historical complicity. Like the poetry of Lisa Robertson, Queyras stitches together a vast and various archive of influence and inspiration. Like the work of Nicole Brossard or of M. NourbeSe Philip, Queyras engages with history in service of the future. Some of Queyras's future-oriented work is rooted in digital space which, while no longer "new," certainly warrants consideration as a point at which literary culture once again shifts. As Kate Eichhorn, Tanis MacDonald, and Karis Shearer and Jessica Schagerl variously observe, the evolutions in digital technologies since 2005 have changed the poetic and indeed literary landscapes significantly.[20] The emergence of social media, blogging, and open journal platforms has (to some extent) made accessing and circulating literary culture easier. And, while the Internet certainly is not an egalitarian utopia, it has undeniably altered the ways in which communication and readership function.[21] Working across digital and print platforms, Queyras exemplifies the poet-critic working across genres, scales, and generations.

Lemon Hound was published in 2006 by Coach House Press and offers a place from which to examine Queyras's formal as well as generational experiments. The collection formulates a persona through which the poet engages with Modernist innovations with grammar, syntax, and perspective. Gertrude Stein's grammatical deconstruction is inhabited and expanded by *Lemon Hound*. Likewise, Virginia Woolf's innovations on perspective and proximity are vivified by the interloping lyric persona. The text also marks a growing attention by Queyras to tenets of conceptual poetics, especially those that involve processional and theoretical questions as the hinge of the poem itself. Some of these experimentations with form come from careful and sustained engagement with the structure of other writers' work. For example, Queyras returns to Woolf's path-making work *The Waves*, which is widely considered Woolf's most experimental fiction. *The Waves* consists of six soliloquies offered by six speakers. In Queyras's work, Woolf's prose is whittled down further. The connective tissue of grammar is removed:

> Him Rhoda go under myself how Jinny
> Rhoda go under myself how Jinny Him
> go under myself how Jinny Him Rhoda go
> myself how Jinny Him Rhoda go under
> how Jinny Him Rhoda go under myself
> Jinny Him Rhoda go under myself how
> (101)

By removing so much grammatical material, Queyras's unmaking of Woolf's work invites the reader to reconsider both. This attentiveness to writers across generational time and space is again evident in Queyras's syntactical and rhythmic inhabitation of Gertrude Stein's prose. Queyras's syntax is stylish. The poem begins with a complex sentence and a dependent clause, which is complicated, then pared down to simple sentences, and built back up again:

> She is feeling brisk at the heel. She loves feeling brisk at the heel. She is feeling brisk at the heel and rivering her thumbs. She is at the edge of cool. She runs her thumbs along the hinge of the river. She loves running her thumbs along the hinge of the river. She feels river. She feels thumb. She is brisk and thumbing. She is numb and loving. She is feeling loving. She is feeling loving about feeling. She loves feeling about loving. She loves feeling about feeling. She loves feeling about feeling loving. Her loving feels. Her loving loves rivers. She is feeling loving about rivers. She is feeling rivers about loving feelings. She rivers about loving. She rivers about feeling. She rivers about the hinges of rivers.
> (12)

The tenets of the traditional lyric are here, though verbs change places with nouns, the subject of the poem remains stable. "She" is the subject who "feels" "loves" "rivers" and "thumbs." This meandering unfurling and refurling poem struck a chord in my memory. With this in mind, consider another except, this time from Gertrude Stein:

> She was telling some one, who was loving every story that was charming. Some one who was living was almost always listening. Someone who

> was loving was almost always listening. That one who was loving was almost always listening. That one who was loving was telling about bring one then listening .... Trembling was all living, living was all loving, someone was then the other one Certainly this was Ada then.
>
> (Stein, *Ada*, 123)

This is an excerpt from Stein's portrait of Alice B. Toklas, which she wrote in 1910. Though not as lyrical as the work in *Tender Buttons*, the tenets of the lyric are present here as well. Stein's text also hinges around the pronoun "She," but here "she" masks the central subject, the "someone" "the other one" who was "Certainly ... Ada." It is a difficult little lyric, to be sure, but as Heather Cass White notes, Stein's lyrical experiments are purposefully difficult (124). Stein's lyrics of this period are concerned with reorienting the traditional lyric voice (126). White suggests that Stein's reoriented lyric turns away from the conversational and back towards an earlier description of the lyric as "overheard conversation by the poet to [him]self" (Mill, 348). In so doing, Stein's lyric opens the possibility of crosstalk by allowing the poet to step away from a position of power. "Poetry is concerned with using and abusing, with losing and wanting, with denying with avoiding with adoring with replacing the noun" (Stein, 165). In these two excerpts, separated by decades, denotations, and archiving, what gets adored, abused, avoided and replaced is the female subject. The women—that's the second place we'll settle. Stein's lyric draws attention to the destabilized and abstracted female subject. Queyras's lyric inhabits Stein's syntax to bring the woman back into focus.

The female subject is of central concern to conceptual writing. In one iteration, conceptual writing is described as "writing that mediates between the written object (which may or may not be a text) and the meaning of the object by framing the writing as a figural object to be narrated" (Place and Fitterman, 25). Unlike the traditional lyric structure, conceptual writing exaggerates the reading process insofar as its "excessive textual properties refuse ... the easy consumption of text and the rejection of reading in the larger culture" (25). Thus, the similarities and resonances between Stein's portrait and Queyras's poem gesture towards a conceptual poetics that has its roots in modernism to be sure. Moreover, Queyras's poetics, their crosstalk with Steinian syntax plots a feminist genealogy that moves rhizomatically across time and space. Inserting itself in the interstices between current literary historicism and conceptual poetic practice, I suggest that Queyras's collection is a kind of generative trespassing into Stein's modernist poetics that demands a rearticulation of the processes that go into tracking Canadian literary history. Queyras's poetics can be situated within a Canadian literary history of *excentriques* that has direct connections to the expatriate work of the modernist period.

An early attempt to sketch out these modernist excentriques came in 1984 when Barbara Godard posited that the creation of a thorough literary history in Canada would require understanding women. Specifically, Godard calls for a rearticulation of literary history that takes into account women's transgressions. She figures Canadian feminist writers as "ex-centriques," meaning outside the centre. They are also "'telling it slant', in Emily Dickinson's words", and in so doing "they are transgressing literary codes in a manner approximating madness—hence eccentric" (58). Godard suggests that the history of positioning feminist writers as colonial subjects in relation to patriarchal culture is of especial import when attempting to understand the literary history of Canada. Godard's thesis identifies a "causal link" between a feminist's relationship to established literary discourse and the:

> role of women writers in this country, most specifically to the advent of Modernism and Post-Modernism in Canada's literary tradition. The more forcefully they have asserted their feminism, the more disruptive their literary productions have been. Ex-centriques, thus avant garde. (57)

In short, Godard proposes a genealogy of feminist writing in Canada that is both viscerally connected to oral tradition's marginalized status in relation to the archive, and between Canadian feminist literary production in relation to the Modern and Post-Modern periods. Importantly, Godard underscores the problematic conditions of creating this genealogical literary history that is specific to Canada. The problem is that unlike countries where feminist literary and theoretical production has been formative and visible in reacting against the overt exclusion of non-male subject from the national canon, in Canada non-male subjects have been uncannily present. Rather than being a cause for celebration, however, this presence has created a false sense of equality and valuation where there is not one (58).

Queyras attends to but does not heed borders and boundaries. Born on the West Coast of Canada, raised in the back of a station wagon criss-crossing the country, a poet, a blogger, an essayist, a teacher, Queyras is an interloper welcome in conversations about conceptual poetry as well as a leader in lyric circles. Queyras's speaker asks, "Who understands trespassing?" The question is posed as the speaker considers both gender and genre. Who understands trespassing better than a queer subject, a feminist, perhaps, trying to forge a line in a poem from language that does not always validate their reality? Queyras's speaker poses the question in a cultural moment that has been defined both as post-secular and as post-human, a moment more apt to "try Advil" than to "try Stein" as a means of navigating contemporary cultural production (Queyras 2006: 58). In her introduction to the co-edited special issue of *Open Letter* on Poetics and Feminism Today, Eichhorn suggests that the current generation of Canadian feminist critics are, "if anything, collectively suspicious of origins" (7). "'We' are more suspicious than our 'foremothers'," she continues, for two reasons. For Eichhorn, previous generations of women dealing with feminist poetics have worked at the two-pronged project of "deconstructing patriarchal Oedipal dramas" while simultaneously maintaining a commitment to a "project of recalling models, figures, and histories that might provide a lineage for their intellectual and creative invention" (7). On the other hand, "we" have come to writing and theory "after Haraway's myth-rejecting cyborgs. 'We' are ironic. 'We' are also nostalgic" (ibid.).

Eichhorn's use of "we" is itself a kind of temporal trespassing, as it connects rhizomatically to Dorothy Livesay's "We Are All Alone," itself a poem taken up by Godard and Di Brandt in 2009 to organize their *Wider Boundaries of Daring: The Modernist Impulse in Canadian Women's Poetry*. Of the 16 essays in this collection only Lianne Moyes's addresses a contemporary writer. Moyes reads Anglo-Montreal experimental prose writer Gail Scott through Gertrude Stein's experimental poetics. Moyes begins her article by citing Dorothy Livesay's poem "We Are All Alone" in order to make the case for a transnational literary network that reorients linear and narrow histories of writing and writerly influence. For Moyes, Livesay's focus on the "we" pronoun "reinforces the idea in the final lines that 'we are *not* alone' and that something more may come of a writer's work than can be seen or imagined" (163). Building on Kristeva's notion of intertextuality and Foucault's cracking open of the term genealogy, Moyes makes the case for reading national literary histories otherwise. Genealogy offers a "critique of teleology" and a "displacement of origins" while simultaneously attending to the "heterogeneous assemblage of discourses and practices" which make up the history of literary texts (173). Intertextuality allows the critic and new literary historiographer to "reconceptualize the writing subject—as an agent and an effect of intertextual relations" (173). Eichhorn's use of "we" differs from Livesay's insofar as they speak to different generations. While Livesay's "we" places emphasis on the "not"—we are *not* alone—Eichhorn's pronoun speaks in a different register. If the "we" of Eichhorn's present continue to organize literary history in a linear fashion then women and other Others will continue to be siloed or left out of wider possible genealogies. One of the intergenerational ties that bind, for Eichhorn, is the fact that there are now "at least two generations of innovative Canadian women writers who have been overlooked by Canadian literary critics" (Eichhorn, "Beyond Stasis," 8). Or, as Louise Bernikow puts it, "What is commonly called literary history is actually a record of choices," and those choices need to be both articulated and questioned regularly (3).

The dearth of criticism on Queyras's—as well as their contemporaries'—work is notable for two reasons. First, like Stein, Queyras is a prolific publisher, significant figure in Canadian and American avant-garde and feminist poetry and poetics. Their blog—think of it as an atelier—was the locus of intellectual engagement with avant-garde poetries and art. Indeed, as Andrea Bennett points out in conversation with Kevin Spenst, *Lemon Hound* the blog served as a vital hub for cross-country conversation between and about poets and poetry (npag).[22] The blog operated as a single-authored endeavour for five years, during which time Queyras engaged in current debates around poetry and poetics, as well as reflecting on art, literature, and poetry. The site changed in 2010 when Queyras opened the space to make room for emergent voices in poetics and art—specifically, the site became part of the Writers Read series at Concordia University where Queyras teaches and was edited in collaboration with their students. During this period, Queyras also continued to write and edit for the site, and reflection on crucial issues included equitable representation in book review culture, literary gatekeeping, and toxic spaces in literary culture. Second, like Stein, critics have been quick to engage with Queyras's public intellectualism, and slower to engage with Queyras's own work. The poetry collection *Lemon Hound* has been discussed by few scholars and critics, as has *Expressway*. Subsequent collections have yet to be addressed in scholarly writing.[23]

Queyras's poetics move across genre boundaries in generative ways. They also engage with poetic innovation across generational boundaries. Starting with *Lemon Hound*, each of their collections keeps company with the thinking and writing of specific women.[24] In the acknowledgments to *Lemon Hound*, Queyras states that this text is, "among other things, a direct response to and engagement with the work of Virginia Woolf." It is Queyras's qualifier "among other things" that catches my attention and hearkens to Godard's claims and Moyes's rearticulations of genealogy and intertextuality. Queyras draws lines of affiliation with that simple preposition "among." Prepositions are "doing" words used to indicate temporal, spatial, logical relations. This one, "among," is used to mean "being in the company of," "being surrounded by," or "being in a large set of." The poetry collection *Lemon Hound* performs a prepositional modernist poetics. Situated among modernists such as Woolf and Stein, as well as Canadian avant-garde poets Lisa Robertson and Anne Carson, *Lemon Hound*'s poetics are generative disruptions, generative genre, and spatio-temporal trespassings that complicate and extend potential readings of Canadian women in modern, post-modern, and conceptual writing communities. Moving between the United States and Canada, from page to site, between the Poetry Foundation's blog and their own, Queyras is a prepositional poet whose poetics enact the possibilities of among that recites Stein, which inscribing a legacy that "thinks back through mothers," as Woolf encourages. Queyras's citation is "disruptive" in Lynette Hunter's sense of the term: Queyras's mothers are queer doers who, through crosstalk and disruption, establish a literary network of excentriques that stretches into the twenty-first century (Hunter, iii).

Their public literary work, meanwhile, bears echoes to the epigraph that opens this chapter: "the women with their pickaxes, unmaking." Queyras's focus—on the page and in the digital public sphere—is on women and other Others, as well as on limits: so-called limits of genre, of gender, and of dubious narratives of "progress." In *Expressway*, lyric subjectivity is stranded in the medians of modernity. Everywhere the highways and roads meant to connect are in ruin. There is grief for labour, unrecognized. There is grief for the environment, which is under constant threat. There is grief for communities and connections that are fraying, straining, and fracturing under the pressures of the present. And yet, there is also hope in the form of women wielding pickaxes. "Go forth and undo harm," prescribes Queyras's aphoristic lyric voice in the closing set of "Proverbs from hell." "Go forth and do."

The imperative to "go forth and do" bears deep resonance with other modes of engaged poetics, such as the work of poets engaged with the environment and climate crisis. Like Queyras's *Expressway*, which troubles twenty-first century dependence on unrenewable energy and petrocultures, much environmental poetry of recent decades works across lyric and conceptual lines. Poets such as Don McKay, Don Domanski, Adam Dickinson, Di Brandt, Rita Wong, Stephen Collis, a.rawlings, and Harry Thurston have been writing at the intersections of poetics and nature with an eye to ecology for decades. Anthologies such as Nancy Holmes's *Open Wide a Wilderness* (2009), Madhur Anand and Adam Dickinson's *Regreen: New Canadian Ecological Poetry* (2009), and Kathryn Mockler's *Watch Your Head: Writers and Artists Respond to the Climate Crisis* (2020) gather poets who attend to climate change, ecology, and nature and demonstrate that this work, though it has some ties to the Romantic interests in sublime nature, is more squarely working in the mode of what Milne names a poetics of engagement. It is meaningful in the context of this chapter that Queyras and Lubrin each have work in *Watch Your Head*, underscoring the increasing intersectionality of contemporary poetic work by many poets.

Case Study: Anne Carson

In the previous chapter on Indigenous poetics, I addressed literary scandals in the form of both appropriation and literary celebrity. Thus far, in this chapter, I have considered a few of the additional tensions and debates in poetic contexts during the early-twenty-first century. In addition to continued discourse—sometimes quite heated—around aesthetics that are reminiscent of the aesthetic debates of the 1930s, there have been important (again sometimes quite heated) clashes around issues of gendered representation. In addition to the latest iterations of cultural appropriation in literary spheres, the last decade has demonstrated the ongoing asymmetry of gender-based representation in literary spheres. In the United States, poets Juliana Spahr and Stephanie Young published an essay in the *Chicago Review* entitled "Numbers Trouble." In it, they address scholar Jennifer Ashton's claims that "by the mid-80s efforts to 'redress the imbalance'" of gender representation in literature "had apparently succeeded—women seemed to make up more or less half of the poets published, half the editorial staff of literary magazines, half the faculties of creative writing programs, and so forth" (160). Following Ashton's claims, which were built on a refutation of an earlier essay by Spahr and Young, Spahr and Young proceed to review women's presence in literary anthologies and come to a resoundingly different set of conclusions. The Vida Count, an annual audit of gendered representation in literary book reviews in America, debuted in 2011.

In Canada, the "Numbers Trouble" debate did not get the same kind of public attention immediately, though as we have seen over the course of this book, feminist poetics have been a constant presence in this country. In their introduction to *Prismatic Publics: Innovative Canadian Women's Poetry and Poetics*, editors Milne and Eichhorn cite Young and Spahr's text as one inspiration for their own anthology. And, as we have just seen, Sina Queyras has been asking in poetry, essay, blog, and social media "where are the women?" for nearly two decades.[25] A change occurred in 2012 when, after the Vancouver 125 Poetry Conference, discussions arose once again around gender representation in literary contexts. One result of these discussions was the formation of CWILA: Canadian Women in the Literary Arts. Founded in 2012, the organization's aim was to offer a space for discussions about representational justice in literary culture in Canada, as well as to run an annual CWILA Count. Like the VIDA Count, CWILA's Count was volunteer-based and audited hundreds of publishing venues at the height of its function. Original spokesperson for CWILA Gillian Jerome noted that it was also a blog post by poet and writer Natalie Zina Walschots that was instrumental in galvanizing the formation of the organization. In the post, entitled "Closing the Gap: Reviewing Books of Poetry by Canadian Women," Walschots conducts her own audit of *The National Post*'s poetry reviews and determines that of the 14 books of poetry reviewed that year only 2 were written by women. Walschots goes on to outline her attempt to discuss this trend with *Post* columnist Michael Lista. Discussions about the culture of book reviewing in Canada grew heated culminating in a series of public statements between Lista and poet Jan Zwicky.[26] The same year, Donato Mancini published *You Must Work Harder to Write Poetry of Excellence*, which is a thorough cultural history of literary review culture in Canada since 1961. In his study, Mancini proposes that 1961 marks a palpable point in which postmodernity began to affect the production of poetry in Canada. And, while poetics began to change, Mancini tracks the ways in which the modes of literary reviews—from concepts to tropes to metaphors—have remained fairly stable. Citing Steven Laird, who observes that "the books that made the short list for the Governor General's Award for poetry indicate that poetry is in the same place," Mancini connects this to the same concerns issued by the founders of *TISH* in 1961.[27] Namely, the concerns are with "lyric poetry's nearly uncontested dominance of literary prizes" (Mancini, 2). And, while the last several years of prize-winning poetry tells a different story, the statement is significant for it marks a moment in time in which tensions—between lyric and conceptual, between poets and literary critics, between academic and popular responses to poetry—were especially clear.

One of the through lines this book attempts to follow is the ways in which historical and cultural contexts effect poetic production. And, while it is nearly impossible to reproduce the simultaneity and constancy of some contexts such as colonialism and capitalism, there are rupture events that make these intersections more demonstrable. Many sets of events have occurred across intersections of gender and, more specifically, patriarchal structures. The formation of CWILA was one example, with its focus on representational justice and review culture. A short two years later, CBC radio host Jian Ghomeshi was fired for allegations of sexual misconduct that reverberated across the country. And while Ghomeshi was found not guilty, the allegations were the first wave to articulate what came to be called the #MeToo Movement in Canada.[28] The movement gained global traction through the use of social media and picked up speed as allegations against media mogul Harvey Weinstein broke nearly simultaneously with Alyssa Milano's use of the term. In Canada, UBC's suspension and eventual dismissal of Professor Steven Galloway occurred in 2015 and resulting discourse included allegations of sexual misconduct. Literary communities in Canada were divided around the allegations as well as the creation and circulation of an open letter in protest of the dismissal under the heading "UBC Accountable." Allegations of sexual harassment and assault emerged against other prominent literary figures as well as members of creative writing faculties at universities across Canada.[29] And, while systemic oppressions such as misogyny are not new, this set of events has once again shifted the contexts in which literature, including poetry, is produced, read, reviewed, and circulated. Perhaps of note here is the ways in which creative writing pedagogy became a subject of wider concern. With these contexts and events in mind, let us consider the work and reception of Anne Carson.

"It is easier to tell a story of how people wound one another than of what binds them together," writes Anne Carson in an early collection entitled *Plainwater* (34). While Carson's speaker may well have diagnosed some of the stories of poetic ruptures in the twenty-first century, the story that Carson's poetic oeuvre tells is quite different. Instead of rupture, Carson's poetics track a steady trajectory of attentiveness to history, formal innovation, and deep curiosity. Her capacious poetics have earned her international recognition as well as some deep distrust that bears some uncanny resemblance to the rifts we have just considered. And yet, Carson's own poetics both attends to power asymmetries and at the same time transcends them.

Carson entered the literary scene in the late-1980s. Trained as a classicist and employed for a time at McGill University to teach in that field, Carson's work pushes the bounds of literary taxonomy. Her PhD dissertation was published as a long treatise on desire that has garnered both critical and popular acclaim. It was followed by collections of poetry including *Short Talks* (1992), *Glass, Irony, and God* (1995), and *Men in the Off Hours* (2000), and *The Beauty of the Husband* (2001).[30] In an early interview, Carson told John D'Agata that she kept two desks. One was for her scholarship on the classics, while the other was for creative writing. The work got better as those two desks became closer together and papers from each began to mix (13). Carson's poetics are constantly evolving, and she has since published several novels in verse, as well as librettos, hybrid essay collections, and a vast number of poetic translations of classical works by Sappho and Euripides. In the excerpt from *Plainwater* quoted above, Carson's speaker observes that the easier story to tell is the one of wounding. This is a characteristically insightful line that says as much about Carson's reception—at least initially, in Canada—as it does about the poem from which it was taken.

When Anne Carson received the Griffin Prize for *Glass, Irony, and God* there was something of a critical uproar. Rather, several poets took exception to Carson and made their exception known by publishing it in literary journals. At the heart of these concerns—if one can manage to peel back the vitriol and grandstanding on the part of the writers—seems to be a two-sided question. Who is this woman poet gaining such sudden and significant success? And what is this writing that she is calling poetry?[31] For example, in an essay titled "The Trouble with Annie," Montreal-based poet David Solway lambasts Carson as a failure as both an academic and a poet. The title is remarkable: note that Solway refers to Carson not by her given name, but by an infantilizing diminutive. What gives Solway the right to refer to Carson as "Annie"? It is unclear. The dismissive tone of the title gathers force as he offers explanation for his two pronged critique. He notes he has begun by critiquing "the scholarship because Carson constitutes a special case in which the double lack of fibre and talent is exemplified by a charlatanism more readily ascertainable in the academic work than in the poetry" ("The Trouble with Annie," 24). Poetry, Solway continues, "can always take refuge in murkiness" (24). He goes on to call her "a phony as a scholar and a poet" (26).[32] In a similar vein in an article for *The Globe and Mail* entitled "Who's Afraid of Anne Carson?" Carmine Starnino refers to Carson as well as her work as "primitive" and "unaccomplished" and does not deserve to have her writing considered poetry (Martin, R3). As we have seen in earlier chapters, the question of difficulty and poetic excellence is not new. It is notable, then, that when confronted with a trifecta of poetic innovation, critical and popular reception, and an identity that is other than white and male, an uproar can almost be automatically anticipated. Again, this is not new. Rather, the vitriolic response by some writer-critics to Carson's work serves to remind readers of the ways in which literature and literary production operates within structures such as patriarchy, racism, and capitalism. In an essay entitled "Canadian Literature and the Dying Temporality of Colonialism," poet, critic, and scholar Jeff Derksen historicizes cultural appropriation in the twenty-first century by looking at artefacts of appropriation from the 1990s.[33] In so doing, Derksen demonstrates the ways in which the death throes of oppressive systems have long lives and require alternative modes of engagement to name, refuse, and in so doing, dismantle them. In addition to anti-Black racism and anti-Indigenous racism, the late-twentieth and early-twenty-first centuries in Canada continue to be marked by misogyny. Literary culture is not exempt; rather, it offers a discrete site in which to observe the ways in which these systems continue to play out. With these contexts in mind, it is worth spending more time with Anne Carson's poetics.

Carson's poetry has been described as electrifying, as working with both sides of the brain, and as a series of dazzling hybrids.[34] Her collections bring together classical references with literary texts to navigate abstract concepts such as love and death. The gulf between the two textual contexts is typically bridged by an enigmatic yet deeply compelling lyric speaker. One compelling example is "The Glass Essay," published in *Glass, Irony, and God*, a collection which did not receive as much critical recognition as some of Carson's subsequent books. Despite this, the poem has been highly anthologized. It is in

Canadian anthologist Gary Geddes's *15 Canadian Poets x 3* (2001). Significantly, it also appears in Sharon Thesen's *The New Long Poem Anthology* (2001). Inclusion in an anthology goes some way in cementing a poem or poet's place in a literary canon, in spite of the inevitable bias of the anthologizer, as Robert Lecker has shown.[35] What is perhaps even more instructive is the poem's inclusion in Thesen's *New Long Poem Anthology*, for this already does the work of situating Carson's experimentation within an extant poetic genre. Despite some critics' confoundment over how to classify Carson's poetics, Thesen's decision to include the poem in its entirety is significant because it signals editorial approval and underscores Thesen's belief that the entirety of the poem is required reading for understanding the long poem as form.

In his work on Carson, Ian Rae asserts that her poetic trajectory can be situated within a Canadian tradition of poet-novelists as well as an American tradition of the lyric essay.[36] He posits that "The Glass Essay" employs the structuring logics of the lyric essay, the paratactic qualities of modernist lyric poetry, and the hypotactic logic of the essay, which develops an argument using classical techniques of rhetoric to persuade the reader. The structure of the poem depends on movement. The setting oscillates between a stark household managing the decline of the patriarch, the life and death of Emily Brönte, and the heartbroken reflection of the lyric speaker. Movement in the poem comes from the cognitive leaps required of the reader. Consider the following excerpt from the first half of this long poem:

> "All tight and right in which condition it is to be hoped we shall all be this
> day 4 years,"
> she wrote in her Diary Paper of 1837.
>
> Yet her poetry from beginning to end is concerned with prisons,
> vaults, cages, bars, curbs, bits, bolts, fetters,
> locked windows, narrow frames, aching walls.
>
> "Why all the fuss?" asks one critic.
> "She wanted liberty. Well didn't she have it?
> A reasonably satisfactory homelife,
>
> a most satisfactory dreamlife—why all this beating of wings?
> What was this cage, invisible to us,
> which she felt herself to be confined in?"
>
> Well there are many ways of being held prisoner,
> I am thinking as I stride over the moor.
> As a rule after lunch mother has a nap
>
> and I go out to walk.
>
> (34)

This selection opens with a citation from Emily Brontë's diary. Brontë was the second youngest sibling of the Brontë family. In her short life, she published both poetry and a novel, *Wuthering Heights*. An enigmatic and solitary figure, Brontë appears in Carson's poem as an interlocutor for the speaker's own condition. The speaker, figured in this section as the "I," has returned to her mother's home after the breakup of her marriage. Ostensibly there to help her mother keep watch over her father, who has dementia, the speaker is dislocated and further isolated. This excerpt offers a sense of Carson's facility with intertextuality and fabulation. The excerpts from Brontë's diary springboard her into considering Brontë's literary reception during her lifetime. Noting that critics fail to understand her sense of imprisonment, the speaker observes that there are "many ways of being held prisoner." The internal logic of the poem emerges in the movement from Brontë, to the present, to the speaker's broken marriage and back again. The movement is itself an emergent thesis, an attempt most properly aligned with the root definition of the essay, or *essai*, from the French "to try." The attempt made by "The Glass Essay" is to suture together three things, and in the suture, evoke the threads that tie loneliness, solitary women, and forced stasis together. Put another way, Carson's use of conceit draws lines between disparate issues, but resists clarifying the connection.[37] Her use of evocation, allusion, and structured repetition has led some critics to compare her poetic structure to that of A.M. Klein and Leonard Cohen.[38]

Anne Carson's poetic innovation and excellence is at this point undeniable. Her work is celebrated internationally, and she holds or has held numerous significant positions including both Guggenheim and MacArthur Fellowships, two Griffin Poetry Prizes, the T.S. Eliot Prize, the Governor General's Award for English-language poetry, the PEN/Nabokov Award, and has been appointed a Member of the Order of Canada for her contribution to Canadian letters. Her poetic innovations have altered both the lyric voice and the poetic essay and poet's novel. Yet her reception history has something to teach us about the internal logics of literary gatekeeping. If a poet of Carson's acclaim and stature can be lambasted for her experimentation using dismissive and misogynistic language, there can be no doubt that poets at different stages of their careers have experienced this kind of dismissal and worse.

From Reorientation to Rerooting

There are many ways to restrict belonging. Gender is one way. Citizenship is another. One of the tasks for careful readers is to discern the tools and how they are put to use. In her study of diasporic citizenship, Lily Cho observes, "citizenship does not come from nowhere, and yet its process of emergence remains strangely obscure. Diaspora makes this process visible. Specifically, it reminds us that there is a process of becoming attendant upon citizenship" (527). A citizen is someone who has been recognized by the state as having met the legal requirements to participate in the political community of that place. The citizen is expected to follow the laws of that place, and in turn the citizen is granted particular rights and privileges. As Cho explains, citizenship does not come from nowhere, and yet it is complicated and often difficult to ascertain. It is Cho's contention that diasporic subjectivity—that is, the experience and identity of being a member of a diaspora—*precedes* citizenship and as such has much to teach us. Cho cites Donna Pennee's essay "Literary Citizenship" as a useful tool for distilling the "pedagogical function of Canadian literature for citizenship" and points to this excerpt from Pennee as a place to begin. Pennee writes,

> National literary studies, understood as a process, provide for a kind of literary citizenship as a form of cultural and civic participation and cultural and civic legitimation in the social imaginary. Literary studies organized under the rubric of the national create a space to ask civic questions of state policies and inherited notions of nationalism.
>
> (75)

In other words, Cho explains, Pennee suggests that understanding what is qualified as "national literature" can offer a foundation from which to question the formation of the nation itself, especially with respect to the ongoing effects of colonialism on the founding of a country (527). Moreover, Cho highlights Pennee's emphasis on the nuance between citizenship and the ways in which national literature can be "critically acculturated" in a university classroom space. Far from suggesting that the study of national literature somehow acts as a tool for assimilation into the nation, Cho instead underscores Pennee's assertion that *critical* acculturation in a university classroom may in fact foster engaged citizens who have the tools to see and critique discourses that privilege the nation as organizing principle. Thus far, this is the fundamental undercurrent of this introduction to Canadian poetry: that context matters, and that we can develop tools for thinking critically and carefully about context. It is Cho's nuance overlayed on Pennee's argument that will take us to the final section of this text.

Cho hones in on Pennee's attention to *critical* citizenship, noting as she does so that Pennee is working with assertions made by Len Findlay and Smaro Kamboureli.[39] To suggest that citizenship can—and perhaps should—be made critical, Cho explains, is to acknowledge the question of "what comes first: citizenship or critical awareness of the nation?" For Cho, the tacit understanding that there is a *before* citizenship makes important space for modes of belonging and ways of knowing that underscore the useful tensions that arise when we critically engage with the nation. Pointing to critics such as Diana Brydon, Nancy van Styvendale and Aloys Fleischmann, and Lianne Moyes, Cho concludes that there is substantive discourse around "the formation of national subjects."[40]

Cho suggests that *diasporic* citizenship has something vital to add to the process of fostering critical citizenship. Diasporic citizenship puts assumptions—such as family, and nation—into productive question and in so doing foregrounds *that* the nation *as well as* subjects' relationships to belonging—to "Canadianness"—are always in process. While Cho's focus is exclusively on literary instances of diasporic citizenship in prose, her observations translate usefully to poetry as well. Exemplars of this productive tension in diasporic literatures can be found in the poetry of Souvankham Thammavongsa's *Found* (2007), Helen Hajnoczky's *Magyarazni* (2016), and Hoa Nguyen's *A Thousand Times You Lose Your Treasure* (2021). Each of these collections of poetry navigates the tensions between documentation, arrival, belonging, and longing that are central to many diasporic narratives. Collections such as Moez Surani's *عملية Operación Opération Operation 行动 Операция* (2016), Larissa Lai's *Iron Goddess of Mercy* (2021), Rachel Zolf's *No One's Witness* (2021), and Stephen Collis's *A History of the Theories of Rain* (2021) address diasporic citizenship in the tensions around wide historical scope, queer desire, and both global and local climate catastrophe. In work such as Vivek Shraya's *even this page is white* (2017), Mercedes Eng's *Mercenary English* (2018), Rebecca Salazar's *sulphertongue* (2021), and Isabella Wang's *Pebble Swing* (2021), the poets navigate the tensions between their own diasporic experiences and living on unceded Indigenous lands. In short, Cho's formulation offers a cogent way to encounter some of the key poetic innovations in the late-twentieth and early-twenty-first centuries in this part of Turtle Island currently called Canada.

Cho closes her explanation of diasporic citizenship by reminding readers that diasporic identity precedes citizenship. Her project is rooted in the argument that Canadian citizenship is an unfinished process. Understanding diaspora is vital to the project of critical relationships with assertions of a national imaginary. With diaspora at the forefront of our minds, it is useful to root that diasporic thinking in a long history:

> Be loyal, be strong, be free.
> The Loyalists, the Maroons, and the Refugees
> You come from all three teaching you lessons
> About how to get where you need to be.
> Stick together like glue,
> Take care of your crew,
> Stand your ground and don't get pushed down
> And when it's time to get free
> By any means necessary!
>
> (20)

These are the opening lines of El Jones's spoken word poem "Be Loyal, Be Strong, Be Free." Jones, a professor, poet, two-time Slam champion, and former Poet Laureate of Halifax, prefaces the poem by making the connection among "the freedom struggles of African Nova Scotians," "the Motherland," and "the Diaspora." The poem, which was written in collaboration with Rocky Jones for the youth of Mulgrave Park, braids the histories of Black Loyalists who arrived in Nova Scotia between 1783 and 1785 after the American Revolutionary War, the Jamaican Maroons who were deported to Nova Scotia in 1796, and the Black Refugees who escaped enslavement in costal Virginia and Maryland and sailed to Nova Scotia between 1813 and 1816.[41] These intersecting histories of movement have been misrepresented by racist narratives. Jones reminds her audience:

> The way they got their names listed
> Makes it sound like you come from
> Loyalists who served
> Maroons who got lost
> And Refugees who were running.
> They make them sound boring like you came from nothing
> The true story is they were fighters with courage and cunning
> (9)

By reframing the tension of diasporic history, Jones underscores the ancestral vitality and brilliance of Black Nova Scotians. She reminds her listeners that these ancestors "fooled two superpowers through stealth and quick wits" who were "playing master against master" "power against power" (9). Moving between three histories and the present moment of performance, Jones activates some of the unfinished aspects of relation to the nation that Cho identifies. Jones draws the connections among past, present, and future together in the final lines of the poem. "Your ancestry is the root and you are the leaf," she explains. "This is not street knowledge it's revolutionary./ So let me repeat: / Be loyal. Be strong. Get free" (10). In activating tripartite diaspora in the present, Jones points her listeners to the future they carry in their bodies.

In this last paragraph, I have slipped between terms such as "listener" and "audience" as well as deliberately identified myself as outside the intended audience of Jones's poem. In her introduction to *Live From the Afrikan Resistance!*, Jones outlines the roots of her poetics. For, while the collection is printed, the poems that make up the book all have their origins and intent in spoken word. Here is how Jones delineates spoken word:

> Spoken word is an essentially Afrikan art form. Our oral heritage goes back to the griots, preserved through 400 years of capture and enslavement and hybridized, remixed, and revisioned ever since. ... Spoken word does not stand apart from all the other ways we have created orally, from speeches and sermons and spirituals and slang: they are all forerunners of the art of spoken word.
> (ii)

In tracing a lineage of spoken word, Jones acknowledges the long and complex histories of Black Canadian poetry.[42] Liveness, performance, and orality are vital components of what George Elliott Clarke refers to as the exceptional poetics of African-Canadian poetry.[43] And, in their introductory notes to each section of *The Great Black North: Contemporary African Canadian Poetry*, Valerie Mason-John and Kevan Anthony Cameron further detail the nuances among print poetry, dub, spoken word, and slam. In each case, voice and presence are vital components of a poet's craft. They note, for example, that the category of print poetry is troublesome insofar as it is the dominant mode of commercial poetic circulation. And yet, "few poets are commercially published and even fewer Black poets." And while there is a significant catalogue of poets who are primarily print poets—including Olive Senior, Clair Harris, Dionne Brand, George Elliott Clarke, Wayde Compton, Afua Cooper, M. NourbeSe Philip, and Maxine Tynes—print poetry is "in fact an extension of the oral tradition."[44] Dub they describe as "one word said in one breath. There is no gap between dub and the poetry or between the words and the poet" (105). Lillian Allen, one of the key members of Dub poetry in Canada, describes it this way:

> originally based in our political activism. It was an artform meant to do political work. Dub took its cues from Reggae and Reggae took its cues from Louise Bennett who took her cues from the way Jamaican people expressed themselves.
>
> (Mason-John and Anthony, 105)

Anchored in everyday speech, culture, and life, dub was given its name in the 1970s by Linton Kwesi Johnson and Oku Onoru and in Canada dub's foundations are decidedly and revolutionarily matrilineal: Lillian Allen, Afua Cooper, and Ahdri Zhina Mandiela rooted dub in the Canadian context in the 1980s. A new generation of dub poets such as d'bi.young anitafrika continue the work.[45] Spoken word further broadens intersections and influences. In conversation with Mason-John, Tanya Evanson and John Akpata describe it as "the continuation of the African griot tradition," and "the art of speaking, using your voice to educate, entertain, and speak to the public," respectively.[46] Slam is similarly defined by Oni the Haitian Sensation, Ian Keteku, and Dwayne Morgan as "an event with a form of poetry in it," which still depend on "cadence, rhythm and personality."[47]

Edited by Harold Head, *Canada in Us Now: The First Anthology of Black Poetry and Prose in Canada* was published in 1979 and included poetry by Dionne Brand, Harold Sonny Ladoo, Ann Wallace, Austin Clarke, and others. In his introduction, Head states, "the writers in this anthology were schooled in Shakespeare, Wordsworth, Black, Byron, Shelley, Keats, and Byron" (ii). Focused predominantly on writers with connections to Toronto, Head's anthology was an important literary event. It marks a moment in which the multiple routes of arrival to Canada were anthologized together. It also marks a moment of deliberate political presencing of Black writing in Canada. It is noteworthy that while individual books by Black poets were published in the same year as Confederation, Head's anthology was published eight years after Multiculturalism was adopted as the official policy of the Canadian government.[48] While there have been many anthologies focused on Black literature in Canada in the intervening years, as Karina Vernon points out, the publication of Mason-John and Cameron's *The Great Black North: Contemporary African Canadian Poetry* was the first anthology of Black Canadian poetry since Head's.[49] Given the wealth of Black cultural production in Canada, Vernon observes, it is crucial that we ask: why did it take three decades for an anthology of Black Canadian poetry to be published? And what does this teach us about the contexts of Canada for Black poets and other Black cultural producers?

David Chariandy notes that while Black Canadian literature and African Canadian literature are now established terms in academic and public discourses, like other fields such as "Asian Canadian literature and First Nations literature," the arrival of these terms have been both "protracted and complex" (539). He explains that the systemic racism of the nation included but is not limited to "historic reluctance of Canada to officially recognize Blacks, among other racial minorities, as both unique and essential agents within the national cultural landscape" (539). Additionally, states Chariandy, whereas in the United States people of African descent are "powerful focalizers of nationwide laws and debates on 'race'," the same has not been true in Canada. This is, in part, due to the smaller population, as well as to "cultural fracturing" (539). Chariandy underscores that in the specific context of literary studies, critics such as Rinaldo Walcott and George Elliott Clarke began public discourses around Black Canadian literature and culture in the 1990s. Nonetheless, the path to recognition was again complicated. Noting that there were decades of debates about and on Black culture in global contexts, Chariandy explains that the reception of such debates and discourses in the Canadian context was complicated by siloed arguments about multicultural diversity and that there was distinct resistance to discourses that focused specifically on experiences and cultures of racial minorities (540). Critics such as Walcott and Clarke individually navigated scholarly frameworks of both postmodernity and post-colonialism, which offered "new theoretical frameworks for emergent literatures broadly speaking" but there were fewer models for focusing on histories of local cultural politics and contexts for Black Canadian literatures (540). Chariandy suggests that a tension between local and global representation of the cultural and political experience of Black Canadians is ever-more complex. Highlighting two broad methodologies—roots and routes—Chariandy demonstrates the ways in which scholars of Black literature, politics, and culture in Canada are addressing the extraordinary complexities of the field.[50]

Case Study: Canisia Lubrin

This chapter has thus far used case studies to navigate some of the central issues of the last two decades: planetary witnessing, misogyny, grappling for power, systemic racism, and big questions about belonging in another age of diasporic movement. Beginning with poetry that navigates the past from the present, the chapter has considered planetary poetics of witness as a means to address global atrocity, joyful feminist genre-trespassing as an antidote to binary divisions between lyric and conceptual poetries and literary gatekeeping, and poetries that attend to precipitous histories of transit through an attention to orality, history, embodiment, and voice. In this final case study, I turn to the work of Canisia Lubrin, whose lyric innovation draws together these poetic lines. Lubrin's lyric innovation keeps company with poets such as Aisha Sasha John, Sonnet L'Abbé, Ian Williams, Kaie Kellough, and Chantal Gibson. Each of these poets navigate the "lyric I" from sites of embodiment (John), agricultural inhabitation (L'Abbé), mathematical word problems (Williams), hemispheric migration (Kellough), and elementary reading primers (Gibson) to probe complex histories and futures for members of the Black diaspora.

Born and raised on the Island of St. Lucia, Canisia Lubrin emigrated to Canada where she completed undergraduate and graduate studies. At the time of this writing, Lubrin is the author of two critically acclaimed collections of poetry. *Voodoo Hypothesis* (2017) was a finalist for the Raymond Souster Award, and *The Dyzgraph^{x}st* (2020) won the OCM Bocas Prize for Caribbean Literature, the Griffin Poetry Prize, and the Derek Walcott Prize for Poetry. Lubrin was the winner of Yale University's Windham-Campbell Prize for Poetry in 2021. In their citation, the Windham-Campbell jury writes of *The Dyzgraph^{x}st* that it bursts "beyond the confines of legibility and the individual," and "summons up oceans, languages, and the self, the other, and the first-person plural, into a generous baroque project of anti-colonial plenitude" (Windham-Campbell, npag). Lubrin's work with collective and singular pronouns harnesses the power of collectivity within the architecture of poetic engagement.

In each of her collections thus far, Lubrin's work is dense. It is referentially dense, conceptually dense, and aesthetically dense. Bearing some similarities to the documentary mode advocated by Dorothy Livesay, Lubrin's poetry is future-oriented without losing sight of the intersecting histories that inform its lyric speaker. *Voodoo Hypothesis*, for example, opens with a missive from Mars, where a lyric speaker reflects on the centuries of anti-Black racism as well as on physics. Here are the first lines:

> Before sight, we imagine
> that while they go out in search
> of God
> we stay in and become god,
> become: Curiosity,
> whose soul is a nuclear battery
> because she'll pulverize Martian rock
> and test for organize molecules
> in her lab within a lab within
> a lab. She doesn't need to know our fears
> so far too grand for ontology, reckoning.
> (4)

Lubrin frames space travel as a deeply colonial act. Here, Curiosity's "soul is a nuclear battery" and she "pulverizes" in order to explore and test. In this introductory poem, a dichotomy is established between "They" and "we." While "They" go in search of God, "we" become immanent. The poem, which shares its title with the book, ends with an intimate and haunting statement: "I safe," the female explorer consoles. Safe where, and how, and with what certainty? In a world where Black women can be shot by police for sleeping at home in their own beds, Lubrin forges certainty and science with a refusal to explain away anti-Black racism.[51] *Voodoo Hypothesis* subverts "blackness" and refuses the systems that created and sustain racial injustice and inequity. "*Voodoo Hypothesis* is an imperative invocation of black dreams," writes Vivek Shraya in an endorsement on the cover of Lubrin's collection. Sonnet L'Abbé's cover endorsement writes "in the lyric lineage of Dionne Brand and M. NourbeSe Philip, Lubrin raises up language like a shield against European histories and sciences," and raises up "poetry like a sacrifice of sweat and blood." There is an evolution in Lubrin's poetics that is evident. In *Voodoo Hypothesis*, the proliferation of state-sanctioned violence against Black people is documented in relentless detail that elevates the possibilities of the "lyric I" to a place of protector and witness.

In a conversation with poet, publisher, and scholar Dani Spinosa, Lubrin addresses the function of "voodoo" in the collection: voodoo functions "etymologically to understand the relationship between humanity and the earth," writes Spinosa (npag). Whereas other modes of religious practice require intermediaries, voodoo, Lubrin explains, does not. Instead, "voodoo understands that god (read: immanence) is within the practitioner" (ibid.). As such, voodoo operates within rather than outside of humanity.[52] The collection, which is full of poems dedicated to Black writers, poets, and thinkers, situates Black lyric subjectivity in conversation with history, futurity, and modes of collectivity.

In *The Dyzgraph*^{x}*st*, Lubrin pushes this interrogation of the possibilities of the "lyric I" further. The title is a deliberate intervention in the term "dysgraphia," where "x" becomes both an unknowable variable and a reference to its uses and abuses in Black history—from the x that stands in lieu of the signature of someone who has been granted the right to be literate to Malcolm X's choice to incorporate it into his name—x does self-reflexive and referential work. In an interview with the CBC, Lubrin explains "the market asks for narratives of trauma, of oppression. It's constantly flattening—it's that same dysgraphia Christina Sharpe theorizes [in her book *In the Wake: On Blackness and Being*]" (Patrick, npag). Whereas dysgraphia—with an "i"—references a condition in which writing is rendered difficult, in Lubrin's poetry the condition is extended out from individual to world. *The Dyzgraph*^{x}*st*, which is a long poem organized into seven movements or acts, refuses the erasure tactics of white supremacy and colonial legacies. Moving from a regularized form of tercets in the first two acts, the poem then unfurls and becomes tidal in its form. Creole, "an exhumed patios," is woven into languages of capital, of climate catastrophe, and of mass migration, as well as the Englishes of colonialism.

This collection breaks the:

> "I" into three parts, and in each act, the "I" is made multiple even as it is faced with violence and erasure. In the lower-case, "i" represents the first person singular, while in upper-case "I" represents second-person singular as well as Third person plural. A fourth figure, Jejeune. Roughly translated to both "I" and "young" as well as indicating a naiveta, Jejune is the voice addressed, every page. The chorus, the you, the we/unnavigable self.
>
> (1)

Always-already on the page, Jejune is a constant presence who complicates and reinforces the other modes of individuation. Lubrin's response is to bring the mode of lyric address from one person into conversation with another, and then with community. The result is a rupture and reorganization of the lyric voice from and for Black peoples. Consider, for example, this excerpt in which the "I" is stretched to contain one and many at once:

> Here—beginning the unbeginning
> owning nothing but that wounding
> sense of waking to speak as I would
>
> after the floods, then, after women unlike
> Eve giving kind to the so-and-so, trying
> to tell them it is time to be unnavigable,
>
> after calling them back to what
> the tongue cuts speaking the thing of
> them rolled into stone
>
> speaking I after all, after all theories
> of abandonment priced and displayed,
> the word was a moonlit knife
>
> with those arrivants
> lifting their hems to dance, toeless
> with the footless child they invent
>
> (17)

The excerpt opens by locating the reader: here. But where is here, and where is here in the context of colonial Canada? There is resonance both with Dionne Brand's *In Another Place Not Here* as well as with Northrop Frye's complicated query.[53] And yet the poet pushes the reader further back in time and space. Here is specific, and it is also the "unbeginning." Here, the I moves from singular speaker, to the possibility of being spoken by women "unlike Eve" busy with the work of "giving kind." Present participles pile up, moving the speaker further and further from being a singular actant. Time, too, is stretched. Beginning moves to unbeginning. The present tense of here gets relocated to time "after the floods" and again to the "time to be unnavigable." "Speaking I" is rendered a singular and collective act, one that happens here, and there. Before and after flood. Before and after theories. "I" is sharpened into "a moonlit knife" that lands with the "arrivants" who dance. In *The Dyzgraphˣst*, Lubrin routes past, present, and future through the grammatical architecture of the I.

By the final Act, "Ain't I Again?" the lyric voice reorients once more. This time, having pulled the multiplicities of being in its wake, the I coheres around community, connection, and a new place to land:

> on the lawn of a sea-spanning country, a sung-of
> citizen, flung out to freeze, from what formlessness
>
> I was that speck in the halogen confusion of myself
> [...]
> I was that speck in the multiplier of myself
> déjà vu, an early stage, what I have learned, new langu-
> age held in the nowhere of my blood up against the page
>
> and the dread thing is that I forget and must do it
> all again, a dyzgraphˣst, je connais, justement—
> I, (re)done when the world itself awakes again
> (160, 161–2)

Here is reworked through the oceanic movement of the lyric I. The stanzas in the final act return to tercets, but loosen their grip on the left-alignment. The reorientation into self and world must be an ongoing project, done and redone, and in so doing futurity is also written into being. The long poem ends with a centred tercet:

> it is better this way, or I would have no reason at all to write you
> *what folds your ear sideways to my mouth, I slip into,*
> wondering what we might have become were we not so alive
> (164)

Echoing the closing lines of the poem "Voodoo Hypothesis" in which the speaker who has landed on Mars writes to say "*hey, / I'm here. I safe. Wish you were here,*" the speaker of *The Dyzgraphˣst* looks both backward and into the future. Connection is achieved through relationality—writing, folding, slipping into the ear of the other. Histories hover in what "we might have become" but futurity unfurls in the liveness animating "I" and "you" into "we." In Lubrin's long poem, the reader keeps company with the multitudinous and refracting "I" until, by the poem's end, "we" are left together to wonder and in wonder.

Conclusion

Two decades into the twenty-first century, poetry is alive and well in what is currently called Canada. If the mid-point of the twentieth century was marked by the development of infrastructure and, following that, the creation of many small presses, the twenty-first century shows signs of yet another shift. In 2012, Random House of Canada, a multinational publisher, took over sole ownership of McClelland & Stewart. McClelland & Stewart, known colloquially as M&S, was founded in 1906 and while it started out as a library supply house, it soon published literature by Canadian writers including work by Bliss Carman and Duncan Campbell Scott. Jack McClelland became president in 1961 and the press developed a vital and ambitious Canadian book publishing programme that included publishing work by leading writers of the day including Atwood, Earle Birney, Al Purdy, Leonard Cohen, and Irving Layton, as well as establishing the New Canadian Library, a series initially edited by Malcolm Ross, in 1958. M&S went up for sale in 1971 and the government of Ontario loaned the press one million dollars to prevent its sale to American publishers. In 1984, the government again intervened and alleviated the press's debt. The press was then donated to the University of Toronto in 2000. Two years later, the University of Toronto sold the majority ownership to Random House. News of the sale was met with dismay from the Association of Canadian Publishers who issued the following statement: "that Canada's most storied book publisher … will be downgraded to an imprint of a foreign-owned multinational corporation … marks an end of a long and illustrious history of a Canadian cultural institution" (Williams, npag). President of the Association Margie Wolfe added "today we have lost one of our greatest homes for Canadian stories. It's a sad and scary day" (ibid.). And while the sale of M&S to a multinational publishing conglomerate certainly marks a consolidation of publishing power on the one hand, it is not the only shift to occur in publishing.

There is also a redistribution of power that is afoot in publishing. In addition to the small presses that were founded in the era directly following the Massey Report—Coach House Press, Brick Books, Anansi, to name a few—there is a significant group of smaller and micro-presses that are revolutionizing how poetry gets published and circulated. In her Introduction to the *Small Press Interactive Map*, curator Kate Siklosi writes that:

> at its heart, small press is about experimentation and community-building. It began as a cost-effective means of circulating innovative, fringe literatures, and in many ways, this scrappy, humble tradition has been preserved while also inviting new approaches to the craft.

> From basement-produced zine to the carefully handcrafted, formally-interested object.
>
> ("Small Press Interactive Maps," npag)

The small press is not new to poetry publishing in Canada. As explored in earlier chapters of this book, the rise of small periodical presses was integral to a surge of literary and especially poetic publication and circulation starting in at least the 1930s. And now, in addition to organizations such as the Meet the Presses Collective, which administers the bpNichol Chapbook Award, there is a growing list of small and micro-presses whose poetic publications are broadening horizons for poets in this country. In an essay published in *periodicities: a journal of poetry and poetics* edited by poet and small-press publisher rob mclennan, Siklosi and Dani Spinosa reflect on their fidelity to micro-publishing. Siklosi and Spinosa are the founders and publishers of Gap Riot Press, which focuses on small-runs, inexpensive chapbooks with hand-made touches, and publishing experimental, visual, innovative, and genre-blurring work by primarily Canadian poets. In their view, the limited run allows them as publishers to make "more books for more people." Siklosi and Spinosa write,

> while some might claim that limited runs are ungenerous and elitist in their limitation, for us it allows the opposite: it lets us open more spaces for folks to get published, more conversations between our works, and more use of our limited resources. It's also a way of making things freakin' special, of preserving the wonder of works, which is a big part of what we love about small press production.
>
> ("Some Rough Notes in Defense of the Limited Run," npag)

Small presses and even smaller micro-presses have the capacity to decentralize power and produce radically diverse material in a short period of time. And, as the small press map Siklosi initiated demonstrates, there are nearly one hundred operational small and micro-presses in Canada. Some, like knife | fork | book, The Blasted Tree Publishing Co., and Rahila's Ghost Press are extremely small and issue limited runs and chapbooks. Others, like Coach House and Brick Books, have been operational for over three decades. The existence of these small and micro-presses cannot be understated. In addition to broadening the field of poetic publication, small and micro-presses have the capacity to foster discursive communities in real time. Accessibility, craft, and reading communities are vital to the circulation of poetry, and small and micro-presses in Canada are a key part of the ongoing work of literary culture.

Key Terms

Africadia: Coined by George Elliott Clarke, Africadia is a cultural geography that encompasses Black Canadian community, culture, history, and life in Nova Scotia and New Brunswick.

Conceptual poetry: A portmanteau that encompasses visual poetics, sound poetry, and constraint-based poetic practices. Conceptual poetry tends to be non-referential and works with the materiality of language.

Lyric conceptualism: Coined by Sina Queyras, the term refers to poetry that employs tactics of conceptual poetics without eschewing tenets of lyric poetry as well.

Notes

1 See Milne, ibid. Spahr's collection addresses the Occupy Movement, King's addresses the BP oil spill of 2010, the Enpipe Collective is responding to both the Enbridge and Gateway Pipeline proposals (2012), while Wong's poem addressing the collective work of Idle No More was published initially on Occupy Love's Facebook page.

2 Janey Canuck is a fictional "everywoman" created by Emily Murphy. Murphy is known most readily for her membership of the Famous Five—a group of five women who lobbied for and won the Persons Case in Canada. This case guaranteed personhood in the eyes of the law, but only for some women. As discussed in early chapters of this book, white feminists in Canada have routinely built their cases on the exclusion and, in the case of Murphy and her peers, oppression of Indigenous women, and women of colour. Janey Smith is the potty-mouthed radical narrator of American writer Kathy Acker's *Blood and Guts in High School*. Together they form Zolf's Janey who is a "cyborg mash-up" bent on "fracking up history."

3 See Bentley, "Colonial Colonizing: The Long Poem on Canada," and Kamboureli, *On the Edge of Genre: The Contemporary Canadian Long Poem*.

4 I am drawing the term "retooling" from Kamboureli and Daniel Coleman's edited collection *Retooling the Humanities: The Culture of Research in Canadian Universities*. In this collection, the editors as well as contributors consider the shift to market driven research and "knowledge mobilization" demanded by national funding organizations such as the Social Science and Humanities Research Council of Canada.

5 They write, "the bourgeoisie has through its exploitation of the world market given a cosmopolitan character to production and consumption of all countries" (65).

6 See for example Kit Dobson's *Transnational Canadas: Anglo-Canadian Literature and Globalization*, Herb Wylie's *Anne of Tim Hortons: Globalization and the Reshaping of Atlantic-Canadian Literature*, Smaro Kamboureli and Roy Miki's *Trans.Can.Lit: Resituating the Study of Canadian Literature*, Kamboureli and Robert Zacharias's *Shifting the Ground of Canadian Literary Studies*, and Jeff Derksen's *Annihilated Time: Poetry and Other Politics* to name a few. Nick Mount's book *When Canadian Literature Moved to New York* also fits in a longer view of the transnational effects of globalization on the material conditions of literary culture.

7 I have written elsewhere about some examples of poets who centre a planetary poetics in site-specific places. Sachiko Murakami's *Rebuild* (2011), Robert Kroetsch's *The Hornbooks of Rita K* (2001), and Meredith Quartermain's *Vancouver Walking* (2005) can take up this notion of planetarity just as thoroughly as works that aim to directly address globalizations, such as Jeff Derksen's *Transnational*

Muscle Cars (2003), Rita Wong's *forage* (2007), or even Adam Dickinson's *The Polymers* (2013). See Erin Wunker, "Towards a Planetary Poetics."

8 Atwood writes of ghosts in several non-fiction texts including *Survival* (1972) and *Strange Things: The Malevolent North in Canadian Literature* (1995).

9 For an introduction to considering settler status and people of colour see Malissa Phung.

10 M. NourbeSe Philip's *Zong!* (2008) is a book-length collection that addresses and attends to the massacre of enslaved Africans on the slave ship *Zong* when the ship's captain ordered that 150 people be murdered so that the ship's owner could collect insurance on "lost cargo." Zolf's *Janey's Arcadia* (2014) and *No One's Witness* (2021) address settler expansion in the Canadian west and globally with attention hinging on the failures in witnessing, reciprocity, and empathy.

11 See for example Stephen Henighan's *When Words Deny the World*. It is notable here, too, that in the same collection Henighan dedicates a significant amount of energy to documenting his scepticism about the reality of appropriation as well as systemic barriers to funding and publication such as gender and race.

12 I'm thinking here of poets such as those George Woodcock names in his survey of "people's poetry," as well as Milton Acorn for whom the "People's Poetry Award" was created in memoriam (1987), and of Al Purdy. Tanis MacDonald makes a useful amendment to this frame of the "people's poet" when she considers the work of Wayde Compton and Stuart Ross as "experimental poets using urban vernaculars." See MacDonald, 481.

13 See MacDonald, 481–2.

14 Like MacDonald, I would differentiate between anthologies that are working to develop trends and trajectories and those that are engaged in the work of recovery and representation. Examples of the latter would include Armstrong and Grauer, Ruffo and Vermette, and Mason-John and Cameron.

15 See a press release about the event entitled "Two of the best to duke it out behind the podium." *Mount Royal University*. www.mtroyal.ca/AboutMountRoyal/MediaRoom/Newsroom/FTDATA_Cagematch_111909.htm Interestingly, the transcript and video of the event has been effectively scrubbed from the Internet. All that remains of the debate to decide the "future of Canadian poetry" is trace material: 404 dead links to video, a few press releases in the lead up to the event, and some blog posts by people who attended, viewed, or heard about the event. My thanks is due to the colleague who shared their CD ROM of the event so that I could consult it.

16 See Eichhorn and Milne (iv). The editors are drawing on the work of American writer Lyn Hejinian who has written at length about poetry as a "language of inquiry."

17 Indeed, Betts begins his study with a date and then works backwards to consider the origins of the term avant-garde in the context of settler-colonial history in Canada. Starting with the International Exhibition of Modern Art in Toronto, which brought together over one hundred active contemporary artists, Betts then considers the origins of the term "avant-garde" in the Canadian context. He notes that the earliest example he has located is from 1704 when "Louis Lahontan describes the coureurs de bois … forming an 'avant-garde' with a band of natives" while French troops lingered behind (49). The relevance, for Betts, lies in the avant-garde's "affordability of their sacrifice and loss to the nation state" (ibid.). For a thorough account of the Canadian avant-garde see Gregory Betts, *Avant-Garde Canadian Literature: The Early Manifestations*.

18 It is impossible to name the full scope of writers, critics, and literary and cultural historians who make this point. Readers would do well to look to BIPOC and queer writers, writers of the diaspora, disabled writers, and women writers who are engaged in intersectional modes of analysis for a fulsome discussion.

19 Examples from the twenty-first century include American poet Kenneth Goldsmith's "performance reading" of the autopsy of Michael Brown at a graduate conference in 2015, as well as American poet Vanessa Place's tweeting of *Gone With the Wind* to name but two. Intervention to these and other enactments of "conceptual poetics" can be found in the archives of the Mongrel Coalition Against Gringpo. The Coalition called out both Place and Goldsmith with a significant degree of media attention. See Michael Leung who closely reads Place and Goldsmith's racist conceptualisms alongside the effective use of conceptual tactics by writers including Claudia Rankine and M. NourbeSe Philip to address racial violence and inequity.

20 See MacDonald. See also Eichhorn, and Shearer and Schagerl.

21 Far from being a utopia, many researchers have demonstrated the disproportionate degree of abuse and aggression that women, BIPOC people, queer people, and other minoritized groups experience on the Internet.

22 See Bennett. The conversation between Spenst and Bennett periodically traffics in descriptions that bear similarities to the discourse around the "Cage Match of Canadian Poetry."

23 *MxT* (2014, Winner of the 2015 ReLit Award for Poetry) is a collection that figures memory and time as a mathematical equation for calculating the space-time of grief. *My Ariel* (2017, Winner of the Quebec Writer's Foundation A.M. Klein Prize for Poetry) addresses Sylvia Plath's *Ariel* and navigates issues of gender and poetics. Both have won significant prizes.

24 *Expressway* engages the journals of Dorothy Wordsworth. *MxT* works with the aesthetics of multiple artists and writers, *My Ariel* is a sustained conversation with Sylvia Plath, and in the forthcoming *Rooms* Queyras meditated on the work of Virginia Woolf.

25 This question comes from one of Queyras's earliest blog posts on *Lemon Hound* and is archived in the print edition *Unleashed* (2009). Queyras circles around and reiterates this query across their poetic oeuvre.

26 The public debate took place on the pages of *The National Post, The Malahat Review*, and CWILA with responses happening on social media and in *The Globe & Mail*.

27 See Laird. The full quotation Mancini refers to is as follows:

> The books that made the short list for the Governor General's Award for poetry indicate that Canadian poetry is in the same place. Let's call the prize a litmus test of what our writers have perfected: if so, then these books demonstrate that the lyric is king, all the difficult knots have been mastered, and the "*I*" that loves to speak the poems is alive, alert, and secure in its place. I've read each of these books with varying degrees of pleasure. Yet, in the end, there's something either missing or very tired in the ideas—not the skill—that drives them.
>
> (21)

28 The term "MeToo" was coined by Tarana Burke in 2006. The term was popularized by the American actor Alyssa Milano who posted on Twitter in 2016 "If all the women who have been sexually harassed or assaulted wrote 'Me

too' as a status, we might give people a sense of the magnitude of the problem." See Milano.

29 At the writing of this manuscript, many of the cases including most prominently that of Galloway are at various stages of legal processes. For a thorough assessment of the Canadian legal system's capacity to manage cases regarding allegations of sexual assault and violence see Craig. See also McKeon.

30 To date Carson's most recent publication is *H of H Playbook* (2021).

31 See for example David Solway's "The Trouble with Annie." See also Carmine Starnino who has referred to Carson as well as her work as "primitive" and "unaccomplished" and does not deserve to have her writing considered poetry (see Martin).

32 The choice of terminology—a "phony"—is curious given that Solway later undertakes a series of hoaxes in which he creates a heteronym and passes that poet's work off as his own. See Rae, "Anne Carson and the Solway Hoaxes."

33 See Jeff Derksen. "Canadian Literature and the Dying Temporality of Colonialism."

34 In a *Globe and Mail* interview with Sandra Martin, poet Dennis Lee not only called her work "electrifying" but also cautioned that she should "slow down and let the well fill up." In the same interview, P.K. Page posited that Carson's work is exciting because she is able to work with both sides of her brain. In one of the earliest pieces of scholarly writing on Carson, Ian Rae characterized her particular poetics as a series of dazzling hybrids, but he notes that he is quoting Melanie Rehak's phrase from a *New York Times* piece on Carson. See Martin. See also Rae.

35 See Lecker, "The Canonization of Canadian Literature: An Inquiry into Value."

36 John D'Agata defines the lyric essay as a recombinative genre:

> The lyric essay partakes of the poem in its density and shapeliness, its distillation of ideas and musicality or language. It partakes of the essay in its weight, in its overt desire to engage with facts, melding its allegiance to the actual with its passion for imaginative form.
>
> (iv)

37 See Ian Rae, "Verglas: Narrative Technique in Anne Carson's 'The Glass Essay'."

38 See Rae, see also Simon.

39 See Findlay, "Always Indigenize!: The Radical Humanities in the Postcolonial Canadian University." See also Kamboureli, *Scandalous Bodies: Diasporic Literature in English Canada.*

40 Brydon addresses Dionne Brand. See also Fleishmann and van Styvendale, and Moyes's "Acts of Citizenship" in which she considers the work of Moure.

41 See Dr. Afua Cooper et al., *Report on Lord Dalhousie's History on Slavery and Race.*

42 David Chariandy observes that while there is oscillation between the signifiers of "Black Canadian literatures" and "African Canadian literatures" neither has ossified as the official term. He reminds readers that certain critics have preferences for one or the other, however (539). I will oscillate between the two terms and, when referring to critics who have clear and demonstrable preferences, will follow their preference.

43 See George Elliott Clarke, "Exceptional Poetics."

44 See Mason-John, Afua Cooper, and Wayde Compton. "Print Poetry."

45 See Mason-John, Klyde Broox, and Lillian Allen's "Dub." For discussions of the intersections of Indigenous and Black oral poetics see previous chapter on Kateri Akiwenzie-Damm. See also Lillian Allen and Susan Gingell.

46 See Mason-John, Tanya Evanson, and John Akpata, "Spoken Word."

47 See Mason-John, "Oni the Haitian Sensation, Dwayne Morgan, and Ian Keteku, 'Slam'."

48 George Elliott Clarke cites the publication of Anna Minerva Henderson's chapbook *Citadel* in 1867 as the first collection of poetry to be published by an African-Canadian woman. See Clarke, "Exceptional Poetics."

49 Anthologies include work such as Lorris Elliott's *Other Voices: Writings by Blacks in Canada* (1985), George Elliott Clarke's *Fire on the Water* (1991–1992), Ayanna Black's *Fiery Spirits: Canadian Writers of African Descent* (1994), Wayde Compton's *Bluesprint: Black British Columbian Literature and Orature* (2001), Donna Bailey Nurse's *Revival: An Anthology of Black Canadian writing* (2006), Whitney French's *Black Writers Matter* (2019), and Afua Cooper and Wilfried Raussert's *Black Matters* (2020).

50 Chariandy's study is vital and impossible to adequately reproduce here, hence I suggest reading it in full. A partial list of scholars who Chariandy flags as central to the vital project of Black Canadian literature in addition to those already mentioned include Wayde Compton, Karina Vernon, Winfried Siemerling, Daniel Coleman, Michael Bucknor, Andrea Davis, Leslie Saunders, Cecil Foster, Katherine McKittrick, Jade Ferguson, Phanuel Antwi, and M. NourbeSe Philip. Though outside of the scope of literature specifically, Robyn Maynard's *Policing Black Lives: State Violence from Slavery to the Present* provides indispensable context.

51 This is a reference to Breonna Taylor's death in her own home at the hands of police in Louisville, Kentucky in 2020.

52 Spinosa writes

> voodoo's etymology is hard to trace because its roots in the Niger-Congo family of languages have few early written records; it is linked to early Niger words meaning spirit or possession, distinctly implying an immanent spirit within the practitioner rather than outside of but accessed by the practitioner.
>
> (npag)

53 Brand's 1997 novel is set between Toronto and the Caribbean and considers belonging and exile. Frye's 1965 question closes his conclusion to the first *Literary History of Canada*. The question, Frye proposes, is the central fixation of Canadian culture.

For Further Reading

Eichhorn, Kate, and Heather Milne, Eds. *Prismatic Publics: Innovative Canadian Women's Poetry and Poetics*. Toronto: Coach House, 2009.

Mason-John, Valerie, and Kevan Cameron. *The Great Black North: Contemporary African Canadian Poetry*. Calgary: Frontenac House, 2013.

Morra, Linda, and Sarah Henzi, Eds. *On the Other Side(s) of 150: Untold Stories and Critical Approaches to History, Literatures, and Identity in Canada*. Waterloo: WLUP, 2021.

Weingarten, J.A. *Sharing the Past: The Reinvention of History in Canadian Poetry Since 1960*. Kingston: McGill-Queen's UP, 2019.

Works Cited

Allen, Lillian. "Poetics of Renewal: Indigenous Poetics—Message or Medium?" *Indigenous Poetics in Canada*. Ed. Neal McLeod. Waterloo: WLUP, 2014. 293–304.

Anand, Madhur, and Adam Dickinson. *Regreen: New Canadian Ecological Poetry*. Sudbury: Your Scrivener, 2009.

Armstrong, Jeanette, and Lally Grauer, Eds. *Native Poetry in Canada: A Contemporary Anthology*. Peterborough: Broadview, 2001.

Ashton, Jennifer. "Our Bodies, Our Poems." *Modern Philology* 105.1 (2007): 160–77.

Atwood, Margaret. *Strange Things: The Malevolent North in Canadian Literature*. Toronto: OUP, 1995.

———. *Survival: A Thematic Guide to Canadian Literature*. 1972. Toronto: Anansi, 2012.

Barwin, Gary. "Cage Match of Canadian Poetry: Microwaveable Elizabethans and the Sonnets for Future Memories." *Serif of Nottingblog* (December 23, 2009). http://serifofnottingham.blogspot.com/2009/12/cage-match-of-canadian-poetry.html

Beaulieu, Derek, Jason Christie and Angela Rawlings. *Shift & Switch*. Toronto: The Mercury Press, 2005

Bennett, Andrea. "Looking Back on Lemon Hound." *Maisonneuve* (May 18, 2015). https://maisonneuve.org/post/2015/05/18/looking-back-lemon-hound/

Bennett, Donna, and Russell Brown, Eds. *An Anthology of Canadian Literature in English*. 4th ed. Toronto: OUP, 2015.

Bentley, D.M.R. "Colonial Colonizing: The Long Poem on Canada." *Mnemographia Canadensis: Essays on Memory, Community, and Environment in Canada with Particular Reference to London, Ontario*. Vol. 1. London: Canadian Poetry Press, 1998.

———. *Canadian Poetry: An Electronic Resource*. Ed. D.M.R. Bentley. 2007.

Bergvall, Caroline. "The Conceptual Twist: A Forward." *I'll Drown My Book: Conceptual Writing by Women*. Eds. Caroline Bergvall, Layie Browne, Teresa Carmody, and Vanessa Place. Los Angeles, CA: Les Figues Press, 2012. 18–22.

Bernikow, Louise. *The World Split Open: Four Centuries of Women Poets in England and America, 1552-1950*. New York, NY: Vintage, 1974.

Betts, Gregory. *Avant-Garde Canadian Literature: The Early Manifestations*. Toronto: UTP, 2013.

Birney, Earle. "Can. Lit." 1962. *The New Oxford Book of Canadian Verse in English*. Ed. Margaret Atwood. Toronto: OUP, 1982. 116.

Blaser, Robin. *The Holy Forest*. Berkeley, CA: UCP, 2008.

Brand, Dionne. *In Another Place Not Here*. Toronto: Vintage, 1997.

———. *Map to the Door of No Return: Notes on Belonging*. Toronto: Vintage, 2002.

———. *Inventory*. Toronto: M&S, 2006.

Brydon, Diana. "Dionne Brand's Global Intimacies: Practicing Affective Citizenship." *University of Toronto Quarterly* 76.3 (Summer 2007): 990–1006. https://doi.org/10.3138/utq.76.3.990

Butling, Pauline, and Susan Rudy. "Why Not Be Excessive?: A Conversation with Erin Mouré." *Poets Talk*. Edmonton: UAP, 2005. 43–62.

Carson, Anne. *Short Talks*. Toronto: Brick, 1992.

———. *Glass, Irony, and God*. Toronto: Vintage, 1995.

———. *Plainwater: Essays and Poetry*. Toronto: Vintage, 1995.

———. *Men in the Off Hours*. Toronto: Vintage, 2000.

———. *The Beauty of the Husband*. Toronto: Vintage, 2001.

———. *H of H Playbook*. New York, NY: New Directions, 2021.

Chariandy, David. "Black Canadian Literature: Fieldwork and 'Post-Race'." *The Oxford Handbook of Canadian Literature*. Ed. Cynthia Sugars. Toronto: OUP, 2016. 539–63.

Cho, Lily. "Diasporic Citizenship and De-Formations of Citizenship." *The Oxford Handbook of Canadian Literature*. Ed. Cynthia Sugars. Toronto: OUP, 2016. 527–38.

Clarke, George Elliott. *Whylah Falls*. 1990. Vancouver: Rain Coast, 2001.

———. "Exceptional Poetics." In *The Great Black North: Contemporary African Canadian Poetry*. Eds. Valerie Mason-John and Kevan Anthony Cameron. Calgary: Frontenac House, 2013. 17–24.

Collis, Stephen. *A History of the Theories of Rain*. Vancouver: Talonbooks, 2021.

Cooper, Afua, et al. *Report on Lord Dalhousie's History on Slavery and Race*. September 2019. https://cdn.dal.ca/content/dam/dalhousie/pdf/dept/ldp/Lord%20Dal%20Panel%20Final%20Report_web.pdf

Craig, Elaine. *Putting Trials on Trial: Sexual Assault and the Failure of the Legal Profession*. Montreal: McGill-Queen's UP, 2018.

D'Agata, John. "A ___ with Anne Carson." *The Iowa Review* 27.2 (Summer 1997): 1–22.

———. *We Might As Well Call It the Lyric Essay*. Geneva, NY: Hobart & William Smith College Press, 2015.

Derksen, Jeff. *Annihilated Time: Poetry and Other Politics*. Vancouver: New Star, 2009.

———. "Canadian Literature and the Dying Temporality of Colonialism." *University of Toronto Quarterly* 89.1 (Winter 2020): 37–50. https://doi.org/10.3138/utq.89.1.03

———. *Transnational Muscle Cars*. Vancouver: Talonbooks, 2003.

Dobson, Kit. *Transnational Canadas: Anglo-Canadian Literature and Globalization*. Waterloo: WLUP, 2009.

Dudek, Louis, and Michael Gnarowki, Eds. *The Making of Modern Poetry in Canada: Essential Articles on Contemporary Canadian Poetry in English*. 1967. Toronto: Ryerson Press, 1970.

Eichhorn, Kate. "Beyond Stasis: Proceedings of an Unrealized Conference." *Open Letter Special Issue "Beyond Stasis: Poetics and Feminism Today"* 13.9 (Summer 2009): i–ix.

———. "The Digital Turn in Canadian and Quebecois Literature." *The Oxford Handbook of Canadian Literature*. Ed. Cynthia Sugars. Toronto: OUP, 2016. 500-32.

Elliott, Lorris. *Other Voices: Writings by Blacks in Canada*. Ed. Lorris Elliott. Toronto: Williams-Wallace Publishers, 1985.

Eng, Mercedes. *Mercenary English*. Vancouver: Arsenal Pulp Press, 2018.

Findlay, Len. "Always Indigenize!: The Radical Humanities in the Postcolonial Canadian University." *ARIEL* 31.1–2 (2000): 307–26.

Fleishmann, Aloys, and Nancy van Styvendale. "Introduction." *Narratives of Citizenship: Indigenous and Diasporic People Unsettle the Nation-State*. Eds. Aloys Fleighsmann, Mancy van Styvendale, and Cody McCarroll. Edmonton: UAP, 2011. xi–xlv.

Frye, Northrop. "Conclusion." *A Literary History of Canada*. 1965. Ed. Carl F. Klinck. Toronto: UTP, 1973. 821–49.

Geddes, Gary, Ed. 15 *Canadian Poets x 3*. Oxford: OUP, 2001.

Gibson, Chantal. *How She Read*. Qualicum Beach: Caitlin Press, 2020.

Gingell, Susan. "The 'Nerve of Cree', the Pulse of Africa: Sound Identities in Cree, Cree-Métis, and Dub Poetries in Canada." *Indigenous Poetics in Canada*. Ed. Neal McLeod. Waterloo: WLUP, 2014. 271–92.

Godard, Barbara. "Excentriques, Eccentric, Avant-Garde." *A Room of One's Own* 8.4 (Fall 1984): 57–75.

Hajnoczky, Helen. *Magyarazni*. Toronto: Coach House, 2016.

Head, Harold, Ed. *Canada in Us Now: First Anthology of Black Poetry and Prose in Canada*. Toronto: NC Press, 1979.

Hennighan, Stephen. *When Words Deny the World: The Reshaping of Canadian Writing*. Erin Mills: Porcupine's Quill, 2002.

Hunter, Lynette. *Disunified Aesthetics: Situated Textuality, Performativity, Collaboration*. Kingston: McGill-Queen's UP, 2014.

John, Aisha Sasha. *I Have to Live*. Toronto: Penguin, 2017.

Johnstone, Jim. *The Next Wave: An Anthology of 21st Century Canadian Poetry*. Windsor, Ontario: Palimpsest Press, 2018.

Jones, El. *Live from the Afrikan Resistance!* Black Point: Roseway, 2014.

Kamboureli, Smaro. *On the Edge of Genre: The Contemporary Canadian Long Poem*. Toronto: UTP, 1991.

———. *Scandalous Bodies: Diasporic Literature in English Canada*. Don Mills: OUP, 2000.

———, and Daniel Coleman, Eds. *Retooling the Humanities: The Culture of Research in Canadian Universities*. Edmonton: UAP, 2011.

———, and Roy Miki, Eds. *Trans.Can.Lit: Resituating the Study of Canadian Literature*. Waterloo: WLUP, 2007.

———, and Robert Zacharias, Eds. *Shifting the Ground of Canadian Literary Studies*. Waterloo: WLUP, 2012.

Kellough, Kaie. *Magnetic Equator*. Toronto: Penguin, 2019.

Kiyooka, Roy. *Transcanada Letters*. Vancouver: Talonbooks, 1975.

Kroetsch, Robert. *The Completes Field Notes*. Edmonton: UAP, 2000.

L'Abbé, Sonnet. *Sonnet's Shakespeare*. Toronto: M&S, 2019.

Lai, Larissa. *Iron Goddess of Mercy*. Vancouver: Arsenal Pulp Press, 2021.

Laird, Steven. "Rev. of Poetry Books Nominated for the Governor General's Award in 2007." *Canadian Notes and Queries* 71 (Spring/Summer 2007): 21–2.

Lecker, Robert. "The Canonization of Canadian Literature: An Inquiry into Value." *Critical Inquiry* 16.3 (1990): 656–71.

Lent, Vanessa, Bart Vautour, and Dean Irvine, Eds. *Making Canada New: Editing, Modernism, and New Media*. Toronto: UTP, 2017.

Leong, Michael. "Conceptualisms in Crisis: The Fate of Late Conceptual Poetry." *Journal of Modern Literature* 41.3 (Spring 2018): 109–31.

Livesay, Dorothy. *The Documentary Poem: A Canadian Genre*. Ed. Eli Mandel. Chicago, IL: UCP, 1971.

Lousley, Cheryl. "Witness to the Body Count: Planetary Ethics in Dionne Brand's *Inventory*." *Canadian Poetry: Studies, Documents, Reviews* 63 (2008): 37–58.

Lubrin, Canisia. *Voodoo Hypothesis*. Hamilton: Wolsak & Wynn, 2017.

———. *The Dyzgraph*^{x}*st*. Toronto: M&S, 2020.

Lyotard, Jean-Francois. *The Post-Modern Condition: A Report on Knowledge*. 1979. Trans. Geoff Bennington and Brain Massumi. Minneapolis, MN: UMP, 1984.

MacDonald, Tanis. "Fracture Mechanics: Canadian Poetry since 1960." *Oxford Handbook of Canadian Literature*. Ed. Cynthia Sugars. Toronto: OUP, 2016. 471–94.

maclennan, rob. "Erín Moure's My Beloved Wager." *rob maclennan's blog* (March 31, 2020). http://robmclennan.blogspot.com/2010/03/

Maguire, Shannon, Ed. *Planetary Noise: Selected Poetry of Erín Moure*. Wesleyan: Wesleyan UP, 2017.

Mancini, Donato. *You Must Work Harder to Write Poetry of Excellence: Crafts, Discourse, and the Common Reader in Canadian Poetry Book Reviews*. Toronto: Book*hug, 2012.

Marlatt, Daphne. *Steveston*. 1974. Vancouver: Ronsdale Press, 2000.

Martin, Sandra. "Who Is Afraid of Anne Carson?" *The Globe and Mail* (February 2, 2002): R3. www.theglobeandmail.com/arts/whos-afraid-of-anne-carson/article 4130651/

Marx, Karl, and Friedrich Engels. *The Communist Manifesto*. 1848. Ed. L.M. Findlay. Peterborough: Broadview, 2004.

Mason-John, Valerie. "Oni the Haitian Sensation, Dwayne Morgan, and Ian Keteku, 'Slam'." *The Great Black North: Contemporary African Canadian Poetry*. Eds. Valerie Mason-John and Kevan Anthony Cameron. Calgary: Frontenac House, 2013. 195–6.

———, and Kevan Anthony Cameron, Eds. *The Great Black North: Contemporary African Canadian Poetry*. Calgary: Frontenac House, 2013.

———, Klyde Broox, and Lillian Allen. "Dub." *The Great Black North: Contemporary African Canadian Poetry*. Eds. Valerie Mason-John and Kevan Anthony Cameron. Calgary: Frontenac House, 2013. 105–7.

——— Afua Cooper, and Wayde Compton. "Print Poetry." *The Great Black North: Contemporary African Canadian Poetry*. Eds. Valerie Mason-John and Kevan Anthony Cameron. Calgary: Frontenac House, 2013. 25–6.

———, Tanya Evanson, and John Akpata, "Spoken Word." *The Great Black North: Contemporary African Canadian Poetry*. Eds. Valerie Mason-John and Kevan Anthony Cameron. Calgary: Frontenac House, 2013. 141–2.

Maynard, Robyn. *Policing Black Lives: State Violence from Slavery to the Present*. Halifax: Fernwood, 2017.

McKeon, Lauren. *F-Bomb: Dispatches from the War on Feminism*. Fredericton: Goose Lane, 2017.

Milano, Alyssa. "If You've Been Sexually Harassed or Assaulted Write 'Me too' as a Reply to This Tweet." Twitter (October 15, 2017), pic.twitter.com/k2oeCiUf9n

Mill, K.S. "Thoughts on Poetry and Its Varieties." *Collected Works of John Stuart Mill*. Vol. 1. Eds. John M. Robson and Jack Stillinger. Toronto: UTP, 1981.

Milne, Heather. *Poetry Matters: Neoliberalism, Affect, and the Posthuman in Twenty-First Century North American Feminist Poetics*. Iowa City, IA: UIP, 2018.

Mockler, Kathryn, Ed. *Watch Your Head: Writers and Artists Respond to the Climate Crisis*. Toronto: Coach House, 2020.

Mount, Nick. *When Canadian Literature Moved to New York*. Toronto: UTP, 2005.

Moure, Erín. "About." *Erín Moure*. https://erinmoure.mystrikingly.com. 2021.

———. *My Beloved Wager: Essays from a Writing Life*. Ed. Smaro Kamboureli. Edmonton: NeWest Press, 2009.

———. *Furious*. 1988. Introduction, Sonnet L'Abbé. Toronto: Anansi, 2019.

Moyes, Lianne. "Acts of Citizenship: Erin Mouré's *O Cidadán* and the Limits of Worldliness." *Trans.Can.Lit: Re-Situating the Study of Canadian Literature*. Eds. Smaro Kamboureli and Roy Miki. Waterloo: WLUP, 2007. 111–28.

———. "Discontinuity, Intertextuality, and Literary History: Gail Scott's Reading of Gertrude Stein." *Wider Boundaries of Daring: The Modernist Impulse in Canadian Women's Poetry*. Eds. Di Brandt and Barbara Godard. Waterloo: Wilfrid Laurier UP, 2009. 163–83.

Nancy, Holmes Ed. *Open Wide a Wilderness: Canadian Nature Poems*. Waterloo: WLUP, 2009.

Nguyen, Hoa. *A Thousand Times You Lose Your Treasure*. Seattle: Wave, 2021.

Nichol, bp. *The Martyrology Books 1&2.* Toronto: Coach House, 1972.

Ondaatje, Michael. *The Collected Works of Billy the Kid.* 1970. Toronto: Random House, 2008.

Patrick, Ryan B. "Canisia Lubrin Uses the Language of the Past to Explore the Future in the Poetry Collection *The Dyzgraphxst.*" *CBC* (April 23, 2020). www.cbc.ca/books/canisia-lubrin-uses-the-language-of-the-past-to-explore-the-future-in-the-poetry-collection-the-dyzgraphxst-1.5538588

Pennee, Donna. "Literary Citizenship: Culture (Un)Bounded, Culture (Re) Distributed." *Home-Work: Postcolonialism, Pedagogy, and Canadian Literature.* Ed. Cynthia Sugars. Ottawa: UOP, 2004. 75–85.

Philip, NourbeSe, M. *Zong!* Ed. Setaey Adamu Boateng. Wesleyan: Wesleyan UP, 2008.

Phung, Malissa. "Are People of Colour Settlers Too?" *Cultivating Canada: Reconciliation through the Lens of Cultural Diversity.* Eds. Ashok Mathur, Jonathan Dewar, and Mike DeGagnel. Ottawa: Aboriginal Healing Foundation, 2011. 289–98.

Place, Vanessa, and Robert Fitterman. *Notes towards Conceptualisms.* Baltimore, MD: Ugly Duckling Presse, 2009.

Queyras, Sina. *Lemon Hound.* Toronto: Coach House, 2006.

———. *Expressway.* Toronto: Coach House, 2009.

———. *Unleashed.* Ed. Kate Eichhorn. Toronto: Book*hug, 2009.

———. "Lyric Conceptualism, a Manifesto in Progress." 2012.

———. *MxT.* Toronto: Coach House, 2014.

———. *Barking & Biting: Selected Poetry of Sina Queyras.* Ed. Erin Wunker. Waterloo: LPS, 2015. 61–4.

———. *My Ariel.* Toronto: Coach House, 2017.

———. *Rooms.* Toronto: Coach House, 2022.

Rae, Ian. "Dazzling Hybrids: The Poetry of Anne Carson." *Canadian Literature* 166 (2000): 17–41.

———. "Anne Carson and the Solway Hoaxes." Canadian Literature 176 (Spring 2003): 45–65.

———. "Verglas: Narrative Technique in Anne Carson's 'The Glass Essay'." *ESC* 37.3–4 (2011): 163–86.

Robertson, Lisa. *Debbie: An Epic.* Vancouver: New Star, 1997.

Rudy, Susan, and Pauline Butling. *Writing in Our Time: Canada's Radical Poetries in English (1957–2003).* Waterloo: WLUP, 2005.

Salazar, Rebecca. *sulphurtongue.* Toronto: M&S, 2021.

Shearer, Karis, and Jessica Schagerl. "Faster than a Speeding Thought: Lemon Hound's Archive Unleashed." *Basements and Attics, Closets and Cyberspace: Exploration in Canadian Women's Archives.* Eds. Linda M. Morra and Jessical Schagerl. Waterloo: Wilfrid Laurier University Press, 2012. 47–64

Shraya, Vivek. *even this page is white.* Vancouver: Arsenal Pulp Press, 2017.

Siklosi, Kate. *Small Press Interactive Map.* https://festivalofauthors.ca/small-press-interactive-map/

———, and Dani Spinosa. "Some Rough Notes in Defense of Limited Run." *Periodicities: A Journal of Poetry and Poetics.* March 1, 2021. periodicityjournal.blogspot.com/2021/03/kate-siklosi-and-dani-spinosa-some.html?m=1

Simon, Sherry. "Hybrid Montreal: The Shadows of Language." *Sites: The Journal of 20th-Century Contemporary French Studies* 5.2 (Fall 2001): 315–30.

Solway, David. "The Trouble with Annie: David Solway Unmakes Anne Carson." *Books in Canada* 30.1 (2001): 24–6.

Spahr, Juliana and Stephanie, Young. "Numbers Trouble." *Chicago Review* 53.2–3 (Autumn 2007): 88–111.

Spinosa, Dani. "Give Us the Black Prometheus: Canisia Lubrin's Voodoo Hypothesis and the Anthropocene." Text/Sound/Performance University College Dublin (April 27, 2019). Dublin, Ireland. https://genericpronoun.com/2019/04/30/give-us-the-black-prometheus-canisia-lubrin-and-the-anthropocene/

Spivak, Gayatri. *Death of a Discipline*. New York, NY: Columbia UP, 2003.

Stein, Gertrude. "Portraits and Repetitions." *Gertrude Stein: Writings 1932-1946*. Eds. Catharine R. Stimpson and Harriet Chessman. New York, NY: Library of America, 1998. 165–208.

———. *Ada*. 1910. London: Norbrow, 2010.

Surani, Moez. ةيلمع *Operación Opération Operation* 行 动 *Операция*. Toronto: Book*hug, 2016.

Thammavongsa, Souvankham. *Found*. St. John's: Pedlar Press, 2007.

Thesen, Sharon, Ed. *The New Long Poem Anthology*. 1991. 2nd ed. Vancouver: Talonbooks, 2001.

———. "After-Thoughts on the Long Poem." *The Malahat Review* (2020). www.malahatreview.ca/long_poem_papers/thesen.html

Traill, Catharine Parr. *The Backwoods of Canada*. London: Charles Knight, 1836.

Vida: Women in the Literary Arts. www.vidaweb.org

Walschots, Natalie Zina. "Closing the Gap: Reviewing Books of Poetry by Canadian Women." *Natalie Zed: Promiscuous Wordsmith* (2012). https://nataliezed.ca/2012/closing-the-gap-reviewing-canadian-books-of-poetry-written-by-women/

Wang, Isabella. *Pebble Swing*. Madeira Park: Nightwood, 2021.

Weingarten, J.A. *Sharing the Past: The Reinvention of History in Canadian Poetry Since 1960*. Toronto: UTP, 2019.

Wheelwright, Julie. "Women and Words: One Thousand Gather to Celebrate Writing." *The Ubyssey* 11.2 (1983): 1.

White, Heather Cass. "How to Have a Conversation with Gertrude Stein." *Connotations: A Journal for Critical Debate* 10.2–3 (2001): 124–46.

Williams, Ian. *Word Problems*. Toronto: Coach House, 2020.

Williams, Leigh Anne. "Random House of Canada Takes over McClelland & Stewart: Canadian Publishers Unhappy." *Publishers Weekly* (January 10, 2012). www.publishersweekly.com/pw/by-topic/international/international-book-news/article/50140-random-house-of-canada-takes-over-mcclelland-and-stewart-pubs-unhappy.html

Windham-Campbell Prizes. "Canisia Lubrin."(2021). https://windhamcampbell.org/festival/2021/recipients/lubrin-canisia

Wunker, Erin. "Towards a Planetary Poetics." *The Oxford Handbook of Canadian Literature*. Ed. Cynthia Sugars. Toronto: OUP, 2015. 92–109.

Wylie, Herb. *Anne of Tim Hortons: Globalization and the Reshaping of Atlantic-Canadian Literature*. Waterloo: WLUP, 2011.

York, Lorraine. *Literary Celebrity in Canada*. Toronto: UTP, 2007.

Zarranz, Libe García. *TransCanadian Feminist Fictions: New Cross-Border Ethics*. Kingston: McGill-Queen's UP, 2017.

Zolf, Rachel. *Janey's Arcadia*. Toronto: Coach House, 2014.

———. *No One's Witness*. Durham: Duke UP, 2021.

Index

Printed in the United States
by Baker & Taylor Publisher Services